14·99

General Editors: J. R. MULRYNE
and J. C. BULMAN
Associate Editor: Margaret Shewring

Othello

D1331906

Already published in the series

Othello

LOIS POTTER

Manchester
University Press
Manchester and New York

Distributed exclusively in the USA by Palgrave

Published by Manchester University Press
Oxford Road, Manchester M13 9NR, UK
and Room 400, 175 Fifth Avenue, New York, NY 10010, USA
www.manchesteruniversitypress.co.uk

Distributed exclusively in the USA by
Palgrave, 175 Fifth Avenue, New York NY 10010, USA

Distributed exclusively in Canada by
UBC Press, University of British Columbia, 2029 West Mall,
Vancouver, BC, Canada V6T 1Z2

British Library Cataloguing-in-Publication Data
A catalogue record for this book is available from the British Library

Library of Congress Cataloging-in-Publication Data
A catalog record for this book is available from the Library of Congress

ISBN 0 7190 2726 8 paperback

First published 2002

First digital, on-demand edition produced by Lightning Source 2006

CONTENTS

[v]

LIST OF ILLUSTRATIONS

Figures

Plates

Every effort has been made to obtain permission to reproduce the
illustrations in this book. If any proper acknowledgement has not
been made, copyright-holders are invited to contact the publisher.

SERIES EDITORS' PREFACE

Recently, the study of Shakespeare's plays as scripts for performance in the theatre has grown to rival the reading of Shakespeare as literature among university, college and secondary-school teachers and their students. The aim of the present series is to assist this study by describing how certain of Shakespeare's texts have been realised in production.

The series is not concerned to provide theatre history in the traditional sense. Rather, it employs the more contemporary discourses of performance criticism to explore how a multitude of factors work together to determine how a play achieves meaning for a particular audience. Each contributor to the series has selected a number of productions of a given play and analysed them comparatively. These productions – drawn from different periods, countries and media – were chosen not only because they are culturally significant in their own right but also because they represent something of the range and variety of the possible interpretations of the play in hand. They illustrate how the convergence of various material conditions helps to shape a performance: the medium for which the text is adapted; stage-design and theatrical tradition; the acting company itself; the body and abilities of the individual actor; and the historical, political, and social contexts which condition audience reception of the play.

We hope that theatregoers, by reading these accounts of Shakespeare in performance, may enlarge their understanding of what a play-text is and begin, too, to appreciate the complex ways in which performance is a collaborative effort. Any study of a Shakespeare text will, of course, reveal only a small proportion of the plays's potential meaning; but by engaging issues of how a text is translated in performance, our series encourages a kind of reading that is receptive to the contingencies that make theatre a living art.

J. R. Mulryne and J. C. Bulman, General Editors
Margaret Shewring, Associate Editor

ACKNOWLEDGEMENTS

Since *Othello* has a virtually continuous performance history and has been popular in many countries, this is neither the first nor the most complete study of the play in performance. I shall mention only a few important books, all of which I greatly admire, that are devoted either to *Othello*, or to staging or to both. My first Shakespeare mentor, Arthur Colby Sprague, gives excellent accounts of the growth of stage conventions and of some nineteenth-century productions in *Shakespeare and the Actors* (1944) and *Shakespearian Players and Performances* (1953). Marvin Rosenberg's *The Masks of Othello* (1961) is still a fine study of its stage history, informed by intelligent thinking about performance, while Gino J. Matteo's *Shakespeare's Othello: The Study and the Stage* (1974) in some respects supplements it with a more detailed look at the eighteenth century in particular. Carol Jones Carlisle's *Shakespeare from the Greenroom* takes an actor's-eye-view of the leading roles that I found particularly congenial. Julie Hankey's admirable volume in the 'Plays in Performance' series (1987) is both comprehensive and theatrically sophisticated, while Virginia Mason Vaughan's *Othello: A Contextual History* (1994) wisely chooses to examine a few productions in detail, and does it so well that I have mostly tried to avoid overlapping with her work. Edward Pechter's *Othello and Interpretive Traditions* (1999) goes into the critical arguments over the play much more thoroughly than I could possibly do.

Given the existence of these earlier works, each exemplary in its way, each finding a different balance between comprehensiveness and detail, I probably ought to say what kind of contribution I think I have made, apart from simply being the latest in the field. John Gillies, in a lecture at the 1997 meeting of the Shakespeare Association of America, talked about the extent to which Othello was written *as* a tragic hero; though I have not seen a copy of that paper or a published version of it, I feel that it strongly influenced my chapter on the early performance history of the character. In fact, the question, 'What does it mean to act a part?', informs the whole of the first section, an inevitably brief survey of the performance of the three central roles before what I take to be the defining event in the play's modern history, Paul Robeson's Othello. Robeson was important because both his performance and his life established a view (not one that he would necessarily have shared) of the importance of certain kinds of identity between actor and role. Subsequent productions of the play, in any society that considers itself multicultural, have had to come to terms with contemporary social attitudes towards race – and, later, towards gender and sexuality. In most cases this has meant a transformation of the play: through adaptation and cutting, through productions that knowingly play against the original context, or through negotiation on the part of actors and director with the aspects of the play that make them uncomfortable.

Othello has inspired numerous imitations, operas and ballets, and films. The simplicity of its plot, in comparison with those of other Shakespeare plays, has also given it an international appeal. It was the first Shakespeare play chosen for translation into French and Hebrew, the first to be performed in Japan. So my approach emphasizes intertextuality and internationalism. No book of this scope can possibly cover the full range of overseas productions, but, being myself 'of here and everywhere', I wanted to give some indication of the complexity of this story, even if it can best be told in detail by individual experts. Even so, there are many actors I have not discussed: surely no Anglo-American Othello can compete with the Armenian Vagram Papazian who is said to have played the role in Armenian, Russian, Italian and French – over three thousand times in all (Stříbrný, *Eastern*, 82), or the Swiss Leopold Biberti, who played the part for the last time at the age of sixty-nine, after over six hundred performances in German and nearly two hundred in French, which were said to be the equivalent of a religious experience (Kachler, 132). The United States has also had some surprisingly cosmopolitan productions. A polyglot *Othello* in San Francisco, on 5 March, 1868, starred an English-speaking Othello (George Pauncefort), with a cast of French, German and Danish actors, all speaking in their own languages (Koon, 158). In 1929 a Russian director, Boris Glagolin, reinterpreted the play for New York's Yiddish Art Theatre, fusing the Shakespeare text with *commedia* traditions and the Cinthio story. In interviews, he said that he planned to reintroduce Iago's child, mentioned by Cinthio, and to give her a complexion like Othello's; surprisingly, no reviewer mentions this remarkable innovation (*New York Herald Tribune*, 26 January 1929). In 1939 a newspaper reported that a director was searching for an American Indian to play the title role in *Othello* for the 150th anniversary of George Washington's inauguration (*Daily Mirror*, New York, 14 March 1939). Other gaps of which I am well aware include the Liz White film, still not generally available, which fortunately is discussed at length in Peter Donaldson's *Shakespearean Films / Shakespearean Directors*. I should also have liked to write about ways in which the revolution in opera staging in the last thirty years has transformed Verdi's *Otello* – but this would need another chapter, perhaps another book.

Whenever possible, I shall devote most attention to productions I have seen myself, though I have supplemented my own impressions and notes with reviews and promptbooks. Performance scholarship is built on shaky foundations: promptbooks which were not necessarily followed in every detail, productions which changed over the course of a run; reviews and personal recollections that contradict each other; statements by directors and actors about interpretations that sound convincing yet (to judge from reviews) apparently convinced no one. Often productions which audiences found powerfully moving leave behind almost no record of the qualities that made them so. Only productions in a major cultural centre or a major theatre festival are reviewed widely enough for a consensus to emerge, both about what happened and about how it was perceived at the time. One cannot generalize from any single experience to say that a particular way of playing *Othello* does not work. If I make some performances sound better than my readers think they were, this does not strike me as a serious crime: at this date, no one will be deceived into wasting money on them. I naturally tend to value productions from which I feel that I learned something, whether or not the director and actors intended to transmit those particular insights.

I have received much help and courtesy from the British Library, the Mander and Mitchinson Theatre Collection, The Harvard Theatre Collection, The British Theatre Museum, The Schomburg Center for Black Culture, The Shakespeare Centre (Stratford-upon-Avon), and the Folger Shakespeare Library. Completion of the book was speeded up by a short-term Folger fellowship in the spring of 1999. I am grateful to the University of Delaware for letting me take unpaid leave during that period, for the help provided by its excellent library, and for providing me with the many splendid research assistants who have helped with this project at all its various stages: Mark Netzloff, Rebecca Jaroff, Barbara Silverstein, Bradley Ryner, Michael Clody and Darlene Farabee, who also prepared the index.

For help with attending the many productions that I saw in connection with this book, or for talking with me about them, I should like to thank Ashland, Oregon (Barry Kraft, Hilary Tate and Derrick Lee Weeden); Martin Hilský and Zdeněk Stříbrný of Charles University, Prague; the Santa Cruz Shakespeare Festival (Audrey Stanley, Michael Warren and Paul Whitworth); the Shakespeare Theatre in Washington, DC (Mary Hardisty); and the anonymous actor who answered my questionnaire about the Lansburgh production of *Othello*.

For helpful information or for giving me better ideas than I could ever have had on my own, I am also grateful to Emery Battis, Stephen Buhler, Tony Church, Richard Davison, Peter Feng, Richard Foulkes, Jay L. Halio, Russell Jackson, François Laroque, Tom Leitch, Lena Cowen Orlin, Kristen Poole, Donald Reiman, Frances Richardson, Michèle and Raymond Willems and Julian Yates.

For his valuable criticism, I thank Jim Bulman, my editor for this series, who gave me enough praise to keep me writing and enough criticism to keep me more or less lucid. My thanks also to the staff at the Manchester University Press, particularly John Banks and Rachael Bolden.

I quote *Othello* from the edition of E. A. J. Honigmann for the Arden Shakespeare (1997); references to his notes are normally to the passage cited; in other references to this edition it is cited as 'Arden'. Other Shakespeare plays are quoted from the Riverside edition, ed. G. Blakemore Evans (2nd ed., 1997). Where dates are given for other plays of the sixteenth and seventeenth centuries, they are taken from Alfred Harbage's *Annals of English Drama*, revised by Samuel Schoenbaum and Sylvia S. Wagonheim (3rd edn, 1989). Unattributed translations are my own.

A final note of thanks: I am grateful to Sandy Robbins, of The Professional Theatre Training Program at the University of Delaware (PTTP) for talking to me about *Othello*; his own production at Ashland in 1982 was highly praised. Late in 1998 the PTTP produced a splendid *Othello*, directed by Paul Barnes, with René Thornton Jr., David Daniell and Cheyenne Casebier as the three protagonists. Since the terms of this series do not allow for extended discussion of productions technically defined as amateur, I should like instead to dedicate this book to Sandy Robbins and all the members of this programme, from whom I have learned a great deal about theatre.

Lois Potter
Newark, Delaware

INTRODUCTION

Those who call *Othello* the most theatrically successful of Shakespeare's plays do not always mean it as a compliment. In almost any competent production the final scene will affect the audience deeply, but it may also make them feel less like spectators at an ancient art form than like bystanders at a traffic accident. This blurring of the boundaries between life and art, which can seem like a lack of art, has affected the play's performance history from the beginning. Though it is hard to find out how individual actors played its hero, heroine and villain, there are plenty of anecdotes about its powerful effect on audiences: they shouted out their revulsion at Iago's behaviour; they shot the actor of Othello to keep him from committing murder; their outrage at the final scene forced the translators of the first French and German performances to supply alternative, happy endings. Not only audiences but actors themselves are said to have become unable to tell truth from fiction: legends tell of Othellos becoming so involved in their roles that they killed their Desdemonas in earnest. Maria Garcia started screaming in the final scene of Rossini's opera when she saw Otello (in real life, her father) approaching her with a genuine knife instead of the stage property; Ira Aldridge, touring Russia in a series of Shakespeare roles, had to live with the rumour that he had already killed several Desdemonas; in two films, *Carnival* and *A Double Life*, a jealous actor barely prevents himself from throttling Desdemona, played in each case by his estranged wife.

Such stories are usually told less as tributes to the play than as comments on the naivety of its audiences. Yet the outrage felt at performances of *Othello* surely results not from the belief that it is really happening but from a sense that the intensity of its effect is inappropriate for something known to be merely fictional; the spectator wishes, rather than fears, to discover that it is real. Hence, the history of playing Othello is the history of a desire for a degree of identification between hero and role that might almost seem to rule out the need to act at all. In 1811 an acting manual called *The Thespian Praeceptor* declared that no one should attempt to play a hero on the stage unless he was capable of being a hero in real life (26). In 1876 a reviewer of Irving's Othello insisted that 'Othello is not, as Hamlet is, a character of many and diverse readings; there can be but one true Othello' (*The Times*, 17 February 1876). Such emphasis on the existence of a 'true' hero and a 'true' Othello is the more remarkable in the light of the fact that, for some three hundred years, 'black Othello' was a role almost exclusively for white actors. The playing of Othello by a famous black actor, Paul Robeson, created a new dynamic in the history of the play, and, in the English-speaking world, it is now taken for granted that actor and role should be racially identical. Racism has become such an international concern that, even in countries with no strong tradition of black performers, no casting decision can be wholly innocent.

Much recent scholarship on *Othello* has been concerned with a search for origins. Where did Othello, with all that his name now means, come from? Where did racism come from? Is there a point at which the perception of racial difference, and particularly the difference of colour, stops becoming a matter of fact and becomes specifically 'racist'? Similar questions are asked about the perception of sex and gender differences in the play. A theatrical study such as this inevitably looks for origins as well. This chapter will quickly rehearse the limited evidence for the play's early performance history, asking the familiar but still useful questions: What else had the actors played? What else had audiences seen? What might they have been reading? What evidence do we have about reception? The existence of two texts of the play – a quarto of 1622 and the version in the First Folio of 1623 – may be evidence of revision, which is our best evidence, if we can interpret it, of what Shakespeare, or his audiences, may have found unsatisfactory. Finally, evidence of the play's post-Restoration performance and reception is to some extent visible in the other plays traditionally performed in the same repertory with *Othello*, as well as in the acting editions that finally fixed the play in its premodern form.

Casting and early performance

Verses on the death of Richard Burbage (*c.* 1567–1619) name Othello as one of his most famous roles. Although Burbage was praised by contemporaries as a brilliantly protean actor, able to encompass Romeo as well as Richard III and Hamlet, Othello would have been an unusual departure for him, and not merely because of the hero's colour. In his mid-thirties, he played a character who says that he is 'declined / Into the vale of years – yet that's not much' (III.iii.269–70); his next major role in a Shakespearean tragedy was probably the octogenarian King Lear.

The most likely Iago, John Lowin (1576–1653), is first mentioned as a member of the company (the Lord Chamberlain's Men in 1602 and the King's Men after 1603) in 1602 and would eventually become one of its leaders. In 1604 he was twenty-eight, exactly the age Iago gives himself in his cryptic statement, 'I have looked upon the world for four times seven years' (I.iii.312–13). He seems to have played a narrower range of roles than Burbage but to have played them definitively. A large burly man, he was the original Sir Epicure Mammon and eventually took on the part of Falstaff, as several other famous Iagos have done. His name has been linked with Kent in *King Lear* (1605), a character sarcastically described in terms that suggest Iago ('an honest mind and plain, he must speak truth!' – *King Lear*, II.ii.99); he also played Shakespeare and John Fletcher's Henry VIII (1613), Bosola (a cross between Iago and Kent) in Webster's *The Duchess of Malfi* (1613–14) and a number of blunt, honest soldiers in plays by Fletcher and his collaborators. Some of these soldiers are genuinely honest and simple, some carry their 'honesty' to the point of coarseness, and some are as devious as the courtiers they despise. *Othello*, which was in repertory alongside these plays, would have given Lowin a chance to experiment with variations on a popular type.

Most productions have traditionally showed a large, powerful but rather static Othello playing opposite a lighter, more mercurial Iago (reviewers often use the image of the bull and the matador). In this respect, Iago seems more like a Burbage part; scholars sometimes imagine a contrast between him and Edward Alleyn, the original player of Marlowe's heroes, and Martin Holmes goes so far as to suggest that Burbage may initially have been cast as Iago, while Alleyn himself played Othello in some special performance with the King's Men, later relinquishing the part to Burbage. There is no evidence at all for this theory, but the issues it raises are interesting. *Othello* is unusual among Shakespeare's tragedies in that the protagonist has fewer lines than his antagonist. While Othello has a longer part (879 lines, 6237 words) than either Romeo or King Lear, Iago's part (1094 lines, 8434 words) is exceeded only by those of Richard III and Hamlet; in fact, as Marvin Spevack's concordance makes clear, he speaks nearly a third of the words in the play. Only two other Shakespeare characters, Henry V and Hamlet, dominate their plays to this extent. Burbage normally played long roles, as did Alleyn (Barabas in Marlowe's *The Jew of Malta* dominates his play even more than Shakespeare's heroes do theirs).

If the original casting was Burbage versus Lowin, perhaps we need to revise our image of the two characters. It is, after all, Othello who requires the greater emotional range. The length of Iago's part may indicate verbosity, not eloquence: he tells Roderigo, early in the play, 'I have told thee often, and I re-tell thee again and again, I hate the Moor' (I.iii.365-7). Numerous actors, struggling not only to remember their lines but to tell one soliloquy from another, have found that he does indeed, as José Ferrer wrote, say 'the same thing over and over again' (Ferrer, 8). At times, as in the first scene on Cyprus where he improvises rhymes for Desdemona, he is reminiscent of the stock Elizabethan figure, the Clown in dialogue with the Lady. Even in his great scene with Othello he is potentially comic as he intersperses his insinuations about Desdemona with maddeningly longwinded apologies for his suspicions. A few years later, Shakespeare revived the parenthetical style for comic effect: Iachimo in *Cymbeline*, another slanderer of an honest wife, finally confesses his crime in a speech so full of self-interruptions that his listeners almost explode with impatience (*Cymbeline*, V.v.153-209).

Othello and Iago also occupy different places in the linguistic hierarchy: Othello, who speaks mainly in verse, represents, perhaps to an exaggerated degree, the 'high style' of tragedy, whereas Iago's speeches, especially those in prose, normally use the linguistic register of a low comic character. He can sometimes speak in Othello's style, as when, at the end of III.iii, the two men vow revenge on Desdemona and Cassio; Othello can also speak in Iago's, and does so, increasingly, as the play goes on. This kind of dramaturgy has been traced to the divided world of the sixteenth-century allegorical drama, where a character representing humankind can speak both in the frankly unnatural 'aureate' style of the virtuous abstractions and in the coarse language of the Vices. But, although Othello's 'Rude am I in my speech' (I.iii.82) is usually taken as absurdly untrue for someone about to launch into one of

Shakespeare's most eloquent speeches, it is important that this is how he describes himself, just as it is important that Desdemona, before we meet her, is described as 'Of spirit so still and quiet that her motion / Blushed at herself' (I.iii.96–7). The play seems to invite a revaluing of speech and silence.

The original Desdemona is, of course, anonymous. Given the short careers of boy actors, there must have been several different ones during Shakespeare's lifetime. The role may have been something of a departure for its young creator. In the first half of the play Desdemona has much in common with some of Shakespeare's comic heroines; like Rosalind and Cleopatra, she can be histrionic, pretending to be happy when she is not and exaggerating her femininity for effect: after telling Cassio that she will make herself a nuisance until Othello reinstates him, she either behaves shrewishly (as used to be thought) or (in more recent feminist interpretations) plays the part of a shrew with comic enthusiasm. The change of tone in the final acts requires other qualities: if the song in the 'willow scene' recalls Ophelia's mad scene, Desdemona is still more pathetic because she remains resolutely sane. The boy who played the part in 1610 at Oxford seems to have stolen attention even from Burbage. Henry Jackson, who saw the production, wrote a fascinatingly suggestive brief account in Latin, referring to the boy-actor only as 'illa Desdemona' who, although effective throughout, 'yet moved (us) more after she was dead, when, lying on her bed, she entreated the pity of the spectators by her very countenance' (Tillotson, 494). The passage, first published by Geoffrey Tillotson in 1933, has interested critics because Jackson, a sophisticated spectator, shows in his choice of pronouns that he thought of Desdemona as a woman rather than a boy actor. 'Illa Desdemona' (literally 'that Desdemona' or 'Desdemona herself') can also mean 'the celebrated Desdemona'. It would be interesting to know whether the phrase refers to the character or, as seems more likely, to the actor; was the boy already known for this part? Jackson's remark may be evidence that even a drama notoriously dominated by words could produce its finest effects through silence; on the other hand, he may have been remembering a moment that combined a striking image with equally striking words, as Othello directed the audience to look at Desdemona's face: 'Now: how dost thou look now? O ill-starred wench, / Pale as thy smock' (V.ii.210–11).

[5]

Date and contexts

Othello's first recorded performance was 1 November 1604. It may (as Ernst Honigmann argues in his Arden edition) have been finished in time to be acted before the death of Elizabeth I and the plagues that closed the theatres for much of 1603–4, or the recorded performance may have been one of the first in James I's reign, during the relatively good year before the theatres again suffered long periods of closure from 1605 to 1608. In either case it belongs to a period when the London theatres were competing to produce plays of an apparently new genre, domestic drama. Longsuffering wives are central to Dekker's *Patient Grissil* (1599–1600), the anonymous *The Fair Maid of Bristol* (1603), and *The London Prodigal* (1603–4); other plays of revenge and adultery in the period 1603–7 include *The Malcontent*, *The Revenger's Tragedy* and *The Devil's Charter* (Knutson, 115–20). Other Shakespeare plays in the company's repertory included *The Merry Wives of Windsor*, with its comically jealous husband; *The Comedy of Errors*, where it is the wife who is jealous and the husband who visits a courtesan; *Measure for Measure*, probably written very close in time to *Othello*, which includes bawds and whores in its cast. The relationship between Iago and Roderigo is remarkably similar to that between Sir Toby and Sir Andrew in *Twelfth Night*, even to Toby's frequent insistence that Andrew should 'send for more money'; the parallels may have been underlined by the casting (Honigmann, Arden, 346–7).

Othello's indebtedness to comic dramaturgy has often been pointed out, and it has been the source of most of the play's difficulties in the theatre. Two episodes that have been cut almost from the beginning require Othello to eavesdrop on other characters: on Iago and Cassio in IV.i and on the attempted murder of Cassio in V.i. Both scenes involve ingenious, perhaps over-ingenious, misunderstandings. IV.i is technically difficult: in many performances the audience find it hard to tell exactly what Othello is or is not meant to hear. No explanation is given for Othello's entrance in V.i (Honigmann's note on V.i.27.1 wonders whether Iago is supposed to have told him where the attack will take place). It is even harder to understand why Iago sends Emilia to the castle to report the news of Cassio's wounding. He might be trying to prevent the murder of Desdemona, or to ensure that Othello is captured in the act, but neither explanation makes much sense.

Moreover, it is difficult for an audience to understand that when Othello says, 'It is even so' and 'Minion, thy dear lies slain', he is responding to Roderigo's 'O, villain that I am!' (V.i.29), which he takes to be Cassio's dying confession. Webster's *Duchess of Malfi* (1613) includes a scene where complicated mishearing in the dark results in the death of the wrong person; it may indicate that, for one spectator at least, the *Othello* scene was admirably effective on the stage. However, since neither text of *Othello* was printed until after 1616, it is equally possible that Shakespeare revised the play in the light of Webster's scene. In *King Lear*, his next tragedy, he recombined the same plot elements more successfully: Edmund offers to let Gloucester eavesdrop on him and Edgar but, if this happens, it happens between scenes; the fake combat that Edmund stages with his brother, partly overheard by Gloucester, is so rapid as to leave no time to think about its probability; when the dying Edmund decides to do 'some good', sending a messenger to try to save Lear and Cordelia from the death he has arranged for them, the result is to create a false hope that reinforces the emotional effect of the entry of Lear with the dead Cordelia. This 'rewriting' is the closest thing we have to Shakespeare's own criticism of *Othello*.

From the point of view of its dramaturgy, *Othello* recalls the plays that Jonson wrote for the King's Men, some of which tend to have two protagonists rather than one: Volpone and Mosca in *Volpone*, Subtle and Face in *The Alchemist*, Tiberius and Sejanus in *Sejanus*. Jonson's characters tend to collaborate in their crimes, then turn on each other. In the Italian story that Shakespeare used as his source, the unnamed characters corresponding to Othello and Iago collaborate closely on the murder of Disdemona (as she is called here) and actually succeed in making it look like an accident: they are detected only when the Moor turns on his former accomplice and cashiers him, after which the Ensign accuses the Moor of murder. The *Hecatommithi* of Giraldi Cinthio includes this story as one told to a group of fugitives from the Sack of Rome. They react to it by blaming the Moor for his foolish credulity and the heroine's father for giving her a name of ill omen ('the unfortunate one'), but 'all praised God, because the criminals had had suitable punishment' (Arden, 386).

Cinthio also offered the wider background that Shakespeare seems to have considered necessary for tragedy, not only because of the racial difference between Desdemona and her husband –

called only 'the Moor' even in direct address by her – but also because the story is set in the context of wars between Christianity and Islam. Cyprus was a Venetian possession when Cinthio wrote his story, but had become part of the Ottoman Empire when Shakespeare wrote his play. Hindsight may, then, play a part in its depiction of the Cyprus garrison. A common complaint since the Reformation had been that Christians 'were killing each other over doctrinal differences instead of joining forces to destroy Islam. At a time when Catholic–Protestant antagonism was intensifying, while Protestantism itself was becoming more fragmented, Othello's response to the drunken scuffle on Cyprus was topical:

> Are we turned Turks? and to ourselves do that
> Which heaven hath forbid the Ottomites?

> (II.iii.166–7)

The initial phrase is proverbial, a rhetorical question meaning 'Are we barbarians?', but in the context of a war with the Turks the lines which follow have several other meanings. Othello could mean that the Turks had not done as much damage to the Christians as they had just done to themselves; he could be referring to the Islamic ban on drinking alcohol; he could also be reminding his subordinates that the Turks never fought among themselves (Honigmann, *Othello*, 337). The choice of pronouns shows that Othello is identifying himself with the Venetians against the Turk (L. A. Johnson, 172), presumably because the religious conflict matters more to him than the racial one. Iago claims that Othello's love for Desdemona is strong enough to make him 'renounce his baptism' – that is, his religion (II.iii.338) – and it has sometimes been suggested that he does renounce it, at the point where he finally loses his faith in her. But in the final scene his imagery of the Last Judgement and afterlife remains Christian.

Elizabethan attitudes to race, to Venice, to Islam, to gender, are all significant, because Iago's plot depends on the acceptance of a few basic stereotypes: Moors (like Othello) are lascivious braggarts; Venetian women (like Desdemona) have loose sexual morals; Florentines (like Cassio) are accomplished Machiavels; soldiers (like Iago) are blunt and honest – and can therefore be believed when they satirize others. Iago in the course of the play has something to say about all these types, as well as Englishmen, wives, fair women, black women, men who talk in their sleep, and strumpets; no wonder Othello thinks he 'knows all qualities, with a learned spirit' (III.iii.263). Emilia makes similar generalizations about men, especially husbands, and Desdemona follows her example ('Nay, we must think men are not gods': III.iv.149). Othello generalizes, once Iago has worked on him, both about women and about himself: 'we can call these delicate creatures ours / And not their appetites' (III.iii.273–4); cuckoldry is 'the plague of great ones' (277). The fact that it is Iago who makes these generalizations suggests that the audience are meant to recognize them as deceptive and inadequate. But it is impossible to know what Shakespeare knew about the culture from which Othello came, or where he imagined it to be. Indirect knowledge of the Moorish legacy in Spain could have reached England through the visit of Philip II, during the time of his marriage to Mary Tudor, or through travellers after that time. Pamphlets about the Moors and the wars in North Africa inspired a number of plays. Shakespeare might have heard about the kingdom of Kongo (a large area of west central Africa), ruled for over a hundred years by Christian kings who could have been the 'men of royal siege' from whom Othello claims descent (I.ii.22).

But Shakespeare probably got the strongest sense of Othello from literature, especially the Italian epics about wars between Moors and Christians. The *Orlando Furioso* of Ariosto and Tasso's *Jerusalem Delivered* were available to him in good translations by Sir John Harington (1591) and Edward Fairfax (1600), but he might also have read them in the original (Arden, 245, 368). The epics depict a remarkable array of interesting Saracens: 'good' ones (converts to Christianity) or villains who are nevertheless impressive. Both Ariosto and Tasso depicted men who killed women they loved and grieved afterward. Marlowe borrowed for the second part of *Tamburlaine* (IV.ii) Ariosto's story of the love of the Saracen Rodomonte for a Christian woman who, to escape his hands, tricks him into killing her. In Tasso's poem a Christian knight, Tancred, loves Clorinda, a warrior on the side of the pagans, but kills her during a fierce combat while both are concealed by their armour and the darkness. Mortally wounded, Clorinda, who has just discovered that she was born a Christian, asks her lover to baptize her, then dies, leaving him overwhelmed with suicidal grief. In each case, the tragedy is intensified by the fact that the lovers are of different religions. Race is much less crucial as a factor.

[9]

The text: Quarto versus Folio

Whatever else may have gone into the rich contextual background of *Othello*, the result was a long play that sometimes seems to be in need of a final editing by its author. It exists in two different texts that appeared in quick succession: a Quarto of 1622 (Q1) and the Folio of 1623 (F1). Neither was published in Shakespeare's lifetime, though the play seems to have been in the company's repertoire almost constantly; he may have intended to revise it further before sending it to the press. Clearly, the manuscripts that lie behind Q1 and F1, if they are entirely Shakespearean, must predate 1616, but their exact relationship is a matter of debate. Honigmann's recent study of *The Texts of Othello* (1996) argues that many of the discrepancies between them can be explained by a combination of different kinds of incompetence in scribal transmission, compositorial error and alteration, all caused in the first place by Shakespeare's deteriorating handwriting. It is generally believed that the Folio text is the later of the two, since, following the 1606 act against profanity on the stage, it removes more than fifty oaths (Honigmann, *Texts*, 3) – among them, the first words spoken by Roderigo ('Tush') and Iago ("Sblood'). The Quarto is about 160 lines shorter than the Folio. If the lines that appear only in the Folio are *additions* to the text, it is reasonable to assume that Shakespeare or his actors considered them improvements. But many of the Quarto omissions look more like cuts. They cannot have been made simply to save time (according to Nevil Coghill's calculations, they would shorten the play in performance only by some eight minutes: Coghill, 177–8); their purpose might be aesthetic or political, or even, as scholars are coming increasingly to think, the result of minor tinkering by the author in the course of copying.

The most intriguing discrepancies between the two texts occur in lines spoken by or about Desdemona. Cinthio's story introduces the heroine with this sentence: 'It happened that a virtuous Lady of wondrous beauty called Disdemona, impelled not by female appetite but by the Moor's good qualities, fell in love with him, and he, vanquished by the Lady's beauty and noble mind, likewise was enamoured of her' (Arden, 371). This initial denial of the Lady's sexual appetite, combined with the information that she had fallen in love with Othello before he fell in love with her, seems to linger in the language of I.iii, as if the author or reviser had difficulty in reconciling the two facts. As has often been noted, her father's description of her as 'a maiden never bold' is almost immediately contradicted by Othello's story showing that 'she was half the wooer'. The two texts sometimes contradict each other in the same way. At the end of his speech in Q, Othello says,

> My story being done
> She gave me for my pains a world of sighs
>
> (I.iii.159–60)

whereas in F the last word is 'kisses'. Possibly 'kisses' is simply a misreading of 'sighes'. But then, Cassio's wish (in Q) that Othello may 'swiftly come to Desdemona's arms' (Q: II.i.80) becomes (in F) 'make love's quick pants in Desdemona's arms'. Either F is concerned to heighten the sexual element in Q or Q is attempting to tone down this element in F. The contrast can work the other way: Desdemona says, in Q, that her heart is subdued 'Even to the utmost pleasure of my lord' (I.iii.252); in F, she says, 'to the very quality of my lord'. The first reading need not refer specifically to sexual pleasure, though it can be understood that way; the second leaves no room for such an interpretation.

The biggest discrepancy between the texts, however, comes in IV.iii. Q gives only a short version of what is usually called the 'willow scene', consisting only of Desdemona's forebodings and part of the debate between the two women as to whether any woman would cuckold her husband. Desdemona, though she talks of the maid Barbary and her 'song of willow', does not sing it; Emilia does not suggest that there might be a justification for women's infidelity if their husbands are cruel or unfaithful. Did Shakespeare shorten a scene that had been found too daring, or did he write up the roles of Desdemona and Emilia for the sake of two popular and gifted boy actors? Honigmann argues that the Q text was revised at the last moment because the boy actor's voice had broken – a view that does not, of course, explain the cutting of Emilia's speech at the end of the scene. F, moreover, makes Desdemona suddenly go out of her way to say something that might justify Othello's suspicions of her: 'This Lodovico is a proper man' (IV.iii.35). Though unwilling to conclude that someone omitted this part of the dialogue from Q in order to make Desdemona's behaviour less equivocal, two Arden editors have reassigned the line to Emilia, and Honigmann further suggests that Desdemona's 'he speaks well' should be delivered with indifference, so as to show that she is 'not interested' in this man (Arden, 55). In a passage found in F only, Emilia, who has already said 'my husband?' three times, is given a fourth question, to which Othello replies with the irritated 'Dost understand the word? / My friend thy husband, honest, honest Iago' (V.ii.149–50). Was Shakespeare intensifying the ironic parallel between Iago and Emilia, both of whom irritate Othello by echoing him, or does Q reflect his sense that he was laying the irony on too thick?

Early stage history and intertextual evidence

The play was clearly a great success from the first. Verses by Leonard Digges, first published in the 1640 edition of Shakespeare's *Poems*, say that 'Honest Iago, or the Jealous Moore' are more popular with audiences than the protagonists of Jonson's *Sejanus*. (Digges's language suggests that the two protagonists were already seen as nearly equal in interest.) Its success meant frequent revivals. Perhaps these may explain the differences between the Quarto and Folio texts. *Othello* was, for instance, one of the plays chosen for court performance in 1612–13 during the celebration of Princess Elizabeth's wedding to Prince Frederick of Heidelberg. A surprising number of these plays dealt with disastrously unhappy marriages (even, in *Much Ado*, a blighted wedding ceremony): perhaps the royal audience were less sensitive about topical meanings than we sometimes assume. Still, it is tempting to speculate that the Quarto *Othello* may preserve revisions made for the court performance. In particular, the exchange between Desdemona and Emilia, concluding with Emilia's suggestion that a wife's adultery can often be the husband's fault, might have been considered unsuitable for a young married couple.

Othello's popularity is further indicated by the fact that it seems to have been the first Shakespeare tragedy to be revived at the Restoration and that it was allocated to the King's Company, along with most of the other prestigious prewar plays. The most respected actor of the age, Thomas Betterton (?1635–1710?), the star of the rival Duke's Company, did not have a chance to play the part until 1682, when the two companies merged and most of his rivals retired from the stage. *Othello* may have been the first play in which the heroine was played by a woman, though her identity is still a matter of speculation; the first Othello and Iago were probably Nicholas Burt and Walter Clun, with Charles Hart,

[12]

a romantic comedy lead, as Cassio (he later took over as Othello). Clun had been a successful actor of women's roles who graduated into comic parts and was famous as both Falstaff and Iago (*Egley*, 30–1). His career ended prematurely when he was murdered in 1664, and the next Iago was Michael Mohun, a highly regarded actor but not, apparently, a comedian. Unfortunately, there is little information as to how these actors played their roles. Pepys's comments are purely evaluative and comparative (he thought Mohun much less good than Clun as Iago on 6 February 1669), although he confirms what everyone knows about the play's powerful effect on audiences: when he saw it on 11 October 1660 a woman near him 'called out, to see Desdemona smothered'.

Information about *Othello* in the theatre effectively begins only in the early eighteenth century. However, something of its effect can be gathered from the two other plays with which it was often linked. In the post-Restoration period Othello was one of three famous black roles: the others were the title character of Thomas Southerne's *Oroonoko* (1695), based on a novella of 1688 by Aphra Behn, and Zanga, the villain of Edward Young's *The Revenge* (1721). These plays remained in the theatrical repertory well into the nineteenth century, and the same actor tended to play all three roles. After Edmund Kean's great success in *Othello* in 1814, *The Revenge* was revived for him in 1815 and *Oroonoko* early in 1817. Southerne's play deals only with the latter part of Behn's novel, in which Oroonoko is a slave in Surinam, but Behn had also described his existence as an African prince and his winning his love Imoinda against the rivalry of his own father. In the novel Imoinda is African as well, but in the play she is white. One would expect the black–white marriage to provoke some comment from the other characters. That it does not suggests that Imoinda's colour is only a contrivance to allow the actress to avoid the need for black makeup. Its effect, nevertheless, is to create a parallel to *Othello*, particularly when Oroonoko kills Imoinda – although he does so with her consent and help, since they have taken part in an unsuccessful slave revolt and know they are about to be recaptured by the white Christians. The play is structured on a system of oppositions in which race is much less important than religion and social class. Like many Restoration authors, Southerne uses the natural goodness of his non-Christian hero to condemn the hypocrisy of some of the Christian characters. For their part, the 'good' white characters are socially conservative. They do not question their right to buy and sell human beings, but make an exception in Oroonoko's case, because they recognize his princely qualities and because he was betrayed into captivity rather than sold into it. 'Natural' class-distinctions, in other words, override 'natural' racial hierarchies.

The Revenge has always been recognized as *Othello* with the racial roles reversed: the wicked Moor Zanga deceives the trusting Spaniard Alonso into killing his wife and best friend ('an alteration', Hazlitt wrote, 'which is more in conformity to our prejudices, as well as to historical truth': Hazlitt, V: 217). Yet, if it appealed to race prejudice, *The Revenge* also glorified blackness; by the end of the eighteenth century it held the stage only because actors wanted to play Zanga. The end of the play shows why he was its most powerful and interesting character: far from sinking into enigmatic silence, he explains that his motive was revenge for his father, an African king whom Alonso killed before making Zanga a slave. Prevented from killing himself and assured that he will be tortured, he triumphantly anticipates still greater opportunities to display his strength of character. Young even invests him with something like militant black pride, as when he gloats over his success:

Let Europe, and her pallid Sons, go weep,
Let Africk, and her hundred Thrones, rejoice.

(V, p. 241)

For William Hazlitt this line summed up the effect that *Othello* himself ought to produce (Hazlitt, V: 338). The speech in which Zanga calls himself one of the 'children of the sun / With whom revenge is virtue' (p. 243) was once widely quoted, and the phrase 'Child of the Sun' was used not only by admirers of the black American actor Ira Aldridge, who frequently played the part of Zanga, but by Aldridge himself. During the long debate over slavery in Britain, its colonies and its former colonies *Oroonoko* too was regarded primarily as an anti-slavery play, and, as Thomas Cartelli has shown, inspired adaptations which emphasized its political meaning (Cartelli, 144–5); Hazlitt expressed surprise that 'the piece is not prohibited' (Hazlitt, XVIII: 217). These plays about enslaved African princes had some influence on how *Othello* was perceived in the late eighteenth and early nineteenth centuries. Though Othello mentions being 'sold to slavery' as only one of many episodes in a long and rich life story, the very brevity with which he speaks of it came to signify depths of stoic endurance.

The acting text after the Restoration

It is possible that by 1660 *Othello* already existed in an acting edition, though the earliest surviving example of one is a marked-up copy of the third Folio (1663/4), as used in performances at the Smock Alley Theatre in Dublin in about 1678–82 (Evans, 3–5). Since the effect of most cuts was to soften the language and make the characters less morally ambiguous, Marvin Rosenberg, whose *Masks of Othello* (1964) gives the first detailed discussion of this important document, attributes them to the desire for decorum. Yet, as he notes, virtually all Iago's coarseness remains. A play as long as *Othello* is likely to have been shortened from the first; given the nature of its subject matter, almost *any* cut is likely to remove something indecorous. Several pages of the Folio volume are unfortunately missing, but it has been estimated that the play was in fact given in a rather full text, with only some 421 lines cut, as against twice that number in most eighteenth-century prompt-books (Evans, n. 23, 11). Many of the cuts, moreover, seem intended to get rid of obscure rather than obscene passages. As is well known, Shakespeare's writing is characterized by 'prolixity': that is, his characters often say things that are not directly necessary for the plot or for their immediate situation. It is precisely this prolixity that gives the illusion, so often noticed, that they have a life independent of their play. Almost every major character in *Othello* has moments of talking too much: both Othello and Cassio can sometimes be called bombastic, while Iago, Desdemona, Emilia and even Bianca tend to make the same point at excessive length. Many of the lines omitted from acting texts after the seventeenth century are easily cut parenthetical remarks.

Some other cuts may result from the changed nature of the post-Restoration theatre companies. The Clown is often cut from even the fullest modern texts of *Othello*, but he appears to have been present in London productions of the play until the end of the seventeenth century. Despite the Restoration contempt for the lowbrow Shakespearean Fool, who epitomized everything embarrassing in the prewar theatre, the low comedian remained a popular member of the company. The missing pages of the Smock Alley text include the first scene in which he appears; he was originally present in the entrance direction for III.iv, but then cut, evidence that probably suggests an early removal from the play. While Brabantio lost no significant lines (perhaps because every acting company had dignified elderly actors who needed to be kept employed), small parts got even smaller in the course of the eighteenth century. At Smock Alley the opening of II.i still included the dialogue between the gentlemen and Montano, though the three gentlemen were reduced to two and the dialogue was somewhat trimmed; by 1755 the scene began with Cassio's entrance, perhaps (as Francis Gentleman suggested in 1770) because the other speeches were considered too flowery for inexperienced minor actors. Although the theatre after 1660 needed all the female roles it could get, to supply its most popular actresses and fulfil the demand for 'female interest', all three of the female roles in *Othello* suffered considerably from cuts. The most damaging of these was IV.iii, the 'willow scene', which was initially played in something like the short Q version, then omitted altogether. In 1770 Francis Gentleman described it as 'trifling' and Emilia's speech as 'contemptible', adding that 'if Desdemona was to chaunt the lamentable ditty, and speak all that Shakespeare has allotted for her in this scene, an audience ... would not know whether to laugh or cry' (Gentleman, 146).

Bianca in the early eighteenth century was a part often used to introduce a very young actress, to judge from those whose names have survived from playbills of the period. She is last found in a cast list of 1740 and referred to in 1770 as 'totally excluded from the stage' (Gentleman, 145). She does not reappear until the end of the nineteenth century. The implications of her disappearance were far-reaching. Not only did Cassio become a blameless young man, apart from his easily forgivable lapse into drunkenness, but the end of the eavesdropping scene, when Othello actually receives the 'ocular proof' for which he has been asking, had to disappear. Thus when, in the final scene, Othello told Desdemona, 'By heaven, I saw my handkerchief in 's hand!' (V.ii.62), the line might easily have bewildered audiences unfamiliar with the play; a footnote in Edwin Forrest's published promptbook explains, 'This alludes to a scene always omitted in the representation' (Forrest, *Othello*, 65). It is not in fact clear whether the eavesdropping scene was cut because of Bianca or, rather, that Bianca's part was cut because the disappearance of this scene made her, as Gentleman put it, 'a mere excrescence of the plot' (145). Somewhere in the early eighteenth century the greater part of IV.i seems to have become unplayable. Some of Othello's speech before his fit is already marked for deletion in the Smock Alley text and the entire episode of the fit was removed later, since critics comment on the fact that Garrick restored it in 1746; it disappeared again between Garrick and Irving.

Alteration, as opposed to cutting, of the text might have a number of different motives. Eighteenth-century audiences heard such editorial emendations as Pope's replacement (in 1725) of the too-enigmatic 'I am not what I am' (I.i.64) with 'I am not what I seem'; acting editions even used the wild conjectures of Thomas Hanmer's 1743 edition, such as his attempt to solve the play's first textual crux, the line about Cassio's wife (I.i.19–20), by altering it to

One Michael Cassio (The Florentine's
A fair fellow, almost damn'd in a fair phyz).

The greatest controversy arose over the famous line 'Put out the light, and then put out the light' (V.ii.7). Most of the alterations, like the notes and editorial paraphrases accompanying them, were designed to make clear that the second half of the line is metaphorical, a fact that spectators were apparently not thought capable of understanding without assistance. In Henry Fielding's *Journey from this World to the Next* (1743) Shakespeare, in the Elysian Fields, is asked to adjudicate a debate between Thomas Betterton and Barton Booth over whether the line should be 'put out the light, and then – put out the light' (Hanmer's reading, which is here ascribed to Booth) or 'put out *thy* light' (as Fielding himself suggests) or, as another speaker suggests, 'put out *thee*, Light'. Shakespeare, who no longer remembers what he meant, says that he would never have written the line if he had realized how much trouble it was going to cause (Fielding, 39–40).

The omission and alteration of unacceptably coarse language began in the eighteenth century, though successive nineteenth-century acting texts refined on it. In fact, they go farther than Thomas Bowdler himself (or his sister, who was apparently responsible for much of the work), in the *Family Shakespeare* of 1818. Recognizing that the moral of the play was inextricable from its depiction of the degrading effects of jealousy (Bowdler, X: 241), Bowdler cuts but does not rewrite the text, and includes passages, like a somewhat shortened version of Emilia's speech in IV.iii, that were never performed. Acting texts, on the other hand, soften the language (replacing 'whore' by 'wanton', 'drab' or 'false'), or delete unacceptable phrases, making characters break off or interrupt each other, as when Edwin Forrest's Othello told Emilia,

'Cassio— ; ask thy husband else' (Forrest, 66; cf. V.ii.134). One writer praised Junius Brutus Booth for having 'chastened' Shakespeare: while retaining the words of Iago's obscene pun ('It is a common thing ... To have a foolish wife': III.iii.306–8), he repunctuated them, omitting Emilia's interjection, and the line became the harmless 'It is a common thing to have a foolish wife' (Gould, 89–90).

It was in the last two acts of the play that most changes were made, and at this point it is difficult to know which of several possible motives lies behind them. One, certainly, was the desire to move as quickly as possible from the onset of Othello's jealousy to his murder of Desdemona and the discovery of the truth. In 1878, when William Winter urged Edwin Booth to restore at least part of IV.i to his acting edition, the actor wrote that, in his experience, 'the quicker tragedy can be acted the better is the audience pleased' (Watermeier, *Letters*, 168). To maintain a rapid pace, the scenes were generally divided into those played in front of a curtain (usually representing a street, like I.i and ii and V.i) and the more spectacular ones (like the Venetian Senate of I.iii) revealed when the curtain was drawn. More revision was required when the play's scenery became more elaborate. When Booth partly restored the willow scene in 1869, Desdemona sang the song at the end of IV.ii; in Fechter's production, it was heard offstage at the beginning of V.ii. Both arrangements were designed to avoid an extra scene change.

The attack on Cassio and stabbing of Roderigo were sometimes cut from nineteenth-century productions, partly to avoid another scene change and partly on the grounds that Emilia reports them later in any case. The action evidently implies an outdoor setting, since characters come and go at will and respond to calls for help. But the fact that Iago leaves the stage after stabbing Cassio and then returns almost immediately 'in his shirt, with light and weapons' as Gratiano describes him (V.i.47), naturally led to questions about where he had been in the meantime. It made sense to place the scene at or near his lodgings, so as to explain what Emilia was doing there, although the absence of Bianca meant that there was little for Emilia to do once she had entered except to be sent off again. Booth's version avoided a scene change at an exciting stage of the play by conflating the Iago–Roderigo dialogue in IV.ii with the attack on Cassio in V.i, thus allowing time to set up the bedchamber scene. The two men met in the invaluable

'dark street', now located in front of Iago's house, and Iago explained, in a slightly adapted version of IV.ii.235–9, 'He sups to-night
with his mistress and this way he will come: he knows not yet of
his honourable fortune. You may take him at your pleasure ...' As
early as the Edmund Kean prompt-copy of 1831 there is a note
that a nightgown and candle should be ready for Iago in this
scene; like Macbeth, evidently, the early nineteenth-century Iago
pretended to have been roused from his bed (Folger promptbooks, no. 17). George Frederick Cooke also entered as if from his
own house, and at the end of the scene, since he had decided that
Iago's lodgings were separate from the castle, sent Emilia off in
the opposite direction (Hare, 191). When Booth and Irving played
together in 1881 Irving's Iago made an effect at this point by
vanishing from the stage fully clothed and reappearing almost at
once, at a window above, looking half-dressed. He did not bind
Cassio's wound with his shirt; Cassio sometimes bound it himself
(Sprague, *Actors*, 219) – with Desdemona's handkerchief – so that
Othello could later point to it when he asked, 'How came you,
Cassio, by that handkerchief / That was my wife's?' (V.ii.317–18).
Othello's brief appearance in V.i was always cut, and remains one
of the most frequently cut moments of the play. It is understand-
able that actors, with the exhausting murder scene still to play,
should happily forgo uttering the couplet:

> Forth from my heart those charms, thine eyes, are blotted,
> Thy bed, lust-stained, shall with lust's blood be spotted.
>
> (V.i.35–6)

It is also true that the entrance is more difficult to play on a realistically darkened stage than it would have been in the Jacobean
period, where the audience could have seen what was going on
while the darkness was coded by the use of lanterns and torches.

Some of the changes made in the final scene were theatrical
necessities: the eighteenth century obviously found difficulty in
understanding why the other characters learn of Desdemona's
murder only after they have already been onstage for sixteen lines
(something that can easily be explained on a large stage with a
curtained bed), so Emilia's crucial statement, 'My mistress here
lies murdered in her bed' (V.ii.181), was moved to an earlier position. Twentieth-century directors have usually been anxious to
end as quickly as possible after the murder, but what now looks
like an obsessive tying up of loose ends struck Francis Gentleman

as an 'interesting train of explanations' which he approved because 'they lead to strict poetical justice' (Gentleman, 146). Thus, Emilia was given plenty of opportunities to make an impression when she revealed the truth, even though she might temporarily steal the scene from Othello and Iago. She was not, however, allowed her death scene, or even her request to be laid beside her mistress. There would in fact have been little point in carrying out her request, since its purpose was to allow her to echo the willow song for Desdemona's ear alone, and the song was no longer part of the play. The surprising cut of Othello's 'I kissed thee ere I killed thee' couplet (V.ii.356–7) may, as has been suggested, result from nervousness about depicting a black man and a white woman on a bed together (Neill, 'Unproper', 407). It may also reflect an aesthetic reaction against the use of rhyme in drama; a critic in 1791 called it 'a trifling conceit in the mouth of a dying man' (Vickers, 565). The play ended abruptly with Othello's suicide, sometimes followed by his gasp of, 'O, Desdemona!', and perhaps Cassio's 'This did I fear' or the tribute, 'he was great of heart'.

As Virginia Vaughan has shown in a comparison of a number of nineteenth-century acting texts, both English and American, most productions of *Othello* in this period used largely the same text, with the same traditional business; they needed to do so, if star actors on tour were to play with a number of different companies after minimal rehearsal (Vaughan, 147–53). Most spectators probably did not realize how much the play they were seeing differed from the original Q and F texts. Some actors, like Forrest and Booth, tried to keep up with new Shakespeare editions and to read the notes; some, like Edwin Booth, even contributed to them or grumbled about having to give up a favourite reading that had been superseded (Watermeier, 176–7). Actors also prepared, or sponsored, acting editions enabling readers to visualize their performances. They were often urged to restore more of the original text, and, towards the end of the century, some began to do so, though, ironically, German productions, often in scholarly venues, were more likely than English ones to give the full Shakespearean text.

It was an actor's, not a director's theatre; if a production achieved a sense of wholeness, it was because of the general consensus of the performers as to what kind of play *Othello* was. The most important factor in any performance of *Othello*, the relative weighting of the two leading male roles and (to a lesser extent) the heroine, depended almost exclusively on the power of the actors playing them. The actors did not change their interpretations according to the production in which they played, except when they found that the scenic arrangements required a change in blocking. Part One of this book will therefore look separately at the playing of each of these three characters in the pre-twentieth-century theatre, with a final chapter about the transitional era when the consensus about their 'real' natures began to be questioned. Part Two will deal with a period in which directorial control affected the interpretation of all the play's characters, and it will then be appropriate to examine productions as a whole.

PART ONE

Othello before Robeson

CHAPTER I

Othello's play

Being a hero

The early history of Othello on the stage is the history of tragic acting, and particularly of a recognized theatrical type, the tragic hero. Perhaps overcompensating for the early association of actors with rogues and vagabonds, the post-Renaissance theatre has always been one of the most hierarchical of professions. As late as 1899 it could be taken for granted that 'The greatest actor is of course he who is greatest in the leading department of his art – viz. Tragedy' (Dechmann, 41). It is not surprising that Julie Hankey's extensive research on the play's theatrical history left her in no doubt that the nobility of Othello was 'the background assumption in every performance from Betterton to Robeson' (Hankey, 110). A theatre dominated by actors, and one in which the leading tragedian was usually the most powerful voice offstage as well as on, would not be likely to stage an *Othello* in which the title character was anything but noble and impressive.

Othello belonged so completely to the category of tragic hero that virtually everything said about the type can apply equally well to him. Indeed, it is sometimes hard to distinguish classical definitions of the heroic from Othello's own self-definition in the first part of the play. Just before his descent into misery, he declares that 'to be once in doubt / Is once to be resolved' (III. iii. 182–3). *The Thespian Praeceptor*, an acting manual published in 1811, must surely have had these words in mind when it insisted that, although 'The heroic mind has frequently doubts', it quickly deals with them; it 'pauses, examines, and determines: for the thing which it most abhors is indecision. The hero vanishes, whenever indecision appears.' In order to embody such a character, the actor must avoid certain mannerisms – taking short steps, swinging his arms in the air, holding his head back, or indeed doing anything that might suggest a state of confusion – 'for ordinary minds only are confused' (26–7). The most explicit advice on how to make Othello heroic came from playwright Aaron Hill. Writing in 1734 to an actor who had just made his debut in the role of Othello, he urged him to 'assume, from your very first step upon the stage, all that warlike boldness of air, that arises from keeping the nerves as well of the arms, as the legs, strongly braced, and the visage erect and aweful; carrying marks of that conscious superiority, inseparable from a character, so dignified as *Othello*'s' (Hill, I: 273). Hill also urged the actor to give more significance to Othello's lines: 'He says nothing, that is not *important*; therefore, *weight* should never be *absent*, in the *tone* that expresses it, no more than in the look that accompanies, or in the action that imprints it' (275). If this advice makes heroic acting sound intolerably pompous, it can perhaps be explained by the fact that Hill was writing to an inexperienced actor of modest social origins, Samuel Stephens, a London citizen and button-maker, whose success as Othello in his first stage appearance did in fact lead to a moderately successful theatrical career. But its emphasis is characteristic of the period.

Othello was not merely a hero, he was also a lover, the type, Hill maintained in his 'Essay on the Art of Acting', that comprises 'all serious dramatic characters, that an actor can expect to shine by' (Hill, *Works*, IV: 400). As Carol Carlisle has pointed out, what differentiated eighteenth-century Othellos was the degree to which they emphasized the hero or the lover (Carlisle, 197). Furthermore, the character embodied the passion of jealousy, which Hill considered the most demanding in the repertoire. He wrote about it at some length, in a passage that would be extensively borrowed by later writers:

> *Jealousy*, which is a mixture of passions, directly contrary to one another, can only justly be represented by one who is capable of delineating all those passions by turns. Jealousy shows itself by restlessness, peevishness, thoughtfulness, anxiety, absence of mind, &c.: sometimes it bursts out in piteous complaint and weeping; then a gleam of hope, that all is yet well, lights the countenance into a momentary smile. Immediately, the face clouded with gloom shows the mind overcast again with horrid suspicions and frightful imaginations. Then the arms are folded upon the breast, the fists violently clinched, the rolling eyes darting fury …

In parentheses, after the last sentence, Hill added Othello's name, indicating that this description was based either on what he had seen in the theatre or on what he thought ought to happen. The actor was expected not only to express each passion to the full but also to indicate its distinct stages. Hill insisted, in advice that would be repeated well into the next century, that the actor should make sure he feels each passion and makes it visible *before* he speaks, and that when he moves from one passion to another he should allow time for the audience to appreciate the transition between them.

While the emphasis here is mainly on facial expression, it is clear that much more than this was required. In Young's *The Revenge* (1721), the Iago-figure Zanga observes Alonso in a situation similar to Othello's: 'his knees smite one another; ... his Eye-balls roll in anguish'. A few lines later, he adds that Alonso is 'On the ground!' (IV, pp. 224–5). An acting manual of 1827 shows that such action was still expected of the actor a century later:

> As he must frequently fall upon the ground, he should previously raise both hands clasped together, in order to denote anguish, and which will at the same time prevent him from hurting himself ... This fall must be repeatedly studied, it being also necessary in *madness*, &c., and indeed jealousy may be termed madness.
>
> (Rede, 82)

Thus, the stately, dignified heroic actor, conscious on all occasions of his own superiority, was also obliged to depict extremes of mental anguish through a highly physical mime of self-abasement. Translating a German work first published in 1785, Sarah Siddons's son Henry, who had himself played Othello as well as seeing his uncle, John Philip Kemble, in the role, found nothing to change in the author's account of a highly pictorial depiction of passion: 'Whilst Othello, staggering from one side to the other, lifts one hand to his head, as if conscious of his approaching fit, and strikes the other upon his convulsed and agonised heart – whilst his tongue can only utter broken, half-connected sentences: we recognize in these external sensations of the *body* the modifications which affect the *soul*' (Siddons, 147). This is still, clearly, a coded language of gesture: the actor's hands touch his head and heart to show the effects of both reason and passion; body and soul are bridged by broken speech.

Appearance mattered more for Othello than for most roles. This is apparently why Garrick, despite his exceptional gifts, was unsuccessful in the part in 1745; he tried it in Dublin and London for another year, but soon gave it up. The comments of his contemporaries suggest that lack of stature, in both senses, may have been one cause. The text never says that Othello is tall, but readers and audiences were convinced that he must be. Perhaps there was an old tradition to this effect. Moorish giants marched in Elizabethan processions, and in Ben Jonson's *Poetaster* a boy who says that he will 'do the Moor' (III.iv.270) from George Peele's play *The Battle of Alcazar* rides on the shoulders of another actor. The 1777 Bell edition of Shakespeare's plays, based on the acting editions used in the theatres, states firmly that 'His appearance should be amiably elegant, and above the middle stature' (I: 10). He was also expected to have a beautiful voice, even though he is the only one of the three major characters not to sing in the course of the play. The actor who most fully incarnated these qualities, and who was thus the eighteenth century's most popular Othello, was the tall, handsome, melodious Spranger Barry (1719–77). His arrival in London in the autumn of 1746 marked an end of Garrick's struggle with a part that even the hard-to-please Francis Gentleman admitted Barry was born to play. Gentleman's praise of Barry illustrates the practice of seeing the character as a series of passions through which the actor was expected to chart a clearly marked course: 'he happily exhibited the hero, the lover, and the distracted husband; he rose through all the passions to the utmost extent of critical imagination, yet still appeared to leave an unexhausted fund of expression behind' (Gentleman, 151). The sense of relaxed power and control is important, as is the choice of the verb 'rose'. Barry evidently made the role an upward, triumphal progression through extremes of beautifully expressed emotion, rather than a descent into brutality, diseased imagination, and self-loathing.

Something of what Barry did can be learned from the analysis in which Samuel Foote, himself an actor and mimic, focuses on his performance in Act III. He begins with Othello's speech, 'This fellow's of exceeding honesty' (III.iii.262):

his Fury begins at,
If I do prove her Haggard.
And subsides at,
Happ'ly for I am black.
Then a sudden Reflection destroys his Coolness, and the Thoughts of her being gone, and that his only Relief was to loath her, hurries him into a fresh Tempest of Impatience and Despair.

Though Foote sometimes writes as if Barry and Othello were one, this is because he clearly feels that the actor fully embodied all the theatrical possibilities of the role, which meant, particularly, its opportunities for startling transitions. At the entrance of Desdemona, the actor has the opportunity for an 'immediate Drop from a Whirlwind to a Calm' (Foote, 30–1). The famous 'farewell' speech is 'finely calculated by the Author for the Advantage of the Actor' – first, because of the contrast between 'the resign'd, calm Despair' of the farewell and the rage with which Othello turns on Iago at 'Villain, be sure thou prove my love a whore' (III.iii.362); second, because Iago's interjections are skilfully used to provide 'breathing Places for *Othello*' in what is really a single long speech (32).

What is important in the way Foote and Gentleman describe Barry is their sense of Othello as a series of magnificent opportunities for an actor rather than a study of pathological degeneration. It is this that explains why the role, despite its acknowledged difficulty, was frequently chosen by actors for their debuts. In this period, completely unknown amateurs with theatrical aspirations (such as Samuel Stephens in 1734) were allowed, for a price, to play leading roles with a professional cast – billed, so as not to embarrass their relatives, simply as 'a Citizen for his diversion' (New Haymarket Theatre, 26 April 1744), or 'a Young Gentleman' (Drury Lane, 17 October 1761). In a performance on 7 March 1751 the entire cast of *Othello* consisted of aristocratic amateurs, the Delaval family and friends, who had been coached by the distinguished actor and acting teacher Charles Macklin. Virginia Vaughan, who gives a full account of this performance (113–34), points out that the Delavals were admired because, being gentlemen, 'they were in reality what they represented' (129) and that their success followed a season in which Garrick had finally given up trying to compete with Barry's immense success as Othello. Both incidents illustrate the degree to which audiences, in the particular case of Othello, insisted on identification between the actor and their conception of the character. 'A really worthy man may perhaps represent strongly the character of a villain,' wrote Gilbert Austin in 1806, 'but the contrary will not hold, that a mean fellow will represent well the character of a hero' (Austin, 98). This view derives from the classical and humanist tradition of oratory, which insists that the good orator is also a good man. It loses sight of the obvious distinction between the orator speaking his own words (or those written for him to speak in his own person) and the actor speaking words written by and for another person. Yet there has always been blurring between the roles of orator/politician and actor, just as there has always been a tendency to identify actor with character. In the second phase of Othello's stage life, the romantic one, the practice would become still more widespread.

Othello's makeup

And yet, of course, none of these actors was identical with Othello in the respect that has seemed most important in recent productions: his colour. From the beginning, the play's stage history has included anecdotes about the problems of getting the right makeup and of keeping it from coming off on the other actors – a problem not only for Othello but for the two other important 'black' roles, Oroonoko in Southerne's play and Zanga in Young's *The Revenge*. Theatrical makeup could be such a nuisance that Leman Thomas Rede, in *The Road to the Stage* (1827), recalls that one actor had it written into his contract that he should never be required 'to blacken his face or to descend a trap door' (Rede, 67). Garrick's friends attributed his lack of success as Othello to the fact that 'the expression of the mind was wholly lost' under his dark makeup (Murphy, I: 106). The anecdotes told about his reception (his rival Quin joked that he looked like a little black servant) suggest that he may even have provoked unintended laughter. In 1770 an admirer of Garrick published a proposal for a temple to Shakespeare and Garrick, which was to include paintings of every other major tragic or comic character. He omitted Othello, supposedly because 'the blacking screens, and renders incommunicable to spectators, all impassioned working of the countenance' (Hiffernan, 6), but really, I suspect, so as to avoid reminding the actor of his one great failure in a Shakespearean tragic role.

Yet those who write of Spranger Barry's emotional impact on his audience never said that makeup prevented him from conveying the transitions from one passion to another. One can only speculate on whether facial expression mattered less to a more statuesque actor than to the quicker and subtler Garrick. Rede himself, perhaps the earliest writer on stage makeup, recommends a layer of carmine on top of the black around the lips and eyes as a way of avoiding a too-uniform look and added that in the role of Othello black makeup, 'as being destructive of the effect of the face, and preventing the possibility of the expression being noted, has become an obsolete custom' (39). This statement has been taken too literally. Shortly before Rede's book was first published, Edmund Kean had lightened the colour of the character's makeup from black to tawny, and his choice influenced many nineteenth-century actors, but there is evidence that black makeup, made from lampblack, continued to be worn for some time; it would have been difficult for itinerant actors to find anything better or cheaper (Lower, 205–15).

Gloves were also important for the actor of this part. They were in any case widely worn from the Renaissance through the nineteenth century; Hankey notes the significance of Macready's promptbook reminder that Desdemona should *not* wear gloves in III.iv, where Othello has to take her hand and comment on its temperature (257). James Quin, in the early eighteenth century, wore white gloves in order to pull one off and reveal the blackness of the hand beneath it (Gentleman, 152). Later, Rede notes with disapproval, some actors of 'black' roles started wearing black gloves or black silk arms, instead of makeup (Rede, 38–9). This practice must have continued for some time. The actor-manager Lena Ashwell (1872–1957) recalled an Othello that she saw as a child: 'His face was very black – he wore black gloves and appeared to be black all over until he waved his arms about, and then, where the gloves ended, he was very white, and that was exciting to watch' (Ashwell, 3).

The gloves were needed more as acting became more physical. Garrick is said to have been criticized for seizing hold of the arm of the person he was talking to, and as late as 1828 someone who called himself 'a veteran stager' was insisting that, 'To preserve what is termed stage effect, actors should never approach nearer to each other, than that by extending their arms, they may be able to take hold of hands' (Grant, 186–7). In the case of *Othello*, the demands of the heroic role coincided with the very practical need to avoid getting makeup on the other actors. One of the play's oldest and most famous bits of business – though one for which there are no stage directions in either the Quarto or Folio text – involves Othello in physically threatening, even attacking, Iago in III.iii, thus providing the motivation for Iago's 'O grace! O heaven forgive me!' (III.iii.376). It came to be called the 'collaring scene', which suggests its violence; if it derives from theatrical tradition, it may have been meant to create a visual parallel between what Othello does to Iago and what Iago vindictively urges him to do to Desdemona. John Coleman, who always refused to act with gloves on, regretted the fact that he let himself get carried away in this scene opposite Macready's Iago; despite attempting to rub off the makeup on his hands before Act III, he found that he had 'left the marks of my ten fingers in his beautiful white cashmere dress' (Coleman, I: 41). Othello thus had good reason to keep everyone at arm's length. Playing Desdemona in 1881, Ellen Terry noted appreciatively that Edwin Booth promised never to make her black (he always held a fold of his robe between his hand and hers), whereas Henry Irving, who was alternating the part with him, generally left her 'as black as he' (Terry, 160). Uneasiness about Othello's physical contact with Desdemona was based on a double vision: in one view, a black man was touching a white woman, yet everyone knew that, on the contrary, a male actor heavily made up to look black was touching a white female actor who might be wearing equally heavy makeup to whiten her skin still further.

Kean and his influence

The insistence that Othello must have a heroic physique finally weakened at the beginning of the nineteenth century, faced with a contradiction too obvious to ignore. John Philip Kemble (1757–1823) had dominated the London stage since the 1780s, both as actor and manager; like Spranger Barry, he was a tall and impressive-looking actor, but Othello was not one of his best roles. In the second decade of the nineteenth century three new actors would appear to challenge his status: Edmund Kean in 1814, William Charles Macready in 1816 and Junius Brutus Booth in 1817. None of them had Kemble's physical advantages: Kean and Booth were both short and Macready, though reasonably tall, could never have been described as handsome. It was Kean, the first one on the scene, who was to remain a reference point for much of the century. As Jonathan Bate has noted, the existence of a 'Kemble dynasty' at Covent Garden made it tempting for critics with radical sympathies, like Hazlitt, to identify the new actor with revolutionary politics (Bate, 137). Moreover, the ambivalence of young English writers and artists towards the diminutive military genius, Napoleon, carried over into their enthusiasm for Kean.

Thus, Edmund Kean (1787–1833) achieved an extraordinary success as Othello – many considered it the culmination of his art – despite his lack of most of the qualities traditionally considered indispensable. He was 5 feet 6 inches, according to his autopsy, and most of those who saw him act thought that he was even shorter than that (Abel, 95). He appears to have compensated for lack of stature, like Garrick, with incessant movement (104–5), while the lighter makeup that he introduced for this role was intended to make sure that his facial expression was visible, as Garrick's had not been, in theatres much larger than those where Garrick played. His costume, which he devised himself, suggested Othello's exotic background. A hostile theatregoer wrote that he resembled not a Venetian general, but 'a little vixenish black girl, in short petticoats', in 'a habiliment as was never seen any where but on the stage' (Robson, 9); even his admirer Hazlitt said that he played the part like a gypsy. This is the costume in the portrait by E. F. Lambert (figure 1); he apparently has bare arms and legs, though in the cheap coloured reproductions I have seen he looks as if he were wearing long sleeves and leggings. Did the artist find the exposed flesh an embarrassment, or did Kean avoid the bother of overall makeup by wearing black 'fleshings'? The discrepancy might explain why, as Carol Carlisle (190–1) points out, the Lambert image looks more 'Negro' than the other portrait of Kean in this role (figure 2), by J. W. Gear. His fingernails are visible, showing that he disdained to wear gloves. The costume was obviously designed to allow freedom of movement, unlike the long robes of the statuesque 'Moorish' Othellos. It emphasized the litheness and agility, but also the vulnerability, of the hero.

The two portraits give some idea of Kean's range. Gear's supposedly illustrates him in his first scene, declaring, 'Were it my cue to fight, I should have known it / Without a prompter' (I.ii. 83–4). Radiating confidence and a malicious recklessness that suggests why Byron and other romantic writers found him so irresistible, he is said to have delivered this line with 'a wonderful mixture of sarcasm and courtesy' that 'always brought down the house' (Vandenhoff, 22). But reviewers generally felt that the first two acts of the play – when Barry or Kemble would have established the character's effortless dignity as a hero and lover – were not Kean's best. Many of his effects came from a sudden drop into the colloquial and naturalistic, after a passage in the grand style, as when he followed his elegant speech to the senate with a quick,

1 E. F. Lambert, Edmund Kean as Othello, reacting to Iago's
'O, beware, my lord, of jealousy!'

2 J. W. Gear, Edmund Kean as Othello, saying 'Were it my cue
to fight, I should have known it / Without a prompter'

casual–'Here comes the lady' (I.iii.171), which struck some as a cheap trick. Some thought that he was too quick, too angry, even when he called Brabantio 'Good signior' (Sprague, *Players*, 79–80). Yet by the time he arrived at Cyprus he had become more subdued. Even in giving the instruction to 'Silence that dreadful bell' (II.ii.171), he apparently spoke 'more in sorrow than in anger' (*Variorum*, 139) and his grief at being obliged to dismiss Cassio set the tone for the rest of the play.

It was in Act III that he came into his own. One spectator, not an admirer, nevertheless said after one performance 'that his speaking of the words "and so she did," was so exactly the voice of nature that it made her jump' (Dyce, 59). The Lambert portrait, if it really does show Kean's reaction to Iago's 'O beware, my lord, of jealousy!' (III.iii.167), indicates that he began to crumble at a surprisingly early point in the play. This portrait seems to catch another habit mentioned by a reviewer in Philadelphia in 1821: 'his hands are kept in unremitting and the most rapid, convulsive movement; seeking, as it were, a resting place in some part of his upper dress, and occasionally pressed together on the crown of his head' (quoted in Hillebrand, 368). Hazlitt too refers to 'the convulsed movement' of his hands as well as 'the involuntary swelling of the veins in the forehead' (XVIII: 394).

The highlight of his performance, the moment for which audiences waited, was his delivery of 'O now for ever / Farewell the tranquil mind' (III.iii.250–1). There is little specific evidence of how he produced such an overwhelming effect of 'utter loneliness of heart'. One writer claimed to have heard that he prolonged the liquids 'l' and 'r', as in 'Farewell-l-l the pl-l-luméd trrroop' (Gould, 28). Perhaps this was the source of the strange echo effect mentioned in 1817: 'his voice seemed to be going away for ever. You felt alone after he had spoken' (*The Champion*, 23 February 1817). Edwin Forrest, who played Iago to Kean's Othello when the latter was in Albany in 1825, regarded the experience as one of the highlights of his life (Alger, II: 559). Like others, he remembered the 'Farewell' best: 'I have tried for years and years to read it as he read it to produce the effect with it that he produced, yet I have never succeeded but once … God Almighty was pleased to inspire me for the one occasion, and for that one only' (Ayers, 24). Kean's earliest biographer remembers the indescribable pathos of 'O Desdemona, away, away, away!' (IV.ii.42): 'His words sunk, by gentle gradations, from reproof into compassion; from compassion into a faint, tender, and indistinct sound; which itself gradually expired, like the sound of a melancholy echo' (Procter, II: 247–8). Where one might have expected rage, as in the last scene, he played much more quietly, with 'Fool! fool!' not howled out but spoken 'with a half smile of wonder' (Sprague, *Players*, 85). When Macready first attempted the role in 1816 and used a 'childish treble' for 'Othello's occupation's gone', Hazlitt described him as whining (Hazlitt, V: 339). John Forster used the same term for Edwin Forrest's Othello in 1836 (Shattuck, 75). Kean seems to have been a dangerous example to follow.

Even Kean's admirers thought that he tended to make every role into his own image; as Frances Kemble put it, 'he intends that all his parts should be *him*' (F. Kemble, *Girlhood*, 430). As Hazlitt wrote, describing his Oroonoko, 'The strokes of passion which came unlooked for and seemed to take the actor by surprise, were those that took the audience by surprise, and only found relief in tears' (XVIII: 216). This capacity to surprise the audience applied only to his first nights; Kean was in fact a very controlled actor who worked out his 'points' with care and differed from night to night only in that sometimes he made them more forcefully than at others. But the point was that his audience wanted to identify him with his roles – as they had not wanted to identify Garrick or Barry. For them he was not merely embodying a series of already existing passions but expressing his own feelings through the roles he played. In the case of Othello he played the part so often that it is not surprising that many of the crucial events of his life should be in some way connected with it. In 1825, when he was found guilty in a sensational adultery case, the lawyer for the plaintiff quoted *Othello* III.iii.341 in speaking of the wife's 'stolen hours of lust' (*Full Report*, 10). It was inevitable that the audience would show their moral outrage during performances of the play: a note written by the prompter on the acting text states that because of 'a great row' one performance in January was over in only two hours and eight minutes, rather than the slightly more than three and a half that seems to have been the norm in the period (Folger promptbook no. 20). It was while he was playing Othello in 1832, with his son Charles as Iago, that he collapsed during the strenuous third act, unable to finish the performance.

Stories about excessive identification with the role are also told about Kean's three near-contemporaries. Junius Brutus Booth (1796–1852), initially accused of being an imitator of Kean, emigrated to America after abandoning his wife and child for another woman. His biographer records that 'Among Jews, he was counted a Jew. He was as familiar with the Koran as with the Hebrew Scriptures, and would name a child of his after a wife of Mahomet' (Gould, 189); the only public reading he ever gave was of *The Ancient Mariner*, another work about an exile (Gould, 186). It sounds as if he was self-consciously identifying himself with the Other in every possible manifestation: his son Edwin recalled that on days when his father was to play Othello he 'would, perhaps, wear a crescent pin on his breast that day; or, disregarding the fact that Shakspere's Moor was a Christian, he would mumble maxims of the Koran' (Woods, 21).

Edwin Forrest (1806–72), who had been a touring player for years, shot at once to the top of his profession after a triumphantly successful debut as Othello in 1826. His approach to the part, as to all parts, was based on his sense of his own nationality as an American. His official biographer, William Alger, saw Forrest as a novelty among actors in that 'he embodied the democratic ideal of the intrinsic independence and royalty of man'; he was particularly happy to be 'the impersonator of oppressed races' (Alger, II: 665) and in 1828, just after his first great successes, he endowed a prize for (and agreed to star in) the best five-act tragedy featuring a native American. Initially much of his effect depended on his remarkable physical prowess. The Editorial Introduction to his acting edition of the play insists that the chief requirement for Othello is 'great physical power in the impersonation ... The passions by which the Moor is torn, are of that intense, explosive description, that no resources of art can supply the lack of extraordinary vocal energy, and that excitability of temper, which fuses the actor's sympathies into the one great emotion he is portraying' (Forrest, *Othello*, n.p.). Although Forrest was of course exploiting his own natural advantages, which he cultivated through rigorous diet and physical training, his emphasis on the body was also political; Alger's biography points out the importance of gymnastics in the great days of Athenian democracy (Alger, II: 560–3). In the text as Alger quotes it, Forrest seems to have omitted the lines in which Othello claims to descend from 'men of royal siege' (II: 769). 'His democratic soul despised courtly fashion and paid its homage only at the shrine of native universal manhood' (II: 474).

Phrases such as 'elemental' and 'natural' are constantly used of Forrest. Some compared him to Niagara Falls (Shattuck, 62). In

Alger's description of the great scene of III.iii the actor virtually becomes a landscape, first classical and then distinctly American. Iago gazes

> on the awful convulsions in the face of his victim as one might look into the crater of Vesuvius. That which had seemed granite proved to be gunpowder. As with the prairie fire: the traveller lets a spark fall, and the whole earth seems to be one rushing flame. (II: 773)

Reviewers compared Forrest (admiringly) to a wild animal; his pacing up and down, which they often mention, is confirmed by the promptbook directions for numerous crosses to left and right in III.iii. As a young man, he used stage tricks to make blood flow on stage, though he later adopted a more restrained approach (Alger, II: 646). The introduction to his edition says that he 'appears like a blinded giant by the side of his crafty tormentor Iago'. The Samson image became still more appropriate in 1851, when he brought an unsuccessful divorce action against his wife for adultery; after that, Shattuck records, 'Othello's fancied wrongs became his real ones, and he underscored every line in the play which conveyed that message' (Shattuck, 85).

Alger, like other reviewers, makes a point of contrasting Forrest with his English rival, William Charles Macready (1793–1873), whom he describes as highly polished but more like an actor than a human being: his Othello 'might secure admiring criticism but could never move feeling' (II: 778). The determination of Americans to treat the two men as symbols, respectively, of effete Englishmen and plain, honest Americans eventually led to the riots of Forrest supporters during Macready's American tour in 1849, which culminated in the death of thirty people outside the Astor Place Opera House in New York. Forrest refused to repudiate the violence that had been committed partly on his behalf. Ironically, Macready himself despised royalty and aristocracy and, though irreproachably Victorian in his private life, was, in the theatre, just as violent and animal-like as Forrest. Fanny Kemble, preparing to play Desdemona to his Othello in 1848, had heard of 'actresses whose arms had been almost wrenched out of their sockets, and who had been bruised black and blue, buffeted alike by his rage and his tenderness' (Kemble, *Later*, 637). Once they got onstage together, she complained that 'he keeps no specific time for his entrances and exits', paces about 'like a tiger in his cage' so that 'I never know on what side of me he means to be', and 'keeps up a perpetual snarling and grumbling like the aforesaid tiger, so that I never feel quite sure that he *has done* and that it is my turn to speak' (*Later*, 642). The finest actor of an age lacking in great actors, this highly intelligent and self-critical man was apparently without an ear for blank verse, and anger came more easily to him than melancholy. After being criticized for 'a pitiful sensibility, not consistent with the dignity and masculine imagination of the character' (Hazlitt, V: 339), he seems to have gone to the opposite extreme, playing Othello in a state of passion almost from the start and becoming jealous almost as soon as Iago said, 'I like not that'. A French critic had heard him described as a wild beast smelling blood (Thierry, 872).

This violent, larger-than-life acting was partly the consequence of the kinds of theatre for which Forrest and Macready played in the first half of the nineteenth century. In London, the growth of the city's population and the Licensing Act of 1743, which allowed only two 'legitimate' theatres in London, had led to the building of increasingly large playhouses. Large theatres meant more seats at lower prices, and hence increasingly large, popular and unruly audiences. Gradually, after Parliament ended the theatre mono-poly in 1843, a change began to be apparent. The giant playhouses were now used only for musical theatre, while a number of smaller ones, with smaller and more comfortable auditoriums, attracted a more select audience, prepared to respond to a more subdued and 'realistic' kind of performance. One interesting by-product was Charles Fechter's *Othello* at the Princess Theatre, London, in 1861. This is the first *Othello* to result in an acting text that reads like a modern play, with stage directions describing the appear-ance of the characters and explaining the subtext of their lines. It was modern in other ways too: there was a good deal of furniture and characters actually sat or leaned on it; Othello was examining papers as Iago began his temptation in Act III (a bit of business, apparently new then, that is still used in many productions), and Desdemona and Emilia were sewing in several of their scenes together. He broke up speeches that had been treated as pure declamation: 'Rude am I in my speech' (I.iii.82) became an apology, after he had said 'No more!' so vehemently as to startle the senators. In IV.ii, with Desdemona, he made a transition of the opposite kind, falling briefly into the 'tones of the old gentle-ness' at line 42 before reverting to jealous fury (Morley, 228, 230). This 'realistic' approach to the tragedy, especially as it manifested itself in Fechter's performance as Othello, was too innovative for many reviewers. G.H. Lewes complained that he was 'unpleasantly familiar, paws Iago about like an over demonstrative schoolboy, shakes hands on the slightest provocation; and bears himself like the hero of French *drame*, but not like a hero of tragedy' (128).

The acting edition exposed Fechter to adverse comment even from those, like Macready, who had not seen his performance (Carlisle, 202–3). Today it may make his production sound more coherent than in fact it was. He may have been the first actor to make racism an important factor in the tragedy, though it is not always clear whether the racism was critiqued or endorsed. He emphasized Othello's dangerous lack of control: though he did not show him falling into a fit, he played the opening of IV.i lying on the ground as if recovering from it, and in earlier scenes suggested the onset of illness in 'convulsive twitchings and involuntary drawings of the corners of the mouth till all the teeth are bare' (Morley, 230). He represented Othello reacting with disgust to the sight of himself in a mirror just before the soliloquy beginning 'Haply for I am black'. At the beginning of V.ii he said 'It is the cause' while looking into a mirror which had dropped from Desdemona's hand when she fell asleep; in disgust, he then flung the mirror out of the window and into the sea. Critic Henry Morley took him at first to be commenting on Desdemona's vanity, and was not placated when he learned from the acting text that Othello was ashamed to name his skin color to the chaste stars (231). Fechter's stage direction for the scene with Emilia after the murder suggests that Othello, far from being disturbed at Desdemona's willingness to lie for his sake, takes her sin as a justification for his own act: he is described as '*delivered from remorse, and returning to his savage nature*'. His playing of the final speech – forcing Iago to act the part of the 'turbaned Turk' and then, at the last minute, killing himself instead of the villain – has been criticized as melodramatic, but it is consistent with the self-disgust that he seems to have made a dominant note of Othello's character. Fechter was a rather unattractive actor who spoke with a French accent, and it is likely that this fact weighed still more heavily against him than any of his directorial concepts. But his intimations of savagery in Othello may have prepared audiences to accept the much more violent interpretation of Salvini, some fifteen years later.

Salvini versus Booth

What Kean's Othello was in the first half of the nineteenth century, that of Tommaso Salvini (1829–1915) was to the second, a reference point to which everyone else was compared. Though Salvini began playing Othello in Italy in 1856, his interpretation was not seen in the English-speaking world until 1874 (the United States) and 1875 (England). To understand the shock he produced, it is important to realize how completely the Anglo-American tradition had emphasized the beauty of Othello's speech and his sufferings at the expense of many of the things he actually said and did. Because Salvini acted in Italian, audiences were more conscious of his actions than of his words. Initially he performed on tour with his own Italian company, but later acted with supporting actors in his host country. Audiences, whether watching the play as a partial dumb-show or following it in a libretto, were in no doubt that they were seeing a man passionately in love with his wife, passionately determined that she must die, and brutal in his killing of her. Henry James, reviewing the production in Boston in 1883, noted that 'some people, apparently, are much surprised to discover that the representation of this tragedy is painful' (James, 174).

The actors with whom Salvini was most often contrasted were Edwin Booth (1833–93) in America and Henry Irving (1838–1905) in England. Booth already had a long career as both Othello and Iago at the time of Salvini's first visit to America, and there is no doubt that he thought of himself – just as did the critics – as representing a contrary tradition. It is relatively easy to compare the two actors because their performances are unusually well documented: both left behind promptbooks and notes on their playing of Othello, both had devoted admirers who recorded their performances in detail, and both commented on some of these observations. The detailed notes made by Edward Tuckerman Mason on Salvini's performances between 1881 and 1882 were translated into Italian and sent to the actor, who returned them with comments in 1883. Mason saw the production again in 1889 and added extensively to the notes on which Salvini had already commented. He saw it again in 1890, when he made a final revision (Mason, v–vii). Booth wrote notes and answered questions for his friend Horace Howard Furness when the latter was preparing his *Variorum* edition of the play; other accounts of his

Othello, which he did not see, were written by Mary Isabella Stone in 1883, and by Kitty Malony, a young actress who played in his touring company in 1887–88. These observers deal mainly with the later years of Booth and Salvini, at which point their interpretations had become firmly fixed. Salvini played the part every year, and insisted on never playing it more than three times a week: 'It exhausts him so, so wears upon his magnetism,' explained the New York theatre programme of 1874, 'that he cannot perform it two nights successively' (*Salvini Programme*). Booth also found the role exhausting, and in fact preferred to avoid it; during his 1887–88 national tour, though audiences were eager to compare his performance with the recent national tour of Salvini, he could be persuaded to act it only once.

Booth's Othello was essentially a continuation of the early nineteenth-century tradition, but, if anything, even more gently melancholic than his predecessors'. Speeches that others, such as Salvini and Fechter, spoke angrily, such as 'If I do prove her haggard', he spoke, as he told Furness they should be spoken, 'more with anguish than with anger' (Furness, *Variorum*, 190). Such a man could never have committed premeditated murder; rather, as one reviewer said, his action seemed the result of 'a sudden access of rage' brought on by Desdemona's weeping for Cassio (*San Francisco Chronicle*, 15 March 1888), and he kept his face averted from what he was doing. To some extent, he was responding to the increased delicacy of audiences. A Philadelphia newspaper in 1863 commented with disgust on Forrest's supposed sensuality: 'That tender meeting of *Othello* and *Desdemona* at Cyprus is transformed by him into a bold, unveiled exhibition of uxorious love. There was not a particle of delicacy in his embraces and oft-repeated kisses, nor did the couple seem to have the slightest objection to hugging each other continually before the assembled citizens of the town' (*Philadelphia Sunday Dispatch*, February 1863). Booth described the same moment to Furness in the opposite terms: 'They embrace, with delicacy. There is nothing of the animal in this "noble savage"' (Furness, *Variorum*, 113).

By contrast, spectators were shocked at what they took to be Salvini's animal behaviour. Yet Salvini himself insisted that Othello's love for Desdemona was 'poetical, not sensual' (Woods, 96), and the evidence indicates that, despite the critics' tendency to treat them as polar opposites, Booth and Salvini were not in fact very far apart in their conception – as opposed to their execution – of the

[41]

part. Both, for example, sought simplicity and modesty in the senate scene; a French reviewer thought that Salvini was almost shy (Thierry, 872). In the senate scene, Booth aimed for an effect of understated modesty, and 'playfully' acknowledged the Duke's 'I think this tale would win my daughter too' (I.iii.172), but turned away while Brabantio questioned Desdemona in case anyone should think that he was attempting to influence her unfairly (Furness, *Variorum*, 62). Both also avoided becoming jealous too early; instead of making 'O misery' (sometimes repeated) into an expression of jealous rage, both men (Booth thought he himself was the first to do so) spoke the line as a comment on jealous men in general rather than as something they considered relevant to them (Watermeier, 170). Booth apparently began to be uneasy while Iago slowly delivered the speech beginning 'Poor and content is rich, and rich enough' (III.iii.174). This was much earlier than Salvini, who let himself be persuaded only by Iago's reminder that he knew Venice better than Othello and that Desdemona had already deceived her father. But Booth also played Iago (something which Salvini attempted only briefly, at the end of his career), and thus probably had a higher opinion of the villain's powers of persuasion.

It was the physical appearance of the two that, more than anything, led critics and audiences to see them so differently. Salvini was, or appeared, large and powerful, Booth small and frail (he complained that people thought him ill even when he was in perfect health: Watermeier, 212). Though Booth had the dark hair and eyes of a southern European, he was of course perceived as American, while the Italian actor was inevitably isolated both by his language and by his vast superiority to most of the actors who were willing to take part in his bilingual touring productions. However, *what* Salvini was saying may also have made a difference, especially to audiences who saw him in the all-Italian version. Though his text was not an adaptation but a translation (by Giulio Carcano), his cuts and interpolated stage business accentuated Othello's importance while making his dominance seem natural and unforced. Many of his cuts were traditional (for instance, the eavesdropping scene; he argued that it was 'not in accord with Othello's character' to remain silent while hearing Cassio apparently confessing to adultery), and although he played the willow scene in Italy he omitted it when playing with Anglo-American actors. But the Italian text also omitted the first two scenes, which establish Iago's hatred for Othello as the frame of the play; Iago, in Salvini's production, was always a minor role. Othello's control of the action is particularly striking in the final scene. Emilia, threatened by Iago, rushes to the others begging them to save her, and it is evidently Othello who stands between her and her husband (she does not in fact die in this version). As she blurts out her explanation, it is, again, Othello who urges her on with interpolated phrases: 'Finisci', 'Parla', 'Or bene?' (Salvini, *Othello*, 84). The reactions of the other characters also help him to retain the respect of the audience. He is never disarmed; he throws down one weapon of his own accord but later wounds Iago with a sword seized from Montano's scabbard. Even when Lodovico tells the others to disarm Othello, there is no indication that anyone has the nerve to do so; instead he replies, 'Deh! Un istante!' ('Soft you!'), and they apparently wait, hypnotized by his words, forgetting until too late that he is still holding a weapon.

In other respects Salvini was the opposite of the passionate Latin his spectators may have hoped to see. His own self-description in his autobiography sounds very much like the Moor that he chose to play and suggests that he deliberately sought to depict contradictory qualities: 'Though apparently self-controlled, I was very violent when my anger was awakened. I was patient in a very high degree, but firm and resolute in my decisions. I was constant when once my affection was seriously given, but changeable in my sympathies. Friendship was a religion for me ...' (Salvini, *Leaves*, 85–6) As Othello, he was self-controlled and happy at the beginning, with no foreshadowing of the later tragedy; Stanislavski thought that he was like Romeo (Stanislavski, *Life*, 266). Mason's detailed account of his delivery of the speech to the senate suggests that, like other actors playing in a language unfamiliar to their audience, Salvini relied extensively on gesture to make himself understood, virtually miming the deserts, the hills, the cannibals ('by a gesture with both hands, as if repelling the man-eaters'), and the 'men whose heads do grow beneath their shoulders' ('by a very graceful action, touching his own head with both hands, and lowering his hands to his breast'). He even imitated Desdemona's voice, as he quoted her words to him, making a dramatic contrast when he returned to his own voice, and 'his own passionate joy', in 'Upon this hint I spake' (Mason, 13).

In Act III he was good-humoured in his conversation with Desdemona, listening to her pleading for Cassio 'as one might attend to the prattle of a favorite child', and attempting at the same time to deal with paperwork, until she finally took the pen from his hand on 'tomorrow dinner, then?" (Mason, 32). At the end of their little scene he was about to kiss her until he saw Emilia and Iago and stopped (Salvini added the note: 'from modesty': 34). Like Fechter, he made Othello do paperwork in III.iii and was initially annoyed with Iago for interrupting him; he made his first 'Indeed' an ironical imitation of Iago's manner, and even when Iago stated his views openly, on 'observe her well with Cassio', he shook his head 'in angry negative' (41). Even though the next part of Iago's speech ('I know our country disposition well') marked the beginning of his anxiety, he was still indignant at the accusation of Desdemona: on 'he thought 'twas witchcraft', his hand went to his sword (42). Salvini's speaking of 'not a jot' was a famous moment in his performance as it had been in Kean's (Archer, 167). But when Mason sent his comments to Salvini for checking, he found that they differed over the motivation behind it. Salvini thought he spoke the line in 'an indifferent tone' while Mason heard it as 'a tone scarcely audible, husky with repressed passion' (42). As Julie Hankey comments, Salvini had become so identified with the role that he 'believed himself to be concealing (as Othello) what, as Othello, he could not help disclosing' (Hankey, 233).

What critics remembered best, however, were the moments of strength and violence. This is not surprising: these are things that cannot be faked. Stanislavski, who saw him late in his career, recalls that in the scene of the fight on Cyprus he looked at Cassio and Montano 'so terribly with his tremendous eyes, he lifted his curved scimitar, making it flash in the air, turned it, and lowered it with such Eastern ease and swiftness, that we understood at once how dangerous it was to play with him ...' (Stanislavski, *Life*, 268). He attacked Iago with violence in III.iii, to the audience's delight, but he murdered Desdemona behind the bedcurtains and, as in classical tragedy, allowed the audience to imagine what had happened. There was a long pause, broken by the sound of Emilia's knocking and calling. Finally, 'the curtains opened a little and Othello's face, wild eyed, was thrust out, and withdrawn. The tension was almost insufferable' (Towse, 163–4). His wounding of Iago was so dramatic that Stanislavski recalled him as having killed the villain 'with one sweep of his scimitar' (*Life*, 272). I have found no other evidence that Salvini changed the ending so dramatically; perhaps, since Stanislavski was not himself looking at Iago during the final moments of the play, he simply assumed that the character was dead. It was himself that Salvini's Othello killed with the scimitar, slashing his own throat and dying with his legs audibly beating against the floor (*Othello*) – a contrast, as Virginia Vaughan notes, with the 'extreme reticence' of concealing Desdemona's murder behind the bedcurtains (Vaughan, 168).

Whereas Francis Gentleman saw in Spranger Barry's Othello a steady upward movement, Stanislavski said that Salvini clearly showed every step of the 'ladder down which Othello descended in the full sight of the spectators from the heights of bliss to the depths of destructive passion' (270). There was no 'poetry' to distract from the sight of a powerful looking man attacking a woman, and, since the role of Iago was normally assigned to a second-rate actor, there was little sense of a diabolical agent forcing Othello to do what he did. On the other hand, when Othello committed some of his worst actions, Salvini made it clear that he repented of them at once: his demeaning request that Iago 'Set on thy wife to observe'; his striking of Desdemona; his physical threatening of Emilia in the final scene. After he had demanded the handkerchief from Desdemona, he went toward Emilia, as if to question her, but thought better of it, thus creating a nice irony as well as yet another example of a hero warring with his better nature (Mason, 68). Above all, when in III.iii he had thrown Iago to the ground and was about to stamp out his brains, he was seized by revulsion toward his own violence; he stepped backwards, 'raising his hands, and exclaiming "O, no, no, no!"' Iago had thrown up his hand 'as if to ward off a fresh attack'; Salvini seized it and raised the actor to his feet, then collapsed, exhausted, on a couch (Mason, 53). This moment was always the highlight of the performance: 'Well roared, lion,' commented one critic; 'the circus rings with applause' (Thierry, 877).

When Booth gave one of his rare performances as Othello for San Francisco audiences who had already seen Salvini, Kitty Malony was convinced that he left spectators in no doubt that he was the greatest living Othello; but most of them, however much they respected the distinguished American actor, would not have agreed with her. A more typical response was: 'Salvini alone is the Othello of Shakespeare. Booth is the Othello of poetry and romance' (*The Argonaut* (San Francisco), 17 March 1888). In 1889 the *Boston Budget*, though acquiescing in what by now was a tradition of praising Booth, added that 'After one has seen Salvini's Moor of Venice no other delineation of the part seems quite the same' (27 January 1889).

Henry Irving played his first Othello in 1876, only four months after Salvini's first visit to London, and received universally negative reviews, many of them unfavourable comparisons with Salvini. F.J. Furnivall of the Shakespere Society was prompted to write to the press. 'Are there to be no more Othellos for us Victorians,' he asked plaintively, 'because an Italian has once played him for us?' (*Daily News*, 28 February 1876). Others wondered the same thing, as Salvini's contemporary Ernesto Rossi and other touring Italians of the next generation brought a continental realism to the playing of Othello. Reviewers began to ask whether English actors could still play the role. Could Englishmen, in fact, act at all, or were they (it was a backhanded compliment) too well-bred and reserved to express violent emotions? A fairly typical comment, though of a later date, was: 'the Moors are akin to the Latins ... Being of the Latin temperament, Othello is played better by Latins than by Englishmen' (Ashwell, 106; see also Vaughan, 170). Thus, when Booth and Irving played opposite each other at the Lyceum in 1881, alternating the roles of Othello and Iago, both were praised as Iago but neither was considered a success as Othello. Reviewer Dutton Cook blamed not the actors, but the current state of the theatre and 'the modern demand for what is known as naturalness on the stage'. He added that 'the poetic drama of the past can only be revived upon the understanding that the actors are permitted a certain heroic or exalted manner, both of bearing and locution, which would clearly be unsuited to a play of modern date' (Cook, 457).

But it was not the play as a whole that was the problem; it was the character of Othello. Carol Carlisle acutely indicates the contradictory nature of the expectations of nineteenth-century audiences and critics who went to see an actor play this role: they wanted 'a naturally majestic, unyielding figure who gave the impression of controlled fury until the breaking point was finally reached and a tidal wave of emotion inundated the scene'. She adds that 'This conception is particularly hard to express in action' (Carlisle, 202). When A. C. Bradley writes, 'The Othello of our stage can never be Shakespeare's Othello, any more than the Cleopatra of our stage can be his Cleopatra' (Bradley, 145), he is referring in part to the acting text, which, in 1904, he could not imagine being performed unexpurgated before a mixed audience. But his paralleling of the two roles is appropriate. Othello is to male roles what Cleopatra is to female ones. The self-contradictory concept of maleness that lies behind the heroic concept of acting – self-control combined with a capacity for passion – is not perhaps so different from the concept of femaleness that, as has often been noted, asks women to demonstrate both chastity and a capacity for passion. Indeed, it is this contradiction that accounts for many of the difficulties which both past and present commentators have found in the character of Desdemona.

CHAPTER II

Desdemona's play

Before the arrival of feminist criticism, English-language critics had little to say about Desdemona: 'a part of no shining qualifications', an example of 'unvarying gentleness' (Gentleman, 154), 'fond, trusting, meek, and unresisting' (Boaden, *Kemble*, I: 257). As late as the so-called 'Henry Irving Shakespeare' edition of 1889, F. A. Marshall's introduction, which devoted a good deal of space to Iago, and somewhat less to Othello, offered only a paragraph about her. She is, it says, 'the very incarnation of purity', whose love 'is as that of a child', but some may find her 'too weak in her very gentleness' (Henry Irving Shakespeare, 18). This rather bored appreciation of her virtues was sometimes countered by harsh criticism. R. S. White, in *Innocent Victims*, has noted how often critics, starting with Thomas Rymer, have wanted to blame Desdemona for what happens (White, 62). Hazlitt may have been the first critic to suggest that Desdemona's love for the Moor reflects on her supposed purity (Bate, 160), and a number of editors blame her for the suffering she inflicts on her father; but these negative views were never, apparently, reflected on the pre-twentieth-century stage. Like the tragic hero, the tragic heroine was a recognized and idealized figure. Salvini was surprised to find that English Desdemonas were generally blonde, since he knew that Venetian women were not (Salvini, *Leaves*, 90). The preference might be justified by the play's many references to the 'fair Desdemona', or by an understandable desire to emphasize the contrast with Othello. Madge Kendall recalled that Ira Aldridge, 'being black, always picked out the fairest woman he could to play Desdemona with him' and got applause when he placed her hand in his so as to draw attention to the difference in colour (Kendall, 28). But blondeness was also associated with vapidity, and this was all that many English and American Desdmonas were required to exhibit.

The English stage: Emilia's play?

That the English-speaking world was unenthusiastic about Desdemona was hardly surprising, since in the acting texts nearly everything that might have made her part interesting (especially IV.iii, the 'willow scene') had been carefully removed from it. Moreover, actors of Othello, reluctant to be identified with unheroic violence, often toned down both their language and their behaviour towards her – cutting, for example, the scene in which Othello strikes her in public, or reducing the blow to 'a very perfunctory one indeed' (Sprague, *Actors*, 203–4). Since most eighteenth- and nineteenth-century Desdemonas were played by actresses who specialized in pathos (Carlisle, 240), they must sometimes have seemed to be feeling sorry for themselves without cause. One exception – about which, however, nothing is known – must have occurred when Kitty Clive acted the part at a benefit in 1734. Clive had played Bianca in her first year on the stage, before the character disappeared from the acting text; she was a fine singer and an immensely popular comic actress, but it is evident that the experiment of allowing a comedienne to play a role defined as tragic could be risked only at a benefit performance, where the object was to attract audiences with unusual offerings.

Far more often, what the audience saw was a tragic actress attempting to make something of a part that years of cutting had reduced almost to nothing. When John Kemble revived *Othello* at Drury Lane on 8 March 1785, playing the title role, his sister Sarah Siddons played Desdemona – 'to serve her brother rather than herself', as her adoring biographer James Boaden put it (Boaden, *Siddons*, 319). Her admirers could not imagine what she could do with the part. Siddons's 'heroic' physique and clear, firm delivery always gave the impression of immense moral and intellectual power, qualities which no one at this period could imagine in Desdemona. But she apparently managed to subdue what was thought of as her natural character, even to the point of looking smaller; perhaps, as when she played Ophelia later, she wore a lower headdress (351). Her performance was highly praised, precisely because it was such a contrast with her astonishing Lady Macbeth, and she herself, recognizing that 'nobody has ever done anything with that character before', wrote in a letter that she was pleased that audiences responded so favourably to 'the innocence and playful simplicity' of her interpretation (Ffrench, 117). Boaden's description suggests that what she found in the part was a character constantly divided in her feelings and intelligent enough to analyse the conflict: her opening speech made a careful 'discrimination' between the duties owed to father and to husband, and in the first scene at Cyprus she combined 'elegant deportment, cordial manners, and smothered anxiety' (Boaden, *Siddons*, 321). When Othello began to show open signs of disturbance, as when he took hold of her hand in III.iv, she traced a progression from 'surprise arising to astonishment, a sort of *doubt* if she heard aright, and that being admitted, what it could *mean*; a hope that it would end in nothing so unusual from him as *offensive* meaning; and the slight relief, upon Othello's adding, "Tis a good hand, a frank one;" all this commentary was quite as legible as the text' (259). Even though Kemble, unlike some later actors, retained the scene where Othello strikes her in public, Boaden, surprisingly, says nothing either about it or about the murder itself: could he not bear to see the magnificent Siddons pleading for her life? He prefers instead to speculate about what she might have done with IV.iii if she had been allowed to play it – which, despite her immense popularity, never occurred to anyone as a possibility.

By contrast, Eliza O'Neill, generally considered the finest Juliet and Desdemona of the next generation, was described by Fanny Kemble as 'expressly devised for a representative victim', gifted as she was with 'the very beau ideal [*sic*] of feminine weakness in its most attractive form' and the power of weeping abundantly without harming her appearance (Kemble, *Girlhood*, 195–6). Miss Kemble's barely concealed contempt is hereditary: she was the daughter of Charles Kemble and the niece of Sarah Siddons. The power of the Siddons image as an icon of tragic acting is evident from another reviewer's comments on O'Neill: her 'chaste, simple, beautiful acting', he insisted, 'did not amount to that which perfect tragedy requires: it deeply interested and affected, but it did not appal, astonish, overwhelm, and reduce all other feelings to littleness and nothingness in its presence' (Robson, 183). It is hard to see how, by this definition of tragic acting, clearly written with Siddons in mind, Desdemona could ever be considered a role worth playing.

By the end of the eighteenth century it was already agreed that Emilia was the better of the two women's parts: as *The Dramatic Censor* noted in 1770, she 'has much more life than her mistress, and shows a well contrasted spirit' (Gentleman, 154). She was also a less morally ambiguous figure on the stage than in the text, thanks to the cutting not only of her defence of women's infidelity in IV.iii but of her coarser expressions elsewhere in the play. The result was that she easily became a sounding board for 'the virtuous indignation of the audience' (Boaden, *Siddons*, 43). She had two great moments. One was, and still is, in the scene following Desdemona's murder, where much of the tragic effect depends on her. But for the late eighteenth and early nineteenth centuries, the highpoint of her part came when, in IV.ii, she voiced her suspicions as to why Othello had turned on Desdemona. As she embarks on the speech that comes closest to the truth –

> I will be hanged if some eternal knave,
> Some busy and insinuating rogue,
> Some cogging, cozening slave, to get some office,
> Have not devised this slander, I'll be hang'd else!

(IV.ii.132–5)

– Fechter's acting edition of 1861 inserts the stage direction, '*suspiciously eyeing* IAGO', though the latter is directed to remain impassive. Edwin Booth's acting edition, published in 1878, insists on the contrary that Emilia ought not to speak with 'intended reference to Iago'. Most critics today would agree with Booth and prefer the ironic effect of Emilia's failing to draw the obvious conclusion from her words, but it is understandable that many actresses chose to be more 'knowing', arguing that her later 'I thought so then' (V.ii.89) was a reference to this moment. Perhaps no rationalization was needed: when acting meant dominating the stage, and making dramatic transitions from one state to another, the opportunity to 'appal, astonish, overwhelm', and so on, was simply too good to pass up. Booth paid (probably unwilling) tribute to the speech's effect when he noted that Iago should not speak his own line 'Fie, there is no such man, it is impossible' (IV.ii.136) until the reaction to her speech has died down (*Variorum*, 266). Emilia's speech continued to build, and the audience eagerly awaited its vehement ending:

> The Moor's abused by some most villainous knave,
> Some base notorious knave, some scurvy fellow.
> O heaven, that such companions thou'dst unfold
> And put in every honest hand a whip
> To lash the rascals naked through the world!

(IV.ii.141–5)

(The speech as written includes another line, 'Even from the east to th'west', but it was cut in the acting texts, apparently for fear of anticlimax.) Boaden even implies, indignantly, that at least one Emilia had stolen the scene from Siddons herself, boasting later 'how she used to get six rounds of applause in the part; and how she beat the gentle Desdemona (perhaps Mrs. Siddons) to a dead standstill by this overstrained and vulgar violence' (Boaden, *Siddons*, 43–4).

In the 1850s a German visitor to London was surprised to find that in English productions, unlike those to which he was accustomed, Emilia 'becomes a leading role in the fourth and fifth acts' (Fontane, 22). In 1845 Charlotte Cushman played the role opposite Edwin Forrest's powerful Othello and succeeded in dominating even him (Shattuck, 91). The actress playing the part was sometimes billed above Desdemona. For instance, in two of Salvini's American performances, the name of Clara Morris appeared equal with the star's and above both Iago and Desdemona. What little we know of Morris's acting indicates that she made the most of every opportunity to control the situation. Her Emilia intended to steal the handkerchief from the outset and even showed some anxiety in case Desdemona should notice that she had dropped it (*Boston Weekly Transcript*, 17 April 1883); in the final scene, she made sure that her offstage shouts for help were not drowned out by the alarm bells, by signalling for them to ring *between* her lines, an effect that always got her a round of applause (Sprague, *Actors*, 217).

Emilia had to make the most of such moments as these, because, of course, her death scene was much curtailed; with no willow song to echo, she could hardly 'die in music' (V.ii.246). Her lines asking to be laid by her mistress's side were also cut. In some productions she was carried off by a servant (partly to save her from having to lie on the stage so long – see Sprague, *Actors*, 217). Fechter had her make signs to a servant to take her to the same prie-dieu at which Desdemona had knelt, and then draw the curtain. Booth, at least in one version, allowed her to die on a couch under the window, to which Iago too was led after his last line, thus showing that Iago and Othello were now 'evened ... wife for wife' (II.i.197). This sounds like a refinement of what Booth's father had done at this point: he 'looked at Othello with a significant gaze, then pointed to his own wife, as if to express that her violation by the Moor was the cause of all his perfidy. He then struck his breast in a triumphant manner, meaning that his vindication was complete and gratifying' (quoted Sprague, *Actors*, 223). Absurd as this sign-language sounds, perhaps it points forwards to the twentieth-century tendency to see the play as the tragedy of two marriages rather than one.

Frustrated heroines: Helen Faucit and Ellen Terry

Comments on the role of Desdemona, from the women who actually played her, are hard to come by. Helen Faucit (1817–98), Macready's most famous leading lady in the 1830s and early 1840s, did however publish (under her stage name Helena Faucit) a book of letters *On Some of Shakespeare's Female Characters* in 1885. Even here she says less about how she actually played the role than about the subtext she imagined for it. Faucit's view of the other characters in her story was notably unsentimental. By contrast with all the critics who shed tears over Brabantio's tragedy, she felt that the old man deserved it for his failure to understand his daughter better ('If he has been deceived, it is by himself and not by her') and for the 'cold malignity' of his final lines (71, 73). She also blamed Othello for not trusting his wife and felt that Iago was far less clever than most people thought. Faucit would have loved to play the willow scene, which she imagined with great vividness, but, even by 1885 when she published her book, she had seen it only in a German production (91). Unfortunately the increasing emphasis on elaborately constructed scenery worked against the reintroduction of a scene requiring a set change. Even so, in the course of the nineteenth century, critics who had appreciated its effect in productions with different acting texts began asking why it was not performed. This was particularly true after Salvini's first visit to England (1875). Perhaps inspired by him, Irving reinstated IV.iii when he produced the play in the following year – but omitted it in the version he did with Booth five years later, when he had Ellen Terry for his Desdemona. The reason may have been the comparative failure of the scene when Isabel Bateman played it in 1876: her singing was inadequate and, according to the *Times* reviewer, she seemed so conscious of her impending doom 'that it was a relief when it came' (17 February 1876). Terry got to play the scene only in 1898, in her own revival of the play, where it was applauded (*The Times*, 23 August 1898). From this point on, it was generally included, though Emilia's speech continued to be omitted or at least considerably shortened.

Most Desdemonas died in a way intended to spare the audience's feelings: the bed was normally placed at the back of the stage; the actor used a pillow rather than his bare hands, then drew a knife on 'I would not have thee linger in thy pain'; increasingly, he committed the murder behind the curtains, as Macready did in Paris in 1828. But Faucit must have pleaded passionately for her life, and with hindsight she could give plausible justifications for her interpretation – as herself, she had a weak chest and was genuinely terrified of smothering (58); as Desdemona, she was determined to live long enough to clear her name and forgive her husband (95–6). Fanny Kemble, likewise, in her last moments rose on her knees in her bed and clutched at Othello ('having previously warned Mr. Macready, and begged his pardon for the liberty': Kemble, *Later*, 631). Kemble had already complained that 'The Desdemonas that I have seen, on the English stage, have always appeared to me to acquiesce with wonderful equanimity in their assassination. On the Italian stage they run for their lives' (Sprague, *Actors*, 213). She was thinking of the productions starring Rossi and Salvini, who, in the (Rossini) operatic tradition, made the murder a violent scene, with Desdemona running to the door and finding it locked, or being dragged round the room by her hair (Sprague, *Actors*, 211–16). The effect of this scene, in the Italian interpretation, depended on the willingness of the Desdemona to be mistreated on the stage. A leading New York theatre critic felt that Salvini's famous Othello was seen at its best only with his Italian company, particularly 'the brilliant Signora Piamonti' as Desdemona. This was because, when he worked with English-speaking casts, 'no actress could be found who was willing to submit herself as Piamonti did to the full fury of his assault' (Towse, 158). Indeed, after Piamonti's early death, a legend grew up, apparently without foundation, that she had died as a result of Salvini's violence ('Nym Crinkle', *New York Herald*, 27 October 1885). Yet even Salvini's production made compromises: Desdemona was still dressed, since the willow scene led directly into the murder scene, and the killing was carried out behind the heavy curtains of the bed. But, before then, he 'slowly circled the stage toward her, muttering savagely and inarticulately as she cowered before him. Rising at last to his full height with extended arms, he pounced upon her, lifted her into the air, dashed with her across the stage and through the curtains, which fell behind him. You heard the crash as he flung her on the bed, and growls as of a wild beast over his prey.' With English actors, Salvini played more traditionally, 'with Desdemona on her couch at his entrance' (Towse, 163–4). Many Desdemonas, even in Britain and America, nevertheless sat up in bed or even arose and cowered beside it, despite the risk of impropriety (see *Variorum*, 298–9).

The other potentially great Desdemona of the Victorian age, Ellen Terry, is constantly described as 'a dream' (Auerbach, 195): she managed somehow to satisfy both male and female fantasies of what woman ought to be. When she played Desdemona in the brief run of *Othello* (1881) with Henry Irving and Edwin Booth alternating the two leading roles, Booth himself later said that she 'was the girl he himself saw when burning his midnight oil over Othello; that she made the tragedy sublime' (Goodale, 278). Terry 'loved playing' Desdemona, and like Faucit she admired the character's courage; but playing opposite two different Othellos in quick succession made her aware of the extent to which her performance depended on theirs. Despite her admiration for Irving, she had to admit that her own interpretation worked better opposite Booth's melancholy Moor, who remained gentle and courteous until the 'brothel scene'. Desdemona's tragedy, Terry felt, came at the end of that scene, when Othello 'destroys her faith'; to create this climax she needed, up to this point, to 'preserve the simple, heroic blindness of Desdemona to the fact that her lord mistrusts her'. This was difficult to do in the face of the emotional, angry figure played by Irving, who was, she said, 'raving and stamping under her nose!' (Terry, 205). Her sense of despair at the end of IV.ii was so acutely felt that it once drew tears even from Irving, as he was playing Iago, but some reviewers, unable to take the character seriously, could accept physical contact between them only when Irving initiated it. Thus, one reproved her for throwing herself, sobbing, on Iago's breast, especially since he was a subaltern, only twenty-eight years old, and she was the wife of the commanding officer (Cook, 458). Another complained that when she threw herself into a chair 'after Othello has left her overwhelmed with grief and shame', 'the effect, to me, was most unlovely'; he suggested that she should look at herself in a mirror and adopt a more graceful attitude (*Illustrated London News*, 14 May 1881). Generally, it is easier to know what Terry looked like than how she played the part.

[55]

The failure, or refusal, of nineteenth-century productions to satisfy either Emilia's desire to be laid beside her mistress or Othello's attempt to 'die upon a kiss' has received a good deal of critical attention. James R. Siemon suggests that the main motive was the star actor's need to keep the audience focused on him (Siemon, 50). Michael Neill, in an essay that was the starting point for many race-focused studies of the play in the last decade of the twentieth century, found behind this motive the insistence that the play's final image should be that of Desdemona in chaste solitude, so that the audience would not see a black man lying beside the two white women with whom he has had, or is said to have had, a sexual relationship (Neill, 407). The questions involved here are complex: did the Jacobean audience see a man and two women or two boys and a man? Would the eighteenth- and nineteenth-century audience have seen, if they had been allowed to see, a black man with two white women, or two white women with a white actor made up to look black or brown? So long as Othello was played by a white actor, sexual propriety was likely to be more important than the possibility of racial scandal. There is a clear similarity between the stage business which made the dying Othello drag himself towards Desdemona's bed but die before he could reach it and the often-used stage business for the death of Juliet, who likewise used to die just as she reached Romeo's body (Sprague, *Actors*, 319), though Juliet was often allowed, even in the nineteenth century, to make physical contact with Romeo at the moment of death. Helen Faucit's Juliet is described as 'laying her face upon her husband's bosom', after which 'she raised his nerveless arms and folded them above her head' (Sprague, *Actors*, 317) – conveniently away from the rest of her body. What seems to have made the end of *Othello* particularly difficult was the fact that husband and wife were seen together not on a tomb but on a bed. The sight of a bed on stage could in itself be improper, which is no doubt one reason why it was often placed in an alcove at the back. As late as 1921, the Godfrey Tearle *Othello* shocked one reviewer: 'The bed is not even half-concealed, as it is in modern plays ... It is wonderful what the public will stand – from Shakespeare' (Harold Layton, unattributed clipping, MMTC: Tearle).

Desdemona in France and Italy:
Voltaire, Ducis, Rossini and Viganò

Meanwhile, however, Desdemona had a very different status outside the Anglo-American world, where she was considered not
only the most lovable but the most interesting character in the
play. Although this emphasis on the heroine is usually attributed
to Jean-François Ducis, whose 1792 *Othello* was the source of
many subsequent translations and adaptations, it can be traced as
far back as Voltaire's *Zaïre*, first performed in August 1732 and
published in the following year. Aaron Hill began to translate the
tragedy as soon as a copy became available, commenting in a
letter that he would like to think that the play's success in depicting
the 'passions' might be due to the author's 'acquaintance with our
Shakespear in his native language' (Hill, *Works*, I: 235). The wish
was evidently father to Colley Cibber's prologue to the play when
it finally reached the professional stage (as *Zara*) early in 1736:

> From *English* Plays, *Zara's French* author fir'd,
> Confess'd his Muse, beyond herself, inspir'd;
> From rack'd *Othello's* rage, he rais'd his style,
> And snatch'd the brand, that lights this tragic pile.
> (Hill, *Works*, II: 28–9)

Voltaire never 'confess'd' any such influence, though he did take
pleasure in pointing out what he thought was an influence in
reverse: the echoing of a line from *Zaïre* in La Place's translation
of *Othello* (1746). Yet it is easy to see why English readers saw a
resemblance. *Zaïre*, like *Othello*, is a tragedy of love and jealousy
in which a Moor murders his beloved, learns that she was innocent
and then kills himself. But in Voltaire's play the misunderstanding between hero and heroine is not fabricated by a villain. Nor
does it appear that, for Voltaire, race played any significant part
in the tragedy, unless one takes the hero's emphasis on his own
passionate nature to be a racial characteristic.

The play takes place in the time of the Crusades. Zaïre, a
Christian captive, is loved by Orosmane, the new and enlightened
Muslim ruler of Solyma (Jerusalem). He wishes to marry her,
promising that theirs will be a monogamous relationship and
offering to free the Christian captives on generous terms. Zaïre
shares his love and is on the point of renouncing her faith; she
knows that she was born a Christian but has lived since earliest
childhood in the Islamic world, believes herself an orphan and

has never really practised her religion. Then she discovers that she is the daughter of the venerable Lusignan, the last Christian king of Jerusalem, and that the French knight Nérestan is her brother. Both men convince her that she is no longer free to choose another religion. The tragedy comes about when Orosmane, already jealous of her and Nérestan, intercepts an ambiguously worded letter saying that she plans to steal out of the seraglio to meet the other man. Orosmane lies in wait for her and kills her. Immediately thereafter, he discovers Nérestan's real identity and learns that Zaïre had in fact been seeking out a Christian priest to baptize her. Full of remorse, he kills himself.

The one real verbal similarity between *Zaïre* and *Othello* occurs in Orosmane's last speech, where, in language that recalls Othello's instructions to Lodovico, he tells Nérestan to return to Europe and give a true account of his actions:

Tell 'em – with this [the dagger] I murdered her I lov'd;
The noblest and most virtuous among women!
The soul of innocence, and pride of truth:
Tell 'em I laid my empire at her feet:
Tell 'em I plung'd my dagger in her blood;
Tell 'em I so ador'd – and thus reveng'd her.

(Aaron Hill, *Zara*, V.i.255–60)

The structure of the speech and its surprise ending as the speaker stabs himself resemble Shakespeare's (and resembled La Place's translation still more), though Hill's translation accentuates the resemblance by its emphatic 'thus' in the final line, for which there is no equivalent in the French.

In making the tragedy result from religious intransigence, always his favourite target, Voltaire was building on something latent in Shakespeare's text. The dialogue between Othello and Emilia after Desdemona's murder shows them both concerned for the state of Desdemona's soul, Othello because she has died with a lie on her lips, and Emilia because Desdemona was 'too fond of her most filthy bargain' (V.ii.153). The significance of their words went unnoticed in England, perhaps because the scene was so heavily cut in the theatre, perhaps because Emilia generally turned it, as we have seen, into an opportunity to 'take the stage'. French audiences were much more alert to such issues: some of Voltaire's early critics were seriously concerned that Zaïre had died unbaptized. In the final moments of the play Nérestan, outraged, insists that Zaïre's death was heaven's punishment on her for wanting to marry Orosmane, while her confidant Fatima retorts that Zaïre loved him and had hoped for heaven's mercy.

But the most important effect of Voltaire's play was that, as its title indicates, it moves the centre of interest from hero to heroine. Instead of leaving her father behind in Act I, the heroine discovers him in Act II. She is then torn between his demands and those of her lover, without being able to confide in either man, a fact that exposes her to suspicion by both. Desdemona's 'I do perceive here a divided duty' might have been Voltaire's starting point, though Zaïre's most famous prototype is Corneille's Chimène in *Le Cid*. It is Zaïre rather than Orosmane who suffers the greatest internal conflicts, because it is she who is most fully aware of the situation. If anything, the English translation accentuated her sufferings: in 1736 Voltaire commented with amusement on the fact that Hill's translation had inserted a stage direction for Zaïre to throw herself on the ground when the sultan attempts to deny his love for her (Voltaire, 417). It has already been pointed out that the English concept of a jealous lover was of someone constantly throwing himself on the ground, so the fact that Hill found such behaviour appropriate for his Zara indicates how completely she was dominating the story.

The adaptation of *Othello* by Jean-François Ducis was a still more important influence on nineteenth-century responses to the play, but its indebtedness to *Zaïre* is obvious: indeed, when Ducis first embarked on the story, perhaps as early as 1782, a fellow writer warned him that his greatest problem would be avoiding an excessive resemblance (Gilman, 73, 85–6). At the beginning of the Ducis *Othello*, Othello has managed both to save the state from an insurrection and to carry off Hédelmone (Desdemona); he is not yet married to her, though the senate do not know this. Her father Odalbert (Brabantio) gets himself into trouble with the senate, from which she attempts to save him; later, having learned that she is not yet Othello's wife, he exploits her concern by forcing her into a signed agreement to marry the Doge's son. As in *Zaïre*, it is Hédelmone's attempt to satisfy the conflicting claims of both father and lover – without informing either of them of her intentions – that leads to disaster. Her request to postpone her marriage naturally arouses Othello's suspicions, though her old nurse, Hermance, defends her with something of the courage of her prototype, Shakespeare's Emilia. In the final scene, although

Hédelmone finally explains herself quite clearly, with none of the ambiguities that further inflame Shakespeare's Othello, Ducis's hero carries out the murder. He then learns, too late, that his supposed friend Pézare has for five acts been betraying not only him but the Venetian Republic, and, only a few lines later, commits suicide. It may have been the arbitrariness of this ending as much as its violence that caused the outrage of audiences at the premiere. Ducis supplied an alternative ending which was used for a while: as in Nahum Tate's Restoration *King Lear*, other characters arrive in time to stop Othello, and all is quickly forgiven.

The play was first performed in November 1792, two months after the proclamation of the French Republic. These dates, as has been pointed out, had noticeable repercussions in the play, especially since the actor of Othello, Joseph Talma, had just been accused by the revolutionary leader Marat of being insufficiently patriotic and pro-revolutionary (Golder, 148–9). Ducis made what he could of the fact that Venice, the scene of all the play's action, is a republic: the characters' patriotic statements about 'la république' were evidently designed to please a Parisian audience. In their advance publicity, Ducis and Talma also pointed out the relevance of the plot to the recent decision of the National Convention to permit universal suffrage without regard to colour, and implied that disapproval of the heroine's mixed marriage was counter-revolutionary (Gilman, 55–8). Ducis's Othello, though he says that he glories in being called the Moor (I.91), seems, still more than in Shakespeare, to have internalized the values of his adopted country, confessing that if he had had the choice he would have preferred to be born in Venice (I.85–6) and begging Hédelmone to pity the passions caused by the African blood that boils in his veins (IV.1137–8). But Venice itself is not always depicted favourably: its senators are aristocratic snobs, and in one of the play's most powerful speeches Othello evokes the sinister side of the republic: its spying on its citizens, its secret arrests and imprisonments. Ducis, originally a fervent supporter of the revolution, had seen several of his friends arrested in 1792 (Campenon, 92).

Ducis had attempted to prepare his audience for the otherwise gratuitous tragic ending by emphasizing his heroine's sense of impending disaster. At several points in the play she recalls her mother's deathbed prophecy of an unhappy death and even wonders whether she will be murdered by her husband. The willow scene in particular makes explicit the fears that are implicit in most of what Shakespeare's heroine says. Retaining this scene was something of a gamble on Ducis's part, since before Le Tourneur's translation (1776) it had seemed just as unnecessary to French translator/adaptors as to English editors (Estève, 291–2). But the song was Ducis's favourite part of the play. Determined not to omit it, he persuaded the well-known composer André Grétry to set it to music simple enough for an actress to sing. It was the most successful and memorable feature of the production, though it is not clear whether it was actually sung by the first Hédelmone, Mme Desgarcins, who had already played Ophélie in Ducis's *Hamlet* adaptation, as well as the twin role of Zaïre. There was no tradition on the continent of actors singing the songs in Shakespeare (cf. Fontane, n., 131). Apparently, audience expectations about musical performance on the stage were too high to allow an actor to sing at the level of an ordinary human being, so some later Hédelmones mimed the song while it was sung and played from the wings (see Ducis, 84–5).

Ducis's tragedy was played seventy times at the Comédie Française between 1799 and 1852; Othello became one of Talma's favourite roles and he continued to play it throughout his career (Monaco, 162). But Ducis's fondness for Desdemona and her 'song of willow' turned out to be even more contagious, both within France (see Estève) and in much of Europe. Since his version had been validated by its success in the theatre, the first Italian, Spanish and Russian translators of the play often based their work on it rather than on the difficult English text. Perhaps most importantly, Ducis was the main influence on Berio di Salsa, the librettist of Rossini's immensely popular operatic version (1816), which in turn influenced even the scrupulously Shakespearean *Otello* of Verdi and Boito two generations later. Like Ducis, Berio keeps the action in Venice throughout; although Berio's Desdemona is married to Otello, her marriage is a secret at the beginning of the play, so that Roderigo, who has the support of Desdemona's father Elmiro, can be a serious rival to the hero, like his counterpart in Ducis. Because Rossini was writing for a company that was unusually strong in tenors (the San Carlo in Naples), all the male roles except Elmiro's are written for the tenor voice. Peter Conrad argues that it is 'psychologically apt' that they should all sound alike, since Rossini's Otello is indistinguishable from the other men in the opera (Conrad, 113), while Desdemona and Emilia (a mere confidante) are sometimes accompanied by a

[61]

female chorus, further suggesting that all women, like all men, are victims of passion. In neither the opera nor Ducis's play is Emilia's counterpart married to Iago, whose motive in both works is unrequited love for the heroine. Qualities like envy and intellectual pride did not lend themselves to opera.

Like the tragedies of Voltaire and Ducis, the opera belongs to its heroine. Whereas Shakespeare's character is marginalized by her own ignorance of most of what is going on, the operatic Desdemona knows from the beginning that Otello has reason to be jealous of her and that Iago is treacherous. Her difficulties result from the tangled web she has woven for herself in failing to reject Roderigo outright because she is attempting to keep her marriage secret from her father. Iago (in a scene which is closer to Shakespeare than anything else up to this point) instils suspicion in Otello's mind and the two men swear vengeance on Desdemona. Left alone, Otello sees Roderigo and they are on the point of fighting when Desdemona enters and urges them instead, 'Strike only at my heart, the cause of so much woe.' This is the moment depicted by an English caricaturist (figure 3): though he obviously finds the heroine and her suitors equally fatuous, he also shows how completely she is the centre of the story.

3   William Heath, caricature of Roderigo, Desdemona and Otello
singing 'Che fiero punto e questo', from Rossini's *Otello*

The final act of the opera is given almost entirely to Desdemona. She broods on the fate of her friend from Africa, Isaure (Ducis's name for Barbara), and sings the willow song followed by a prayer. Though Shakespeare's Desdemona tells Othello that she has prayed, and her last couplet in IV.iii may be spoken as a prayer, it is probably Ducis who is responsible for this aria, since he made Hédelmone pray aloud before going to bed. Otello enters from a secret door at the back and they have a brief exchange, set against the sound of a storm, before he stabs her to death. There is knocking, but not from Emilia, whose grief would compete with Otello's. Instead a servant reports that Iago's villainy has somehow been revealed; Roderigo, Elmiro and the Doge burst in, apparently wanting nothing more than reconciliation with Otello. In a few terse lines he reveals the body and stabs himself, thus achieving the union with Desdemona that her father had finally promised him. The other characters respond with what a London critic called 'A scream of horror' – an ending 'quite new to the Italian stage' (Richard Bacon, *London Magazine*, 1822; quoted Fenner, 152). Although spectators who knew Shakespeare's play well, such as Stendhal (*Rossini*, 293–324), were appalled by the reductiveness of this libretto, *Otello* nevertheless became so popular that it established what was really an alternative version of the story, still well known when Verdi's masterpiece arrived to displace it in 1887.

Like the Berio–Rossini opera (1816), the Othello ballet first given at La Scala, Milan, in January 1818 is essentially focused on Desdemona, though of the two the ballet is much closer to Shakespeare's original. Its creator, Salvatore Viganò (1769–1821), was praised by Shelley and Stendhal, who found his ballets even more moving than Edmund Kean's performances in the English theatre (Shelley, *Letters*, II: 14; Stendhal, *Rome*, I: 109). Viganò's works were not merely ballets; he aspired to something more like Wagner's idea of the *Gesamtkunstwerk* (Dalmonte, 206). The principals sang as well as acting, accompanied by a large chorus expressing itself entirely through gesture, since words would not have been clearly understood if spoken by so many people at once (Ritorni, 38); the whole was beautifully costumed and elaborately staged. Sheer size had a lot to do with the effect of these 'choreodramas', as they were called (Ritorni, 40); even in the final scene there were some thirty people in Desdemona's bedroom. Viganò had visited England and seen Shakespeare on the stage, with the result that his version was much closer than Berio's to the original. He did, however, follow Ducis and Rossini in keeping the action in Venice, and he opened the story some time after the marriage of Othello and Desdemona, thus avoiding the displeasing subject matter of elopement and filial disobedience. As in Ducis and Rossini, the heroine's father is present throughout, but in this version he is on excellent terms with his son-in-law until the latter begins to display signs of insane jealousy. This is also the first adaptation to give Emilia something like her Shakespearean role, though she is Iago's mistress rather than his wife, and her hope that he will marry her gives her a motive for keeping quiet about his villainy. She is not otherwise guilty, since Iago steals the handkerchief himself while Otello is in his fit; the villain then manoeuvres Cassio into presenting the handkerchief to Desdemona, in view of Otello, as an attempt to win her to his side. In an unusual final act, considered a masterpiece of classical pity and terror (Ritorni, 184), Otello stabs her behind the bedcurtains. Perhaps because female roles in ballet were more showy than men's, the original Desdemona, Antonietta Pallerini, was the most discussed member of the cast: 'Her walk is more like the sweepings of the wind than the steps of a mortal, and her attitudes are pictures', wrote one admirer (Clairmont, 89n.). She was said to have been so expressive that even those furthest from the La Scala stage lost nothing of her performance (Ritorni, 195). Because there was no satisfactory language for recording his mixture of choreography and pantomime, which in any case soon became prohibitively expensive, Viganò's extraordinary creations died with him – though the revival of his *Otello* in 1846 deserves attention as a possible influence on Verdi and Boito's conception of the play.

Thus the story of *Otello*, Italian in origin, returned via France to its home in Italy, then travelled in operatic form to much of Europe. By the time a company of English actors made its famous visit to Paris in 1827–28, responses to the play had been heavily influenced by the tradition of Ducis, Rossini and Viganò. In all three works Desdemona was at least as important as Othello and rather more important than Iago; audiences expected to take an interest in her. The fact that she had far fewer lines than the male protagonists was if anything an advantage, since few of her audience understood English. This at least partly explains why, of that group of actors, it was Harriet Smithson, first as Ophelia and then as Desdemona, who most captivated audiences and the illustrators of *Souvenirs du théâtre anglais*, who depicted her in nine of their twelve pictures (Raby, 86). Eugène Delacroix and Théodore Chasseriau (1844), who produced memorable illustrations of the play, gave most of their attention to Desdemona and depicted her singing the willow song, which of course they would have seen only in the Ducis or Rossini versions (see Merchant, 80–4; Fisher, 22). Smithson was a beautiful young Irish actress who, partly because of her accent, had never had great success in England, but she was a perfect visual embodiment of what was becoming the dominant type of female ideal: the self-sacrificing heroine exemplified by Gretchen in Goethe's *Faust*. Part One, which ends with Gretchen's death, was published in 1808; Part Two, in which she becomes a means for the hero's final salvation, in 1832.

The most famous of early nineteenth-century Desdemonas were not actresses but singers. Giuditta Pasta was the first Rossini heroine; in some ways she seems to have resembled Siddons, majestic and controlled. But Maria Malibran, who played the role with enormous success between 1826 and 1836, made her identification with the part clear from the outset: she wept as she sang the willow song and, with a realism unknown to the English stage at this point, climbed the walls in her efforts to escape from Otello (Bushnell, 73). Critics disagreed as to whether this was overacting, but it moved most audiences powerfully. Malibran played many times in London; Macready, one of the many men fascinated by her, was deeply shocked by her early death at the age of twenty-eight. The singer may well have influenced the acting of Helen Faucit, who first played opposite Macready in 1836, the year of Malibran's death. In the operatic willow scene, one of Berio's best ideas was to have Desdemona and Emilia hear an offstage gondolier singing the famous lines from the *Inferno* about the grief of recalling happiness when one is wretched. The lines come from the episode in which Dante meets Francesca in the second circle of hell, whirled about with her lover in endless winds. In 1885 Faucit recalled that, as she lay and listened to Macready speaking Othello's most anguished words –

Whip me, ye devils,
From the possession of this heavenly sight!
Blow me about in winds, roast me in sulphur,
Wash me in steep-down gulfs of liquid fire!

(V.ii.275–8)

– she felt that he was 'a soul in hell, whirling in the second circle of the Inferno' (Faucit, 97). Berio is unlikely to have known the Shakespearean lines, but Helen Faucit probably did know that the opera quotes Dante. It may also have been due to the opera, and to Malibran in particular, that Faucit was, as she reports (95), 'very hard to kill' – though not because, like Malibran, she ran about the stage trying to escape (when Fechter introduced this business in 1861 her husband, Sir Theodore Martin, condemned it, which he would not have done if it had been her practice: see Sprague, *Actors*, 213–14). Faucit's literary and theatrical persona, as English and innocent as Malibran's was passionate and theatrical, prevented her from admitting her determination not to let herself be utterly annihilated by the performance of her notoriously jealous actor-manager.

There are all too many reasons to explain why, of all the female roles in Shakespeare, Desdemona suffered most at the hands of theatre practitioners. An aesthetic definition of tragedy excluded most of her scenes as trivial; the growing elaboration of scenery meant that, even when critics began to ask for the reintroduction of the willow scene, it became technically difficult to make a major scene change so late in the play; above all, well-meaning delicacy towards both the actress and the character reduced Othello's verbal and physical brutality to the point where actresses such as Faucit and Terry, who thought of Desdemona as heroic, had no opportunity to demonstrate what they meant. When Salvini came along, it is hardly surprising that audiences, though they took delight both in his manhandling of Iago and in his violence towards Desdemona, found it hard to accept the obvious sensuality of his love for her because of what it implied about her feelings toward him. On the English stage, women performing in comedy and burlesque could be flirtatious and sexy; the tragic heroine, like the tragic hero, had to represent an ideal. In Britain and America there was obvious discontent with what Desdemona was traditionally thought to be, but no willingness to experiment with the role, perhaps for fear of what might be discovered about it. Precisely *because* audiences and critics idealized Othello and Desdemona, they were much more interested in Iago and Emilia.

Outside Britain and America, however, *Othello* in the nineteenth century was primarily the tragedy of Desdemona. Although the adaptations and translations of the period softened the sexual implications of the play's language, they gave Desdemona a much bigger role than she had on the English-speaking stage – literally, because they did not cut her best scene, and metaphorically, because they took greater interest in her situation. Whereas the other major characters – Othello the 'tragic hero', Iago and Emilia the male and female 'confidants' – did not quite fit the classical tragic roles for which they seemed intended, Desdemona was reminiscent of such classical heroines as Corneille's Chimène and the clear-headed, absolutely upright Junie and Aricie of Racine; some of the best nineteenth-century comments on her character came from French critics (e.g., Bertrand, 5–6). So long as Ducis and Rossini held the stage, moreover, her story was inevitably seen through their interpretation of it. Even in Salvini's production, a few interpolated lines vaguely based on Shakespeare's "Tis meet I should be used so, very meet' (IV.ii.109) make her sound much more like Ducis's or Rossini's heroine:

> Giusta, è ben giusta,
> La pena mia. La casa di mio padre
> Figlia immemore, ingrata, abbandonai

(Salvini text, 100)

[My suffering is just, utterly just. A forgetful, ungrateful daughter, I abandoned my father's house.] A biographer of Ducis claimed in 1835 that the French adaptation was superior to its original in the clarity with which it subordinates everything in the play to punishing Desdemona's sin against paternal authority; Shakespeare, he noted with regret, had merely confused the moral effect by giving so much attention to less interesting characters such as Othello and – especially – Iago (Leroy, 156, 159).

CHAPTER III

Iago's play

The iconography of villainy

In 1844 Théodore Chassériau, a French engraver, published a set of fifteen etchings illustrating *Othello*. The final image in the series, which closely follows Shakespeare's text in the Benjamin Laroche translation, gives a dominant role to Lodovico and his final gesture towards 'the tragic loading of this bed'; a beautiful, un-shrewish Emilia lies beside Desdemona, while Othello, who may or may not have succeeded in dying upon a kiss, has collapsed into a sitting position just below the bed (figure 4). This is not an illustration of the play in performance: nineteenth-century *Othello*s never gave Lodovico the closing speech or allowed Emilia to die on the bed where she had asked to be laid; they ended with the hero's suicide, sometimes followed by one (rarely both) of the lines in which Cassio reacts to the event. A viewer familiar with the play will inevitably look round the picture in search of Iago. He is indeed present at this final moment – another break with performance tradition, since in many productions he has made a dramatic exit before Othello's suicide. But Chassériau has positioned him at the extreme edge of the scene, half hidden in shadow; although the contorted position of his legs may indicate that he is writhing in pain, it also makes him look as if he has been crammed into a space too small for him.

As Jay Fisher points out in his edition of the series, Chassériau's consistent difficulty with Iago contrasts with the delight he evidently took in depicting Othello and Desdemona, who appear together in ten out of the fifteen etchings (Fisher, 21). In an earlier illustration, for instance, it seems that the artist began with the conventional image of a villain, with the diagonal lines and humbly stooping gesture of a hypocrite, but later gave the character a more four-square pose and a more honest appearance (Fisher, 52). The result, however, is bland and uninteresting. The viewer sees what

4 Théodore Chassériau's illustration of the final lines of *Othello*

the other characters presumably see, but not what the audience is permitted to glimpse. Even after he has been detected and no longer needs to conceal his true feelings, he shows virtually no emotion.

Chassériau's difficulty with the depiction of hypocrisy might seem to be a problem peculiar to the visual arts. As has been pointed out, the essence of expression is movement: a smile that is fixed soon ceases to be a smile (Montagu, 3). If the essence of Iago was his constant *movement* from hypocritical bonhomie to passionate hatred and envy, any attempt to picture him was likely to fail. But the eighteenth and nineteenth centuries were dominated by a pictorial, even iconographical, approach to acting, which found its way into all the handbooks on the subject. The ultimate source of this approach was a lecture on expression by Charles le Brun, first published in 1698 and translated into English in 1734. Its illustrations, showing how the various passions should be depicted in facial portraiture, had enormous influence not only on artists but also on actors. Up to the end of the nineteenth century, aspiring actors continued to read manuals showing them how to represent the various passions by breaking down each emotion into manageable units. As late as 1882 Gustave Garcia (Maria Malibran's nephew), drawing heavily on earlier tracts, reprinted illustrations based on Le Brun and explained that the passion of anger, for instance, 'is known by an inflamed visage, the eyes darting fire, the teeth sometimes gnashing, the whole body, and the arms in particular, thrown into a violent emotion' (Garcia, 149). Such uncontrolled behaviour sounds too extreme for Iago to adopt even in soliloquy, yet this is also the emphasis given in Francis Gentleman's note on the character in Bell's Shakespeare (1777). Rather than requiring Iago to give a convincing portrayal of goodness and occasionally reveal his 'true' evil, Gentleman says that Iago needs to be able to mark the traits of villainy and occasionally assume those of goodness. The definition of 'Hypocrisy' found in *The Thespian Praeceptor* (1811) likewise shows that evil is meant to dominate the impersonation: `HYPOCRISY has generally a smile on the face when the person to be deceived is present, but when alone in his soliloquies, the villain is then to be pourtrayed in the countenance' (47).

However, it is clear from Garcia's manual that he does not believe that villainy can really be concealed:

> Although the hypocrite assumes a soft, persuasive tone of voice and has a smile on his lips, yet his attitude does not inspire confidence; for notwithstanding his art at concealing his feelings, the state of his soul is reflected in his features, which assume a restless and deceitful expression. The face of the hypocrite is often pale: he never looks others in the face, he seems to be afraid of their searching glance; his manners are calculated and insinuating; he rarely makes an impetuous movement; his walk is silent, almost mysterious; his action uncertain, his attitude humble, so as never to raise suspicion. (Garcia, 145)

Paradoxically, even though he is writing an acting manual, Garcia is clearly reluctant to acknowledge that acting might indeed be totally successful. Although in practice the success of the actor playing Iago was generally measured by his credibility as a deceiver, this credibility needed to be limited. Even in the late nineteenth century there was something too disturbing to contemplate in the idea that good acting might actually deceive the audience as well as the victim. For this reason, villains were traditionally given an appearance that could be decoded as villainy by the audience but seem harmless to the other characters. As early as 1650 a stage villain (in Thomas Killigrew's *Cicilia and Clorinda*) is described as 'clothed in black, with black Feathers, black Perriwig, his person is crooked and ugly, with a Dagger by his side' (pt. 1, I.i). The practice of putting villainous characters into black wigs continued into the Restoration, and Charles II, himself a swarthy man, commented on it (Cibber, 78). That villains were still stereotypically dark fifty years later can be deduced from Addison's 1709 definition of 'The Complexion [that is, makeup] of a Murderer' as consisting of 'a large Piece of burnt Cork, and a Coal-black peruke' (quoted in Odell, I: 290. Was the 'burnt Cork' intended to make the rest of the facial hair match the peruke?).

The early history of Iago suggests, however, that a variety of physical types could be accepted in the role. Both John Lowin and the Restoration actor Walter Clun were famous Falstaffs, likely to have presented a bluff, honest appearance. But in the 1620s and 1630s the part was taken by the good-looking Joseph Taylor, Burbage's successor as the star of the King's Men, and Clun was succeeded by another handsome actor, 'Major' Michael Mohun. However, when the great Thomas Betterton inherited Othello, after the union of the theatres in 1682, his Iago was Samuel Sandford, a stage villain so crookedly shaped that Colley Cibber was sure that Shakespeare would have wanted him for Richard III (Cibber, 77). Cibber argues both sides of the question about type-casting villains: on the one hand, it is better that they should be unattractive so that the spectator, 'not being misled by a tempting Form, may be less inclin'd to excuse the wicked or immoral Views or Sentiments of them' (75). But he also questions whether it would be wise 'to employ, in wicked Purposes, Men, whose very suspected Looks might be enough to betray them' (78). Cibber himself, a scrawny actor with an undistinguished face and an unimpressive voice, first played Iago in 1708, after the death that year of the actor to whom the role had belonged; but between that year and 1715 he shared it with another actor, Theophilus Keene. When Keene left the company in 1715, Richard Steele reported in his journal The Town Talk that Cibber was reluctant to mount a revival of Othello at Drury Lane because he knew he would have to play Iago. That Cibber was right when he wrote in his Apology of the audience's tendency to hate the actors of villains' roles is borne out by the jibe of the critic John Dennis, who insisted that the actor could play fops and villains only because he really was both these things – 'and sometimes in Tragedy he blends the Fop and Villain together, as in Jago for Example, in the Moor of Venice'

(Potter, 156). Nevertheless, Cibber carried on as the Drury Lane Iago until 1732, by which time he was over sixty. Most people agreed that he was excellent in comic roles, but contemporary comment on his Iago often describes him as an obvious villain who would have fooled no one. However, similar comments were made about Charles Macklin, probably the best Iago of his time; his clear, unstagy and intelligent delivery were highly respected; but, like many Iagos, he was both praised for his 'seeming openness, and concealed revenge' (Cooke, 407) and criticized for looking too villainous (Foote, 37–9). It sounds as if Iago, like Othello, was a role demanding such opposing qualities that no one actor was likely to strike an audience as sufficiently villainous or sufficiently plausible.

David Garrick should have been superb in both capacities. His failure as Othello was followed by a brief period during which he played Iago to the popular Spranger Barry. That his biographer Arthur Murphy praised his generosity in doing so is sufficient evidence that Iago was still regarded as a secondary role. Garrick may have hoped to make it something more. But, although Murphy says that 'the attention of the public was equally divided between the two great performers' (Murphy, II: 173), once Barry had left Drury Lane for Covent Garden in 1750, Garrick lost interest in Iago, playing him only once more, in 1753. There is no evidence as to what he did with the part, and he does not seem to have altered the tradition of treating it as a supporting role, though given by preference to actors who, like Macklin, spoke clearly and intelligently. Indeed, the distinction that Virginia Vaughan sees in Victorian productions between emotional Othellos and intellectual Iagos (Vaughan, 158–9) seems already to have been present a hundred years earlier. One of the most highly praised Iagos of the late eighteenth century was Robert Bensley, an ex-soldier with a plausibly honest appearance. A favourite with Charles Lamb, who praised him for looking to the audience just as he should look to Othello, he first played the part in 1771, partnered the great Barry in 1772 and ended by playing opposite Kemble in 1794.

John Henderson (1747–85) was not only a famous Iago but a successful Hamlet and a still greater Falstaff. Like Garrick, he began to play Iago only after he had failed as Othello (Ireland, 117–18), though, unlike Garrick, he seems to have liked the role. Clarity was one of his greatest virtues, and his best roles were those for which elegant verse-speaking was not an important

5 Johann Heinrich Ramberg, John Henderson as Iago

criterion (Boaden, *Siddons*, 257). Boaden, the biographer of Kemble
and Siddons, wrote that Henderson's Falstaff 'made his audience
for the time as intelligent as himself', and that his Iago was
'profoundly intellectual, like the character. Anything near this I
have never seen' (74, 245). He is credited with several innovations
that later became customary: skilfully varying the constantly
repeated phrase 'put money in thy purse' (246) and making the
rhymes in II.i sound genuinely improvised. The contemporary
theatrical portrait by Johann Heinrich Ramberg (figure 5), partly
based on a portrait head by Gilbert Stuart, may illustrate his
'unrivalled' ability to bring out the character's jealousy (quoted in
Highfill, VII: 260). His crooked eyebrows may be modelled on
those with which envy and anger are indicated in the illustrations
to Le Brun's lectures on the passions. His contorted gesture may
serve the same purpose, though it might also result from the
belief, derived from Quintilian, that gestures should be made only
with the right hand (Roach, 53–4). Or perhaps the artist simply

captured Henderson's notorious ungainliness. 'To the last,' one admirer wrote rather proudly, 'he never possessed an action that was elegant'; as Hamlet, he was always in danger of losing the fight at the end, and he was said to have been so indifferent to appearance that he boasted of having worn the same costume for three different roles in succession (Anon., *Stage Trick*, 16). From playing Falstaff so frequently, he is said to have acquired a 'fatness of tone' (Ireland, 65) that might have suited the persona adopted by Iago. Henderson may have become a legend only because he was still under forty when he died, but the surviving evidence suggests that he caught the imaginations of his admirers at least partly because he lacked the usual attributes of a good actor and thus seemed more 'real'. His clearly spoken, unpoetic Iago may have been one of the first to subvert the kind of style associated with the tragic hero, thus foreshadowing the theatrical rivalry between Othello and Iago.

One might have expected Edmund Kean, whose first London Iago, on 7 May 1814, came only two days after his debut as Othello, to go still further in this direction. B. W. Procter, his first biographer, comments tantalizingly on his interpretation: 'He took for his model a person still alive'; alas, he does not say whom (Procter, II: 73). Kean played with such a light humorous tone that there was some critical debate about its propriety, and his musical talents helped him make the drunken scene enjoyable; when Junius Brutus Booth later played Iago to his Othello, reviewers who remembered Kean complained of the inferiority of Booth's singing (*The News*, 23 February 1817). But, if Procter can be believed, Kean changed his interpretation after a few nights (were there threats from those who recognized his model?), and his later performances were only 'second-rate'. The actor, who often based his stage attitudes on statues and paintings, seems to have been looking for a different way of 'coding' Iago's villainy than the generalized Le Brun tradition. He may in fact have been the first to exploit a national stereotype. Having carefully studied 'the distinctive characteristics of the southern blood', he 'imparted a peculiarly *Italian* tint to the character of the ancient, especially in that significant action of silently rubbing his hands behind him as his plot satisfactorily progressed' (Hawkins, 249–50). There may have been political motives behind this reading. Since 1815 Queen Caroline had lived abroad and had been accused of adultery with an Italian lover. In 1820, when George IV was trying to ensure that his estranged wife was never crowned Queen of England, a Bill of Pains and Penalties against her was debated in Parliament. Many of the witnesses against the Queen were, inevitably, Italian; the Lord Chief Justice, summing up in her defence, reminded his listeners that Shakespeare always depicted the slandering of an innocent wife as taking place in Italy (Bate, 88); he was presumably thinking of *Much Ado About Nothing*, *Cymbeline* and *The Winter's Tale* as well as *Othello*. At a time when any potentially topical reference could become a cue for an audience demonstration, the theatres took the opportunity to exploit this topicality. In productions of *Othello* during this period, the first cue for audience reactions was Iago's question, 'Where's that palace whereinto foul things / Sometimes intrude not?' (III.iii.140–1). Then, when Emilia indignantly suggested that someone had devised the slander of Desdemona 'to get some office' (IV.ii.132), her words provoked in the audience what one startled spectator described as 'a noise such as I have never heard in a theatre' (Limon, 115).

The idea of Italianizing Iago did not need topical justification, of course; whether accidentally or intentionally, the stereotyping continued throughout much of the nineteenth century. The American ex-president John Quincy Adams, writing in the 1840s, bracketed Iago and Othello together as 'national portraits of man – the ITALIAN and the MOOR' (Hackett, 241). One well-known nineteenth-century Iago, Edwin Booth, had strikingly dark hair and eyes. But even the blond Charles Fechter (1861) is said to have made a 'swift Italian gesture of contempt' towards Othello (Morley, 235); in 1881, Irving's Iago was praised as 'so marvellously Italian' (Dickins, 89). At the same time that critics were praising Italian impersonators of Othello and describing the role as beyond the reach of too-highly-civilized Anglo-Saxon actors, they nevertheless managed to treat Iago's cold-blooded villainy as typical of his country. Writing in 1888, an Italian critic finally protested, pointing out that, apart from Othello, *all* the characters in the play are Italians ('Jarro', 55–6). As late as 1904 A. C. Bradley felt it necessary to deny, in *Shakespearean Tragedy*, that Iago represented 'that peculiarly Italian form of villainy which is considered both too clever and too diabolical for an Englishman' (171).

The Othello–Iago partnership

The unusual relationship of Othello and Iago, not only as characters but also as actors, had been noted at least from the time of Samuel Foote's *Treatise on the Passions* (1747). Drawing on his own experience of playing Othello with Charles Macklin as Iago, Foote emphasizes the importance of taking both roles seriously: 'I defy the greatest *Othello* that ever was born, unless he be well provided with an Ancient, properly to express either the Hero or the jealous Lover: Nor, indeed, can the Skill and Address of *Iago* be placed in a conspicuous Light without the Assistance of a judicious *Othello*' (36). What he stresses here is the interdependence of the characters, not their competition. Macklin, Bensley and Henderson, though highly regarded in the role, did not make anyone think of it as the centre of the play. Moreover, Othello and Iago were not considered so equal in importance that actors wanted to play them both.

In the early nineteenth century, however, the competition between Othello and Iago in the play began to be mirrored in the theatrical casting. George Frederick Cooke (1756–1812), a gifted but erratic actor who was seen as a successor to Macklin and Henderson, originally acted both Othello and Iago but had dropped Othello from his repertory by the time he came to play at Covent Garden opposite John Philip Kemble in the season of 1803–04. Kemble, a tall, handsome, if rather statuesque, actor, normally took heroic roles such as Othello, but it was when Cooke played Iago that spectators had to be turned away. An often-quoted account by Washington Irving shows how the two actors, without benefit of direction or rehearsal (since Cooke had refused to attend one), could act out a competition whose nature must have been obvious to much of their audience:

> they went on the boards without previous rehearsal. In the scene in which Iago instils his suspicion, Cooke grasped Kemble's left hand with his own, and then fixed his right, like a claw, upon his shoulder. In this position, drawing himself up to him with his short arm, he breathed his poisonous whispers. Kemble coiled and twisted his hand, writhing to get away – his right hand clasping his brow, and darting his eye back on Iago. (Sprague, *Actors*, 194)

Though the actors clearly enjoyed playing up to each other, the excitement of the scene came not only from its spontaneity but from the sense that, as Edward Pechter says, 'There are two assaults here – one on Kemble and one on Othello' (97). During a brief period in 1807 while Cooke was absent (he had in fact been jailed for debt) Kemble actually did take over the role of Iago (Wilmeth, 234–5). Possibly influenced by his experience as Zanga in *The Revenge*, a splendid villain who remains triumphant to the end, Kemble played such a sympathetic and heroic character that, 'to a greater part of the audience, *Iago* appeared as an oppressed man, and *Othello* as the real villain'. This odd experiment is known only because the reviewer just quoted insisted on its wrongness: Iago, he argued, 'is no otherwise a tragic character, than as he is rendered such by his superlative wickedness ... It is the jealousy of Othello, not the revenge of Iago, which Shakespeare intended to depict' (*Oxberry's ... Histrionic Anecdotes*, 280–2). But the possibility of an alternative reading had been raised, as had the possibility of alternating the roles. Audiences must have been interested in comparing Kemble's Iago with his Othello. Ten years later, when Junius Brutus Booth began acting in London, the playbill for his first appearance in Woolwich as Othello declared, in increasingly large typeface, that this performance 'must be rendered doubly attractive, from the remembrance that HE ALSO PERFORMS Iago in the same play'.

In 1816 Macready and Charles Young, both of them at the beginning of their careers, may have been the first to alternate the roles of Othello and Iago on a regular basis, deliberately encouraging audiences to compare them. Macready had at one point been intended to alternate these roles with Kean, but Kean had such a strong preference for Othello that he never went through with it; according to Barry Procter, he once made a point of playing Iago as badly as possible when he knew that a provincial theatre manager was in the audience, 'with a view of not being called upon to act a character, to which he seems to have had an inveterate dislike' (Procter, II: 102). Other leading actors felt no such objection. In a period when the theatrical repertory was narrow, audiences must have become restive at the limited fare offered at the only two London theatres allowed to perform 'legitimate' drama; giving the same play with two actors alternating in the leading parts was a good way to revive public interest. When actors were known to be ambitious and jealous of one another, the famous scene in III.iii, where Othello and Iago make physical contact, was bound to be exciting and unpredictable. The performance on 20 February 1817, with Edmund Kean as Othello and Junius Brutus Booth as Iago, was clearly recognized as a 'wrestle of talent'; Kean, who 'seemed to take a pleasure in the struggle', finally (in III.iii, of course) 'beat his antagonist hollow' (*The Champion*, 23 February 1817). The competition reached the point of absurdity in a performance where Edwin Forrest's Othello confronted Gustavus Brooke's Iago. The latter, determined not to be quelled by Forrest's famous physical and vocal power, responded to Othello's attack by drowning him out with the sheer volume of his cry: 'O Grace! O Heaven, defend me!' 'Forrest,' we are told, 'was actually stupefied by the sudden explosion: it was the first time in his career that he had ever been over-matched in volume of tone. The audience was so astonished that it knew not whether to applaud or hiss' (Wingate, 44). One can understand their surprise, particularly since, if the actors followed the usual stage tradition, Othello had just come close to strangling the man who now addressed him at the top of his voice.

Forrest's most famous rival, Macready, was also accused of abusing his power when he alternated the two roles. According to George Vandenhoff, who had played both Iago and Othello with him,

> when he played Othello, Iago was to be *nowhere*! ... Iago was a mere *stoker*, whose business it was to supply Othello's passion with fuel, and keep up his high-pressure ... The next night, perhaps, he took Iago; and lo! presto! every thing was changed. Othello was to become a mere puppet for Iago to play with; a pipe for Iago's master-skill to 'sound from its lowest note to the top of its compass' ... Thus, this great work, this terrible duel between brain and heart, the conflict of intellectual subtlety with all-triumphant love; this Machiavellian victory of the base over the noble, ... was to be in either case a one-sided picture. (Vandenhoff, 208–9)

Whether or not Vandenhoff was being fair to Macready, he shows that the two roles had achieved virtual equality; no actor of Othello could automatically assume that he would dominate the play.

Yet the audience's appetite for rivalry between the two actors sometimes gave way to a desire for some sort of symbiosis between them, like the sinister doubles in the fiction of Dickens and Stevenson. So Thomas Gould, in his almost hagiographic biography of Junius Brutus Booth, wished that his reader could 'imagine Booth's Iago played against his own Othello' (Gould, 94), and the young actress Kitty Malony, on Edwin Booth's 1887–88 tour, found herself imagining something very similar when she watched Booth, whose Iago she had already seen many times, play Othello in San Francisco: 'By shutting my eyes and ears to Mr. Barron [the Iago], it was easy enough to vision the master-actor in both characters – to see them together on the stage. And when I did not so see them, Iago at once dwindled into a despicable hypocrite' (Goodale, 214). Implicit in these words, and even in the Othello–Iago alternations, is the allegorical or Freudian reading of the play, in which Iago is simply an aspect of something already existing in Othello himself. Young's *Revenge* had already suggested some such interpretation in its last line, which warns that jealousy is a condition where 'each Man finds a *Zanga* in his heart' (70).

Iago triumphant: Booth and Irving

A reviewer of Samuel Phelps's Iago is frank – if also perhaps slightly embarrassed – about the pleasure that audiences derived from hating Iago: 'when Othello stabs him, a feeling of delight (if we may so express ourselves) thrilled the bosoms of many present' (Bath *Herald*, quoted Allen, 73). The character attracted hatred because hatred was often the dominant note of the role. When, as in the early nineteenth century, Iago left the stage before the end, Macready was remembered for the rage with which he burst open the doors with his fists (Hankey, 334). Phelps at the same point 'was roundly erect and made his exit with a glance of unspeakable scorn – no ordinary villain's look of hate, but a frighteningly powerful defiance of human sympathy' (Manchester *Sphinx*, 17 November 1869, quoted Allen, 177). In Fechter's 1861 production a crowd who had to be kept back by the guards threatened Iago when he was brought in after his attempted escape, his hands tied behind him. After Othello's death the guards again approached the villain and clapped their hands on his shoulder as the curtain fell. It is evident that the purpose behind these various bits of business was to provide an outlet for the righteous anger of the audience.

But even in Fechter's production one can see the signs of a new attitude that would make Iago not only easier to play but easier for the audience to like. The naturalistic acting style, full as it was of casual details, might be unhelpful for Othello, but it worked in favour of Iago, and Fechter played both parts in succession. Instead of telegraphing villainy through costume and makeup,

[79]

Fechter stipulated that Iago's clothes should be 'Quiet and in good taste; his manner and appearance attractive' (Fechter, 1). Other stage directions indicate that there must have been considerable rapport among the actors. On 'What was he whom you followed', Iago is *uneasy, and scrutinizing* CASSIO, *to find out whether he has recognized* RODERIGO', then laughs when he realizes that Cassio remembers nothing. In his great scene with Othello, Iago shows 'feigned embarrassment' on 'why, say they are vile and false'. With particular subtlety, Iago pretends to misunderstand Othello's actions when he moves away on 'Ha!' – really out of annoyance at Iago's behaviour – and responds with 'O, beware my lord of jealousy!', as if Othello were already showing the attitude against which he pretends to warn him. These kinds of subtleties were easy to achieve in the role of Iago, whereas Othello, by definition, was incapable of them.

Though, as I have noted earlier, many handbooks of acting continued to cling to a mechanistic approach to the expression of coded emotions, this was no longer the only model available for the actor. Joseph Roach, in *The Player's Passion*, has shown how writers on acting draw simultaneously on several theories of the passions. By the late eighteenth century they seem to have been able to imagine not only the alternation of intense passions but also a 'physiology of vibrations' which compared the passions to stringed instruments whose effects subsided only gradually (Roach, 106). This second model made it easier for an Iago to reconcile the two opposing aspects of his character, remaining consistently evil even while he played a variety of roles with others.

Edwin Booth above all was credited with this power:

> At one moment he is the man who unwillingly knows more than he can tell; then he is the indiscreet friend who has told more than he had intended; then he is the thoughtful adviser who tries to curb the impatience of his friend and stem the current of his jealousy; then he is the fool who realizes that he has been placed in a most awkward predicament; and then he is the frank challenger of Desdemona's fidelity. All these he is upon the surface to Othello; but underneath it all there is but one magnificent villain (*The Playgoer*, Memphis, Tenn., 29 January 1888; clipping in Folger Scrapbook, 'Edwin Booth: 2')

The New York critic J. R. Towse also described Booth as 'entirely plausible, with no hint of venomous intrigue except in the soliloquies', but added that he 'somehow seemed to be enveloped in an aura of evil' (Towse, 190). Words such as 'fiendish' are often used of this actor, and Goethe's Mephistopheles surely lurks behind the red costume that he wears in the portrait by Thomas Hicks. Horace Howard Furness, his friend, printed in the *Variorum Othello* many of Booth's comments on the need for subtlety in playing Iago. Another friend, William Winter, writes admiringly of moments at which he sounded utterly convincing: 'his tone of devotional entreaty, at "Do not rise yet"'; 'the speciousness of his tender solicitude and bland sympathy, at "Is my lord angry"'; and what he called 'the sweet serenity and inexorable purpose of evil' in his delivery of 'I'll set down the stops that make this music' (Winter, 197).

Booth apparently played the part rapidly: even at fifty, he made his first entrance with 'such physical vitality that I wonder if Mr. Booth did not intend it for a symbol of his mental vitality' (Goodale, 110). Booth himself believed in a light and comic Iago, suggesting to Furness that the role ought to be given to the company's light comedian rather than to the 'heavy man' (Furness, *Variorum*, 146); some of his comments, as when he notes that he could not prevent himself from pocketing the purse thrown on the floor by Othello in IV.ii, suggest that his own instincts were comic (Furness, *Variorum*, 264). But he knew that he himself lacked 'the soldierly quality' and his naturally gloomy temperament worked against the comic approach. He did not play an affectionate husband to Emilia, believing that Iago 'is rather given to chiding than caressing'; in IV.ii, where she indirectly accuses him, he blended, one spectator thought, hatred of his wife and contempt for the women's ignorance of his real nature (Stone, 193). His most effective accentuation of Iago's villainy (Fechter and Irving also used the business, as do many modern Iagos) came in V.i. The acting text omitted both Othello's entrance and the unheroic dithering of Lodovico and Gratiano about whether or not to respond to Cassio's cries; thus, the line, 'How silent is this town' (V.i.247), which in context is Iago's feigned outrage at the absence of response to his calls for help, became a calm, blood-chilling recognition that there would be no witnesses to his murder of the wounded Cassio. Figure 6 shows Booth as he moves toward his helpless victim, just before the sound of the approaching Venetians forces him to abandon his plan.

Often, when there is an opportunity to compare the actor's impression of what he was doing with the observer's interpretation

6   Edwin Booth as Iago in V.i, photographed by Sarony

of it, one finds that Booth's apparent intention of undermining the villain was often itself undermined, either by his own unconscious unwillingness to make himself really contemptible or by his audience's determination to read him more sympathetically. For instance, although in the notes he made for the *Variorum* (270) he indicated that Iago should be embarrassed and even 'somewhat nervous' when Roderigo threatens him in IV.ii, the notes made by his admirer Mary Isabella Stone indicate that he seemed totally indifferent to the threats and quickly succeeded in dominating his victim ('Iago folds his arms and looks sternly in Roderigo's eye; the latter quails': Stone, 196). From her account one can see that he displayed what sounds like abject terror as he realized that Emilia was able to give him away, 'first perceived in the shaking of the plumes in the hat he holds'; with the aid of the makeup he already wore, he apparently managed to turn pale and then, as if choking for breath, fumbled 'at the fastening of his doublet at the throat' (205). Yet Stone responded sympathetically even to this behaviour from a suddenly vulnerable Iago. Like her, other spectators were especially impressed with his (largely silent) performance after Othello had wounded him and he was struggling 'not to afford his enemies the satisfaction of seeing him overcome' (210). It was only here that he revealed the full extent of his hatred and malignity, 'with a horrible gritting of clenched teeth' (Towse, 191) as he said, 'From this time forth I never will speak word' (V.ii.301). This moment was famous: 'No one doubted that even under torture that jaw would stay shut ... Over forty times I saw that self-imposed lockjaw, and not once did it seem studied, and I never failed to catch Iago's unspoken gloating over those who would try to open his jaw and fail' (Goodale, 110). As Stone describes him, he refrained from scene-stealing during the final moments of the play, standing in silence or, in 1882 and 1884, collapsing on an ottoman, with his back to the audience until Othello's suicide, at which point he twisted round to let them see his face with its look of 'fiendish triumph' (Stone, 211).

Nevertheless, by the time he played the part in London in 1881 he seemed old-fashioned and too obviously villainous beside Irving, with whom he alternated the two roles. Critics mention in particular Booth's pointing in triumph to the dead bodies at the end, a piece of business that goes back to the early nineteenth century. Irving played Iago for only a few weeks, by contrast with the performance that Booth had been refining over many years. Like Booth, Irving was sometimes called Mephistophelian, and both apparently borrowed from the scene of Valentin's death in Goethe's *Faust* the business of knocking up Roderigo's sword in the fight with Cassio in V.i. But Irving was a witty, comic devil, not a frightening one; what made this performance so popular was that he was the most amusing Iago anyone had yet seen (Terry, 205). He made the character a well-dressed gentleman-adventurer: one reviewer, observing that the money Iago got from Roderigo was obviously spent on fine clothes, suggested that his lavish lifestyle explained why Emilia had put up with him for so long (George Augustus Sala, *Illustrated London News*, 7 May 1881). Most reviewers emphasize his comedy and wit (Sala notes that his 'colossal duplicity' in V.i 'provoked a general titter'), but

Irving seems also to have showed a restless fidgetiness implying real tension behind his apparently casual manner. When Booth trembled all over in the final scene, no one ever took this for anything other than part of his characterization; but the mannerisms that Irving gave the character were sometimes taken by reviewers to be his own (Vaughan, 176). His performance may well have influenced the author of an essay on 'The Attitude of Iago' (1905) who declared that 'The real tragedy of *Othello* is not the murder of Desdemona and the suicide of Othello, but the wasting of a first-rate intellect on private and second-rate objects, and the evil use of ability merely for the sake of exercise' (*The Era*, 5 August 1905). Despite the Italian touches, this new Iago was a cool English intellectual dandy; Wilde's Lord Goring, in *An Ideal Husband*, might have resembled him, if he had manipulated bracelets and letters to shatter a marriage rather than preserve it.

Though the two actors played Iago very differently, it is evident that they both exercised a romantic attraction for their audiences. When Booth played Iago, it seemed like the leading role. He greatly preferred it to Othello, and was annoyed when he found on his European tour that German audiences, still wedded to the traditonal concept of heroes and villains, expected their visiting star to play the far more tiring role of Othello (Goodale, 131–2). The fact is that Iago did not seem like a secondary role. While she was acting in Booth's touring company, Kitty Malony teasingly informed him that he was unsuited to the part of Iago because he was too good-looking: 'No new husband who is not a born fool would select such a guardian to escort and protect his young bride.' Her half-flirtatious, provocative yet safe relationship with the famous actor, twice her age, is comparable to that of other spectators, admiring Iago from the safe distance of their theatre seats. But Malony went on to quote a friend, Frank Mayo, who had attempted to debunk the entire romantic conception of the character. Anticipating William Empson's recognition of the slightly condescending connotation of 'honest', as in 'honest Thompson, my gardener' (Empson, 224), Mayo had pointed out that the word 'honest' is not normally used of good-looking people. 'When there is no other adjective people can think of to apply to a man except honest – they mean that he is close to being a fool. I suppose he meant not shrewd enough to be dishonest. That's why every one trusts Iago and calls him honest. Mr. Mayo says Iago should be fat; a blond; almost lazy; even perspiring! No romantic girl would, of course, fall in love with *that* type, and a smart, unscrupulous man could easily be of this type' (Goodale, 289–90). Mayo was probably joking: no one would have seriously expected to see a blond, sweaty Iago at this period, certainly not from Booth, who did not wear a blond wig even for Hamlet. But what may have been a joke at the end of the nineteenth century would become an acceptable interpretation by the end of the twentieth. The iconography of Iago's villainy would draw on an increasingly widespread new code, the Freudian one.

CHAPTER IV

Interval: alternative *Othello*s in the modern age

Hesione. Ellie darling: have you noticed that some of those stories that Othello told Desdemona couldnt [*sic*] have happened? ... Desdemona would have found him out if she had lived, you know. I wonder was that why he strangled her!
Ellie. Othello was not telling lies.
Hesione. How do you know?
Ellie. Shakespeare would have said if he was. Hesione: there are men who have done wonderful things: men like Othello, only, of course, white.

(Shaw, *Heartbreak House*, Act I)

By the late nineteenth century it was recognized that the theatrical *Othello*, the product of two-and-a-half centuries of cutting and re-shaping, was far different from the original text. As one reviewer put it, 'the play has been much refined since its masterful creator breathed into [it] the immortality of genius, and there is left to the theater-goer only the nobility and purity that give romantic and poetic charm to the Moor' (*The Inter Ocean*, Chicago, 9 October 1888). The writer does not say what the play contains apart from 'nobility and purity', but anyone who read the newspapers could find out what he meant. It is implied in the controversy over Salvini and the Italian actors, and stated more explicitly by advocates of the 'new drama', of whom the best known is George Bernard Shaw. The precariousness of Othello's claims to heroism and nobility, at least in the second half of the play, had always been recognized. In *A Treatise on the Passions* (1747) Samuel Foote, who had played the part briefly himself, said that the actor's greatest challenge was the task of 'raising in the Minds of the Audience a Compassion for himself superior, if possible, to that they entertain for his Wife' (Foote, 33). For most of the nineteenth century Desdemona's insignificance and the focus on famous actors had made this task comparatively easy. But near the end of this period growing dissatisfaction with the play and its hero can be traced in a number of reviews. When one reviewer of Ernesto Rossi's Othello in 1881 lamented that the Italian actors had destroyed his illusions – 'It used to be thought that Othello is a very noble, magnanimous, delicate, poetic creation ... It used to be held that the slaughter of Desdemona is a sacrifice, and not the pretext for a melodramatic shambles' (unattributed NYPL clipping) – another retorted, 'Murder, especially when prompted by jealousy, founded or unfounded, is murder and unjudicial' (Towse, 159). In 1887 a reviewer in Pittsburgh declared that 'The nobleness and the stupidity of Othello was [sic] amazing' (*The Pittsburg Press*, 23 November 1887). In 1914 a New York reviewer said firmly, 'Othello is not morally justified in killing her or in thinking her unfaithful, and the best acting in the world can never make it convincing' (unattributed, *Brooklyn Daily Eagle*, 1 May 1914; Folger Scrapbook: Othello). In the three previous chapters I have indicated how the play belongs severally to each of its characters, depending on the perspective from which it is viewed. The heroic play is Othello's, the pathetic one Desdemona's, and the intellectual approach, which of course is the one taken by most critics, is Iago's. In a heavily cut and 'refined' text the Iago approach was not yet so dominant as it would later be, but it is interesting to see Shaw, for example, adopting the character's words when he suggests that *Othello* 'would be a prodigiously better play' if 'it were a serious discussion of the highly interesting problem of how a simple Moorish soldier would get on with a "supersubtle" Venetian lady of fashion if he married her' (Shaw, *Quintessence*, 151). *Heartbreak House* also supports Iago's view, paraphrased in the passage that appears above as an epigraph, that Othello wooed Desdemona by 'bragging and telling her fantastical lies' (II.i.221); Ellie soon discovers that her romantic suitor is a compulsive liar, and married as well. This chapter will look first at the alternatives to the heroic and poetic *Othello*, then at the various ways in which the poetic tradition survived, as it still survives, particularly outside the English-speaking world.

'The fit': Othello diagnosed

The 'new drama' first shows its effect in its interest in one previously overlooked aspect of Othello's character. A distinctive feature of the heroic part was supposed to be its lack of 'glaring exterior oddities. Its individuality consists in mental rather than physical peculiarities. It usually derives its interest from the excessive predominance of one passion' (Dechmann, 66). Othello's blackness did not count as an 'external oddity', presumably since everyone knew that the actor was not in fact black. On the other hand, Othello's 'trance' or seizure in IV.i must have disturbed the heroic image, as it seems to have disappeared by 1725 (Sprague, *Actors*, 203), apart from a brief reintroduction by Garrick in 1745. The episode may have been omitted from the play because of uncertainty as to whether it might be a 'physical peculiarity' rather than yet another example of the intense emotion that often made characters in post-Restoration drama faint or fall on the ground. Most scholars took Iago's lines

My lord is fall'n into an epilepsy;
This is his second fit, he had one yesterday.

(IV.i.50–1)

to be a characteristic improvisation, intended to get Cassio off the stage while incidentally spreading the view that Othello is an unstable character. It is clear that Othello is not foaming at the mouth, since Iago goes on to warn that this is what he will do if disturbed. Henry Irving, who was interested in abnormal psychology, played the epileptic fit in 1876. He was probably the first English actor since Garrick to do so, although Charles Fechter's production had opened the scene with Othello lying in a faint. Julie Hankey notes that it 'sounds more like a faint than a fit' (269). Irving omitted the fit the second time he played the part in 1881, since Booth had never played the scene and would otherwise have had to learn new lines. Furness's New Variorum of 1886 notes that the depiction of epilepsy is accurate, supporting his statement with a quotation from *The Medical Knowledge of Shakespeare* (1860); F. A. Marshall, the editor of the 'Henry Irving Shakespeare' (1889), annotated the passage in some detail, treating it as a realistic, clinical depiction and pointing out that the after-effects of the fit would make Othello particularly susceptible to the insinuations of Iago (Marshall, 98–9). Dostoevsky, the first major writer to depict epileptic characters, died in 1881; his works were already known on the continent and began to be read in England not long after that date (Temkin, 370–82). In the same year as the Henry Irving Shakespeare, the Italian actor Ermete

Zacconi (1857–1948) played an Othello who was a sick man from the start of the play, and whose condition explained his credulity. Zacconi had already made his name in the new realistic drama; in the first Italian production of Ibsen's *Ghosts* he had played Oswald, who goes mad from a condition related to hereditary syphilis, and he would later play Musset's Lorenzaccio as an epileptic. A reviewer from the London *Telegraph* who caught a later performance on tour in Paris failed to understand its rationale but recognized that he was being shown 'an amazing picture of the physical pain of jealousy. It was not dignified or dignifying pain, but unbearable pain of the flesh, and he swooned as if worn out by the rack.' Since Zacconi began with Act III, Othello was 'mad with jealousy from the beginning of the performance'. The sheer violence of the ending seems to have exceeded even that of his predecessors:

> Suddenly he leaped up, sprang like a tiger on to Iago's back, and stabbed him. He sank back again into stupor, then pulled himself together, and stood up for the 'nothing extenuate' speech, sank down again in the middle of it limply on a chair, and looked round him, helpless and downcast. He caught sight of a dagger on the floor, swiftly seized it without making a sound, stood up again with one last moment of energy and speaking rapidly, 'In Aleppo once,' stabbed himself in a flash and fell dead on the floor.
>
> (London *Telegraph*, 23 January 1911)

Characteristically, Zacconi had studied this death in clinical records (Busi, 40–1). The 'epileptic' interpretation was evidently more popular on the European continent than it ever became in the English-speaking theatre; a lecturer on criminal psychology in Rome during 1909–10 concluded his course with a study of Othello as an example, noting that some theories see all criminal behaviour as a manifestation of epilepsy (D'Alfonso, 39). As late as 1944 a Swiss reviewer defined three basic ways of playing Othello: the noble hero, the childlike dupe and the pathological epileptic (Kachler, 135).

If Zacconi's clinical approach now seems excessive, it was at least an actor's attempt to put a traditional heroic role in a contemporary context. Most other Othellos continued to avoid the episode. Oscar Ashe, who first played the part in a successful 1907 production, made a curious compromise between realism and the traditional heroic style: he omitted the fit at the place specified for it, but provided himself with a 'strong curtain' at the end of III.iii

[89]

when, having said, 'Now art thou my lieutenant' (III.iii.101), he fell senseless at Iago's feet (Dickins, 146). He seems to have accepted Iago's statement that the fit in IV.i was Othello's second one (though only scholars could have made the connection); at the same time, he played a conventional stage collapse rather than a realistic attack of delirium such as seems implied by the incoherent lines before it. Godfrey Tearle, one of the last of the 'heroic' Othellos and probably the most successful British Othello in the first half of the twentieth century, never included the fit in any of the four productions in which he starred (1921, 1922, 1948 and 1949). By 1949 he felt obliged to take responsibility for his actions in a letter to *The Times*, because the omission had gone against the wishes of his director, Anthony Quayle. Tearle, who had a fine presence and rich voice, played the role, Jill Bennett wrote, as 'a man of enormous dignity ... even in the jealousy scenes ... Suffering, he never broke. The epilepsy scene would not have been right for such an interpretation' (Bennett, 51–3).

Nostalgia versus 'psychology'

Tearle's success in Britain is paralleled in America by that of Walter Hampden, whose 1925 *Othello* ran for fifty-two performances, setting a Broadway record that was to be broken only by the Robeson *Othello* of 1943. It was clearly a display of old-fashioned heroic acting, praised by the veteran critic J. R. Towse for 'recalling the best days of the theatre' (*New York Post*, 12 January 1925). Though some reviewers felt that Hampden was too bland, even ascetic, and lacked the 'elemental' quality of the character, audience enthusiasm for the production is said to have verged on 'mild hysteria' (*New York World*, 12 January 1925). One reason must surely have been that Hampden was already well known, particularly as that great hero of nostalgic drama, Cyrano de Bergerac; he directed his own company, which had a strong Iago and Emilia in Baliol Holloway and Mary Hall (two Desdemonas alternated). He played a fairly full text (it lasted slightly over three and a half hours, and included Bianca though not the Clown) and the production was visually beautiful. One reviewer contrasted Hampden favourably with some recent performers, mainly from overseas: the 'wild beast' of Sir Herbert Beerbohm Tree and even the American Robert Mantell, apparently 'a worthy and a resonant Elk'. The Italian Othellos came in for even more severe attacks, especially Ermete Novelli (1907), who wore unusually dark makeup for the role: Giovanni Grasso (1910) only 'pawed the white limbs of his Desdemona', but Novelli was 'snorting, rabid, animal and negroid' (*New York Herald Tribune*, 12 January 1925).

The element of what might be called necessary falsehood in the romantic reading of the play was clearly recognized by a reviewer of an Old Vic production in 1935, who called Othello 'a brutish half-wit' and then praised Abraham Sofaer because he 'spared us the brutishness' and 'murdered with discretion' (Ivor Brown, *Observer*, 27 January 1935). It was still more pronounced when Robert Edmond Jones directed Walter Huston for a drama festival in Central City, Colorado, in 1934, then on tour and finally on Broadway in 1937. Jones was one of America's great designers: in Central City, where the production was a great success, the set for the final scene, which got applause when the curtain went up, was described as 'sufficiently magnificent to make the audience forget they were seeing a tragedy' (*Variety*, 24 July 1934). He actually based his acting edition on Edwin Booth's; by the time it reached Broadway it was only two and a half hours long, omitting, of course, Bianca (*Stage*, n.d., 70–1). It goes without saying that there was no 'fit'. One reviewer praised Huston for redeeming the play from the 'tripe of scholarship' that had called Othello 'a murderous brute' (Douglas Gilbert, *New York World Telegram*, 7 January 1937). But most complained that the play seemed dated. Even Iago no longer seemed more modern than Othello. Brian Aherne had been directed to speak his asides directly to the audience, a gesture towards Renaissance theatrical convention that was described as distracting and archaic (Burns Mantle, *New York Daily News*, 7 January 1937; *Variety*, 13 January 1937). Somehow, no one even noticed that the character was supposed to be young; Gielgud recalled that 'In the old days Iago was always acted by a middle-aged leading man' (Gielgud, 82). The play in general, and its hero in particular, had become anachronisms in a period dominated by understated comedy and psychological drama.

The most obvious collision of the older reading of *Othello* with a modern one occurred in the 1938 production directed by Tyrone Guthrie at the London Old Vic, with Ralph Richardson as Othello and Laurence Olivier as Iago. Ralph Richardson was probably the only twentieth-century Othello with experience of playing the title character in *Oroonoko*, now a period piece; seeing him in this role at the Malvern Festival in 1932, and admiring his 'grand sincerity', 'repose and fire', Harcourt Williams thought that he would make a good Othello some day (Miller, 51). It would obviously have been a traditional 'noble Moor'. But Guthrie and Olivier, after talking with Ernest Jones, the author of *Hamlet and Oedipus*, had worked out what they felt was an exciting new interpretation. Olivier says that Iago's motive was to be a subconscious homosexual attraction to Othello (*Confessions*, 113); Guthrie, carefully elliptical, refers to the interpretation only as 'psychological' (Guthrie, 173). The casting was perhaps intended to reinforce this interpretation, since Desdemona was played by an actress (Curigwen Lewis) who had previously been a successful Jane Eyre. One reviewer called her a 'timid, silly, spiritless little doll' (J.G.B., unattributed clipping, MMTC, February 1938); just as 'psychological' meant sexual, so 'spiritless' seems to mean sexless. Olivier and Guthrie, in their autobiographies, manage to suggest both that Richardson failed to understand what Olivier was doing and that he understood but refused to have anything to do with it. In any case, the audience and reviewers certainly failed to understand it, even when Olivier, in the first few performances, responded to Richardson's simulated fit by falling on the ground beside him and simulating an orgasm (Olivier, *Confessions*, 113). The reviewers obviously expected Othello to display emotional power in the central scenes of the play and faulted Richardson for failing to provide it: he was, as one wrote, only 'a clever actor striving to conceal the fact that he is incapable of these storms' (Richard Prentis, *John O'London's Weekly*, 18 February 1938). Everyone also expected Iago to be clever but not comic: as W. A. Darlington wrote, 'Othello seemed to have too much sense and Iago too little' (*Telegraph*, 8 February 1938). If Olivier's concept was missed even by sophisticated theatre reviewers, it is too easy to say simply that they, and audiences generally, were in a state of denial about the sexual component of the play, or even, as Olivier concluded in his account of the episode, that it is impossible to convey anything that is genuinely subconscious. The Lord Chamberlain's role did not come to an end until 1968: the London theatre was unused to modern plays on explicitly homosexual themes and thus audiences lacked experience of recognizing coded references to them. A 'psychological' reading was, at this period, essentially 'unreadable'.

Antitheatricality: the Leavis critique

Though F. R. Leavis's famous essay, 'Diabolic Intellect and the
Noble Hero: or The Sentimentalist's Othello', is generally recognized as one of the influences on the Othello that Olivier played in
1964, the essay was first published in 1937, the year before the
Richardson–Olivier *Othello*. In 1927 T. S. Eliot's 'Shakespeare and
the Stoicism of Seneca' had already described Othello's final
speech as 'adopting an *aesthetic* rather than a moral attitude,
dramatizing himself against his environment' (Eliot, 40). Leavis's
account of this speech starts from the same point, but goes still
farther:

> Contemplating the spectacle of himself, Othello is overcome with
> the pathos of it. But this is not the part to die in: drawing himself
> proudly up, he speaks his last words as the stern soldier who
> recalls, and re-enacts, his supreme moment of deliberate courage
> ... [He quotes V.ii.366ff.] That he should die acting his ideal part is
> all in the part: the part is manifested here in its rightness and
> solidity, and the actor as inseparably the man of action. The final
> blow is as real as the blow it re-enacts, and the histrionic intent
> symbolically affirms the reality: Othello dies belonging to the
> world of action in which his true part lay. (Leavis, 152)

The language makes it clear that Leavis recognized the Renaissance pun on acting and action – but with the difference that, for
him, the double meaning was pejorative. In arguing that there is
something inherently sentimental about wishing to believe that
Othello's achievement of nobility in his last moment was the final
'truth' about him, Leavis is being characteristically provocative.
He wishes to replace this 'truth' by another: that Othello's sense of
himself as a tragic hero is precisely the flaw that brings about the
tragedy and that our temptation to sympathize with him is the
result of identification and hence a sign of sentimental self-
indulgence. Nevertheless, his reading of the play is based on the
formalistic view that the proper focus of study is the tragic hero,
not the villain; 'Othello is the chief personage – the chief personage in such a sense that the tragedy may fairly be said to be
Othello's character in action. Iago is subordinate and merely
ancillary', 'a necessary piece of dramatic mechanism' (Leavis,
138). (Similarly, although he criticizes Othello for his lack of any
real knowledge of Desdemona, Leavis himself takes very little
interest in her and sees no need to 'enquire into the consistency of

[93]

Emilia's behaviour': 157.) He may be writing out of awareness that Iago had increasingly come to dominate the play in the theatre – although this was happening not because the actor playing Othello wanted to make his character seem more noble by stressing the 'diabolical intellect' of his antagonist but because the actor playing Iago wanted to make himself more interesting to the audience.

Most nineteenth-century critics, however much they might deplore the way the plays were performed, had some knowledge of them in the theatre. Much criticism in the first half of the twentieth century, however, was independent of theatrical experience, in a way that has become less common with the accessibility of films and videos and the theatrical popularity of Shakespeare generally. Leavis did a service in drawing attention to lines often cut in the theatre which, perhaps for that reason, had often been ignored by critics determined to see the consistent nobility of Othello. But, precisely because he focuses on a close reading of the text, he ignores everything that is not purely verbal; he condemns Othello for his self-dramatizing without considering the importance of self-dramatization in the theatre; he also implies that 'self-dramatization' is always likely to be 'un-self-comprehending' (152). A postmodernist reply would question the possibility, as well as the value, of self-comprehension. A reply from a theatrical perspective would also ask whether self-comprehension must always express itself in words. It is possible, for instance, that Edmund Kean's quiet, 'O fool, fool, fool!' convinced his audience that he understood everything that Leavis would have wanted him to understand. However, it was just this aspect of the theatre – its ability to produce effects outside the words – that criticism at this period found most suspicious.

The romantic tradition: the Verdi–Boito opera

The Verdi opera, which once sought to be a musical equivalent of the play, now enables us to imagine a theatrical *Othello* that was a spoken equivalent of the opera. Bernard Shaw claimed that Othello's 'forever farewell' speech ought, when spoken, to resemble 'Ora e per sempre addio' as sung by Verdi's first Otello, the tenor Francesco Tamagno (Shaw, *Theatres*, III: 148). Opera-lovers often claim that Verdi's *Otello*, with its libretto by Arrigo Boito, is superior to Shakespeare's; director Janet Suzman has replied that such people 'don't know the play, that's all' (Suzman, 'South Africa', 32). She is right, of course; I once heard someone who knew only the opera express disappointment after seeing the play for the first time, because the production had emphasized everything the opera leaves out: the operatic Jago lacks much of Iago's cynical humour and all of his obscenity; the operatic Otello humiliates Desdemona less viciously; he does not strike her, only forces her to the ground, and the original Jago, Victor Maurel, thought that even this was too much (Maurel, 140–1).

The opera does indeed focus on the 'nobility and purity' of the hero. Boito's preface to the production book of *Otello* refers to him in precisely the terms used by eighteenth-century writers on acting: 'First we should see the hero, then the lover; and we must perceive the hero in all his greatness if we are to understand how worthy he is of love and how great his capacity for passionate devotion' (Budden, 327). Yet, by comparison with the versions available on the English-speaking stage in the 1880s, Verdi and Boito gave a surprisingly full and 'organic' reading of the text, and two of their finest effects came at moments usually cut in the Anglo-American theatre. Although Bianca is absent from the opera, as from all stage versions at this period, the composer and librettist kept the notorious 'eavesdropping scene', which became a brilliant trio for Otello, Jago, and Cassio. Because the opera lets the audience hear Jago and Cassio only at the moments when Otello hears them, the situation is clearer than in many theatre productions; all three singers are clearly distinguished: the purely lyrical music of the tenor Cassio, Otello's more passionate tenor, and Jago's almost cackling high-baritone, much of which is within the tenor range. Furthermore, at a time when most English-language productions still did not allow Othello to speak his final couplet, Verdi and Boito restored it, linking it musically not only to his kiss at the beginning of the scene 'e'er I killed thee' but also to an earlier moment of their own devising, the end of Act I's love duet between Otello and Desdemona. The poignancy of this repetition has been called 'something the spoken theatre cannot achieve' (Osborne, 428–9).

The opera follows European rather than Anglo-American performance traditions. Although, when they began working on the opera, Verdi and Boito thought of calling it *Jago*, this was not because they saw him as the central character but because they hesitated to compete openly with Rossini's famous work; by

January 1886 they finally agreed that Othello was their protagonist and had to be the title character (*Verdi–Boito*, 96). Iago's
role, though brilliantly conceived, shrinks to insignificance after
Act III; Emilia is a relatively subdued character, as in the
continental tradition, and she is not killed at the end. On the other
hand, Desdemona's role is expanded: she appears at the end of Act
I to sing a love duet which gives her many of Othello's lines from
the speech to the senate; in both Acts II and III she dominates an
important ensemble, and in Act IV she sings both the Willow Song
and an Ave Maria in which, as she repeats the last line 'at the hour
of our death', she shows the sense of fatedness that derives from
the Ducis–Rossini tradition. In describing how he envisaged the
complex ensemble at the end of Act III, Boito calls Desdemona
'the chief figure on the lyrical side' and Jago 'the chief figure on
the dramatic side' (*Verdi–Boito*, 55). This dichotomy is actually
present in the play, where Iago refers to the couple as 'well-tuned'
but promises to 'set down / The pegs that make this music' (II.i.198–
9) and Othello, lamenting what he takes to be Desdemona's
degradation, suddenly talks of her musical gifts (IV.i.185–6). But
in the opera, as Peter Conrad puts it, Desdemona's lyrical and
musical impulse is set against Iago, 'the evil genius of spoken
drama' (Conrad, 163–4).

Stanislavski claimed that the tenor Francesco Tamagno, who
created the title role, had studied the part with Salvini (Stanislavski, *Legacy*, 41). This does not seem to be true, but Boito and
Verdi had seen the famous Salvini production; its influence is
particularly evident at the end of Act III, the most theatrical part
of the opera. Boito rearranged the text so that the arrival of
Lodovico and the public humiliation of Desdemona precede
Otello's collapse, which occurs after he has ordered the rest of the
characters offstage; only Jago remains to watch as Otello, after
raving about the handkerchief, falls into a faint (which can also be
played as a fit). Gloating over his success, Jago comments that
there is now nothing to prevent him from setting his foot on the
neck of his general, who is being saluted by the offstage chorus as
the 'Lion of Venice'. At this point, it appears, the librettist Boito
wanted Jago only to contemplate the possibility of setting his foot
on Otello's neck, whereas Verdi wanted him actually to do it. The
original Jago, Victor Maurel, obeyed Boito at the first performance but later decided to carry out the more sensational action
and claimed that his audience preferred it (Maurel, 140–3). Both

librettist and composer may have recognized, with different reactions, the visual echo, or inversion, of the famous moment in Salvini's performance where Othello was on the point of stamping out Iago's brains with his foot. Though Verdi and Boito were much more interested in Iago than Salvini, they eventually chose to end the opera much as he had ended his version of the play: Jago does not kill Emilia, and he is not onstage when Otello commits suicide. There is thus nothing to interfere with the final repetition of the 'kiss' theme and the reaffirmation of the power of love.

Early films: Italian and German

The early silent films of the play, often based as much on the opera as on Shakespeare, provide the visual equivalent to its music. The 1908 Pathé film gives the sequence of events as Boito arranged them in Verdi's Act III – that is, the striking of Desdemona precedes Othello's collapse, and the scene ends with Othello writhing on the ground as Iago watches and laughs in quasi-operatic style. In the final scene, as in the Salvini tradition, Emilia denounces Iago but is not killed by him, and Othello commits suicide by slitting his own throat. The film made by Ambrosio in 1914, which keeps the action in Venice throughout, may draw on Rossini's libretto for its treatment of the elopement of Othello and Desdemona, precipitated by the news that Brabantio has presented Roderigo to Desdemona as a suitor. The film's final scene, in which Desdemona is seen praying in front of an image of the Virgin, recalls the importance of the 'Ave Maria' for Ducis, Rossini and Verdi; the flame in front of the image flickers and dies at the moment of the heroine's murder.

By contrast, the 1922 Buchowetski film, made with Emil Jannings and Werner Krauss, is played in the exaggerated style associated with German Expressionism. Jannings, once considered the greatest actor in the world and certainly one of the most over-the-top actors to be seen on film, plays Othello almost like an animal; Krauss is a grotesquely grinning, skipping Iago. The programme for the US premiere of the film (Criterion, New York, 25 February 1923) gives the acting credentials of the two stars (declaring, incredibly, that Krauss's Iago is in the tradition of Edwin Booth), but pays even more attention to the fact that Ica Lenkeffy, the Desdemona, had won a beauty contest in her native

Hungary and had the 'measurements of the Venus de Milo'. The sheer length of the English captions, unusual for a silent film, looks like excessive homage to the source, yet in fact the adaptation is extremely free. The existing print seems to have been cut down from a longer version, which may explain the presence of a few loose ends. Robert Ball suggests that Othello's surprising declaration to the senate that he is the son of an Egyptian prince and a Spanish princess was inserted to prevent American viewers from taking offence at the depiction of miscegenation (281). The source of this idea may be someone's knowledge of the Moorish occupation of Spain and Othello's reference to the 'Egyptian' who supposedly gave the handkerchief to his mother, though I am told that the word is generally translated as 'Zigeuner', or gypsy (Werner Habicht, personal communication); no one seems to know what the caption said in its German version. It has always been tempting to read the performances of Jannings and Krauss in the light of subsequent events in Germany, especially since both actors were to have their brilliant careers tainted, if not destroyed, because of their popularity with the Nazi leaders to whom they willingly lent their talents. The Expressionist tradition of playing Othello as an animal stopped only when, as Wilhelm Hortmann notes, directors recognized that the approach reinforced Nazi racism (Hortmann, 151–2). Werner Habicht cites a Nazi ideologue who saw in Iago a case of 'tragically inverted Nordic potential' (Habicht, 'Shakespeare', 115). Performances of *Othello* were later banned by the Nazi government in 1940, though the ban appears not to have been rigidly enforced.

Stanislavski and the Russian tradition

Probably the most important event in the 'international' history of *Othello* occurred in 1901, when Konstantin Stanislavski saw Salvini's performance and immediately determined to direct the play, taking the title role himself. His 1904 production was only a partial success, and his extensive notes for a Moscow Arts Theatre production in 1930 remain unfinished, whilst the production based on the notes was short-lived. Yet the play is so pervasive in his posthumously published writings on the theatre (at one point, indeed, he thought of making it the central text for all of them) that it had a disproportionate effect in central and Eastern Europe. Some of the visual effects he envisaged, such as Othello's first entrance in I.ii carrying armfuls of flowers, became something of an icon, imitated or parodied in later productions (Stříbrný, *Eastern*, 80–1).

Moreover, despite his apparent romanticism, as early as 1904 Stanslavski was already bringing out the play's sexual and political implications in a way that had no parallel in the contemporary Anglo-American theatre. It would be several decades before the western theatre paid as much attention as he did to Desdemona's sexuality. Salvini's passionate greeting of Desdemona in II.i had been controversial; Stanislavski was so conscious of the passion implicit in this reunion that, when he was working on his production in 1928, he proposed delaying her entrance (as in the opera) so that Othello could deal first with his duties to his comrades and the people of Cyprus (Stanislavski, *Legacy*, 165–6), an idea that was actually carried out in at least one Soviet production (Nels, 207). He wanted the couple to show a difference in their behaviour after Act II, which ended with their wedding night: when Desdemona hears that Othello has a headache and says, 'Faith, that's with watching' (III.iii.289), she ought to show that she is alluding to 'that unforgettable love night' and that she feels not only 'anxiety about his health' but also 'the pride of love' (*Stanislavski Produces*, 175).

Stanislavski also took a new line on the Cyprus plot. A nineteenth-century French pantomime version based on the Ducis adaptation had depicted the Turkish maltreatment of the Cypriots, who rejoice to hear that Othello is coming to their aid (Gilman, 86). Stanislavski saw the episode from the opposite angle. Deeply impressed by a friend's comment that the senate was sending Othello to Cyprus as 'a blackamoor against blackamoors' (Stanislavski, *Life*, 280), he emphasized the status of the Cypriots as an occupied people who, in II.i, can barely conceal their desire for the success of the Turkish invasion. In *Creating a Role* he shows drama students registering their awareness of the play's political significance: 'Cyprus, Candia, and Mauritania are conquered provinces, under the heavy heel of Venice ... The arrogant Doges, Senators, and aristocrats do not look upon the conquered people as human beings and do not allow intermarriage with them' (Stanislavski, *Creating*, 168–9).

Even before Stanislavski *Othello* had a special place in the Russian Shakespeare repertory, not least because Pushkin had a special admiration for the play and identified himself with its hero; of partly African descent, he died in a duel over his wife's honour. After 1917, at a time when the play seemed an anachronism to audiences in London and New York, it was the most popular of Shakespeare's works in the Soviet Union. Though the treatment of the hero and his love in Soviet productions was intensely idealistic, it was also carefully historicized: Iago's obsession with money and his ruthless individualism made him an obvious representative of the rising capitalist culture of the Renaissance; though he destroyed Othello and Desdemona, the play's ending was not despairing because the hero's death was not seen as meaningless. At the Maly Theatre in 1935 (dir. Sergei Radlov) Alexander Ostuzhev, who had acted with Salvini in 1900, played an Othello who was meant to inspire love; in an interview, he stated his conviction that the killing of Desdemona was 'more the tragedy of Othello than the tragedy of Desdemona', since Othello believes that in killing Desdemona he is destroying 'a source of evil' and his suicide is his punishment of the source of evil in himself. 'Only in this way can the eventual triumph of Othello's humanism and the downfall of Iago's misanthropic philosophy be made to appear inevitable' (Ostuzhev, 162–3). Zdeněk Stříbrný points out the 'colossal discrepancy between utopian illusion and cruel reality' at the end of this interview, which took place in 1938, in the midst of Stalin's terror: 'The Soviet people love Othello, as I do,' the actor insisted, as the country was devoted to establishing a society based on the love of man (Stříbrný, *Eastern*, 83). Other famous *Othello*s (at the Rustaveli Theatre in Tbilisi, 1937, and the Mossovet Theatre in Moscow, 1948) stressed the racism of the Venetians and their exploitation of Othello, an important negative example for a regime trying to establish a multicultural society; they also made Othello and Desdemona an exemplary couple (Nels, 183, 200). The play was considered so inspirational that in 1942 an abridged version was prepared to perform for troops at the front (Morozov, 61–2).

The Yutkevich film

Some of the effects of the 1956 *Othello* by Sergei Yutkevich – for instance its use of the wordless chorus as background music – have caused it to be dismissed as a 'lush color imitation of Welles's *Othello*' (Jorgens, 26). But the Russian approach to the play has always laid a good deal of emphasis on music; both the Rustaveli and the Mossovet productions had emphasized Desdemona's associations with song and surrounded her with musical accompaniment (Nels, 183–4, 201). The film is undoubtedly beautiful, partly thanks to a special new kind of film, Sovcolor (Manvell, 73). But since Yutkevich derived some of his ideas from Stanislavski, who was in turn inspired by Salvini, he used modern technology in the interest of a reading which preserves the Russian concept of the optimistic tragedy, and, incidentally, gives Desdemona an unusual degree of interiority.

Desdemona is an important symbolic figure in the Russian tradition: Ostuzhev considered her statement 'I saw Othello's visage in his mind' as 'truly revolutionary' (163), and Mikhail Morozov notes how often the word 'free' is used to describe her (Morozov, 65). Yutkevich's pre-credit sequence begins as Othello, having told his story with the aid of a turning globe, says farewell and leaves with Brabantio. Desdemona remains, half in a dream. As she gazes out her window, the wavy, dappled light on the walls is 'read' as the reflection of water on the Grand Canal. A sphere on one side of her and a carved Pietà on the other represent the conflicting impulses of adventure and piety between which she is pulled; then the film's title is superimposed on the silhouette of Othello's ship as she remembers, or imagines, the story he has just told. The flashback is a composite of every adventure film one has ever seen, and includes a glimpse of a caged Othello (figure 7) who appeals to Desdemona's pity as well as to her love of freedom. When the distraught Brabantio searches for her, he too is seen gazing from the window: the wavy light becomes a ghostly reminder of her romantic *wanderlust*. When he arrives on Cyprus, Othello runs up flight after flight of stairs to reach her, but this symbolism of the upward-beckoning ideal does not prevent her from being a companion, since she also seems very much a 'fair warrior' (Yutkevich may have been the first to make Desdemona arrive in man's dress, which was much less commonly worn in the 1950s). Images of music and water are constantly associated with her. Her singing is heard in the background as Othello resists Iago's insinuations and again in IV.i when Othello recalls her beauty and her musical skill. Like Welles, Yutkevich sets the great central scene of III.iii near the water; fishermen's nets nearby, then between them and the camera, indicate the trap in which Othello is becoming enmeshed. Iago, on the other hand, is seen near fire (Dorval, par. 13), which is obviously his element. The

7   Sergei Bondarchuk as Othello in slavery, from the film by Sergei
Yutkevich, Mosfilm, 1955

final scene, almost too mannered in its effects, parallels the
reflections of water in the opening sequence: the candle flame
rebounds off Desdemona's red-curtained and red-covered bed,
casting an eerie light over the whole scene. As Othello lunges
toward her with his bare hands, the camera shows him from her
point of view, with the whites of his eyes startlingly visible and his
hands already blood-coloured. After the murder, recalling the
Salvini tradition, he re-emerges backwards through the drawn
bedcurtains; when he turns round, we see that his hair has turned
grey (later, when he learns the truth from Emilia, his eyes will
glow red). Throughout this final scene he maintains his dignity
and the sense of his love for Desdemona: he is thinking of her
reputation when he whispers to Emilia the secret that 'She's like a
liar gone to burning hell'. After Emilia has drawn the bedcurtains
to show her mistress's body, he redraws them to protect her from
the gaze of the others ('Nay, stare not, masters'). While the others
go in chase of Iago, he carries Desdemona's body out of the lurid
atmosphere of this chamber and on to the terrace of the castle, as
if recalling the scene of their reunion in II.i. The others arrive to

find that he has arranged her body with care, and he kills himself in the clear light of dawn. The final image is of Lodovico on board the funeral ship carrying the bodies back to Venice, with Iago tied to the mast; the viewer looks through the snare-like rigging into a sky irradiated with light.

It should be possible to reissue this beautiful film in colour and in the original Russian version, since I have seen both. But at present it is available on video only in black-and-white, with a soundtrack dubbed in English. The dubbed text, sometimes rewritten in a feeble attempt to improve the lip-synchronization, is not only awful in itself but creates some weirdly comic effects when – since Khatchaturian's musical score could not be dubbed – English speech is followed by Russian songs. This is one reason why it is not as well known in the Anglocentric world as it deserves to be, although some echoes in Oliver Parker's film have been pointed out (Dorval, par. 11, par. 13), and Herbert von Karajan's film production of the opera plays in a similar way with the symbolism of reflections. Yuktevich's film has, however, been extremely influential elsewhere: one leading Chinese Othello, Zhu Li, saw it ten times before playing the role (Zhang, 189).

It would be easy to say that in the first part of the twentieth century all western productions of *Othello* gradually became cynical while those in the east remained romantic and idealistic, and to explain the difference in terms of idealistic socialism and cynical capitalism. In fact, as we have seen, the most successful revivals in the west were also, on the whole, romantic, while some Russian productions attempted to bring out the harsher side of the play. A more accurate generalization might be that the less text-based productions – whether musical, filmic or the product of a less verbal theatrical tradition – are likely to be the most romantic ones. Theatre in the Soviet Union was taken seriously, and was thus under pressure to provide a reading of the plays that would inspire a popular audience with optimism about the future, whereas in the west theatre was largely left to an intellectual community whose view of life was often cynical and even despairing. It took the coming of the Second World War to give the play a contemporary meaning again. For the English-speaking theatre, Paul Robeson's playing of Othello was a turning point in its history, because it restored the romantic and tragic reading of the play while at the same time bringing it back into contact with real life.

PART TWO

Robeson and after

CHAPTER V

Othello becomes contemporary: Ira Aldridge and Paul Robeson

The modern performance history of *Othello* begins with Paul Robeson, whose mere presence transformed and re-politicized the play. But the 'Robeson effect' was not merely the result of his impressive personality and presence: when he played Othello, audiences believed that they were gaining, for the first time, privileged access to a racial consciousness which would otherwise have been closed to them.

Robeson was not the first black actor to play Othello, as he himself well knew. As Errol Hill has documented in *Shakespeare in Sable*, African-American actors played Othello and other roles in Britain in the nineteenth century; and Haitian actors (some of them in whiteface) performed scenes from the play in New York in 1888 ('Grimwig', *Courier*, 8 January 1888). A newspaper reference in 1848 to 'the long looked for *début* of a native amateur in the character of Othello' in Calcutta (*Bengal Hurkaru and India Gazette*, cited in Solomon, 343) apparently refers to a production with an otherwise all-white cast (Singh, 32–3). An African-American company gave the play in New York, Boston and Philadelphia in 1916 for the three-hundredth anniversary of Shakespeare's death, opening with a gala variety evening for which the invited audience included Sir Herbert Beerbohm Tree, Mrs Patrick Campbell, the British ambassador and a Russian prince (Unattributed clipping in Folger Scrapbook: 'Othello', dated 8 April 1916; *New York Tribune*, 24 April 1916). In 1930, the same year that Paul Robeson acted the part in London, another black Othello, Wayland Rudd, appeared with a non-black company at the small but well-respected Hedgerow Theatre in Pennsylvania; he later emigrated to the Soviet Union, where he made a career as an actor and playwright. Hill notes that Rudd's attitude to Russia anticipated Robeson's (E. Hill, 101–2), but there are other reasons for the parallel. Rudd –

and perhaps whoever invited the Russian prince to the 1916 gala – must have known something about the career of Ira Aldridge, the most famous nineteenth-century African-American actor.

Robeson probably had heard about Aldridge while Robeson was starring in *The Emperor Jones* in London in 1925, and he and his wife became friends with Aldridge's daughter, now a singing teacher. As if handing on a torch, Amanda Ira Aldridge presented Robeson with the earrings worn by her father in *Othello*, hoping 'that he would someday wear them when he, too, played the role' (Duberman, 91). Though Robeson does not seem to have worn the earrings (at least, not in photographs of the 1930 *Othello*), he felt indebted to Amanda in other ways; both in the programme and in newspaper interviews he thanked her for reading through the play with him and helping him acquire the right accent for a British production. What his daughter would have remembered best about Aldridge were the last twenty years of his career, when he was constantly on tour in Germany and eastern Europe and something of a hero to actors and artists in Czarist Russia. Shortly after the close of the 1930 *Othello* production, Robeson took up serious study of the Russian language (Duberman, 149). He must have heard still more about Aldridge on his first visit to Russia in 1934. It was a Russian, Sergei Durylin, who published the first full-scale Aldridge biography in 1940, and, at a much later date, Robeson considered narrating a Russian film about him, to be written by Aldridge's biographer Herbert Marshall (Duberman, 492). Aldridge was not only a role model but also a contributing factor in the passionate love of Russia that was to be so significant in Robeson's life.

Ira Aldridge (1807–67)

If this theatrical history of *Othello* has so far excluded the one nineteenth-century black actor whose career is well documented, it is because Aldridge was largely excluded from that history even in his lifetime. Though Eliza O'Neill and Maria Malibran, the famous dramatic and operatic Desdemonas of the early nineteenth century, wrote admiringly of his Othello, most of his contemporaries in England seem to have regarded him – if they mention him at all – as a curiosity rather than as part of an acting tradition. The fact that so much of his later career took place outside the English-speaking world, and that the best accounts of his acting are not in English, makes the task of retracing his career a particularly difficult one. All scholars are heavily in debt to *Ira Aldridge: The Negro Tragedian*, by Herbert Marshall and Mildred Stock, who piece together the scattered evidence of Aldridge's extensive tours in Britain, Ireland and Europe, quoting extensively from translations of German and Russian theatre critiques. In what follows I shall often be referring to this book (by page number only) except where I am quoting a source not cited there: extracts from the Ira Aldridge scrapbook in the Folger Shakespeare Library ('Folger Scrapbook'); from Durylin's biography ('Durylin'); and from a typescript in the Mander-Mitchinson Theatre Collection containing material collected for, but not used in, the Marshall and Stock book ('MMTC').

Aldridge was born in the United States and acted with semi-professional groups in New York before coming to England in 1824 at the age of seventeen. For nearly ten years he performed at small London theatres and in the provinces, developing an extensive repertoire. Though he found and created some roles for heroic black characters, he also took on others – usually those of comic, greedy, cowardly black slaves – that a black actor today would consider degrading. He actively looked for roles in which his colour would be an asset, and (with C. A. Somerset) adapted *Titus Andronicus* (c. 1849) to make Aaron and Tamora hero and heroine rather than villain and villainess. At the same time, he (or the companies with which he acted) experimented with what would now be called multiracial casting, which was perhaps made easier by the fact that he was relatively light-skinned: by 1827 he was already acting white roles in white makeup, whilst in 1829 he played Aboan in *Oroonoko* opposite Charles Kean in the title role: a curious combination of a genuine actor of colour and a white actor in (much darker) blackface (102). At a later stage he himself played the starring role of Oroonoko with John Coleman as Aboan. Coleman, whose theatrical memoirs are usually too good to be true, claims that, when he came on with his coal-black makeup, he could hear the audience debating which of the two was 'the real blackamoor' (Coleman, I: 168).

As an actor who moved easily between tragedy and comedy, Aldridge was not merely employable but successful. But it is clear that he wanted more. To reach the top of the profession, in the age of the Licensing Act, meant starring at one of the two licensed London theatres. In April 1833, less than a month after Edmund

8 Anonymous artist, Ira Aldridge as Othello addressing the
Venetian senate (probably 1833)

Kean's final Othello at Drury Lane, he made his debut in the role
at Covent Garden. As some reviewers noticed, Aldridge's Othello
costume, with its curious tunic, cloak and cap, resembled Kean's
(compare figure 8 with figures 1 and 2, above); he even used the
name Keene, presumably in homage, when he first appeared on
the English stage. Many of Kean's famous roles, including the
black characters of Zanga and Oroonoko, were also staples of
Aldridge's repertory; moreover, Aldridge, like Kean, had a good
singing voice; he could also play the banjo and guitar. He
obviously hoped to do what Kean himself had done in 1814: take
the town by storm and succeed to the position of leading tragedian.
Perhaps it was too soon to make such an attempt. His *Othello*, on
10 April, attracted only a small audience. Some reviewers responded
with lukewarm praise, others with sneeringly personal, and

indeed racist, comments. Even so, most of them admit that his performance went well, to the point where he played *Othello* again on 12 April in place of the two shorter pieces he had intended to offer. Although he had been announced for further appearances in other roles, Covent Garden was closed for five days because of 'the prevailing illness' (129–30), and when it reopened Aldridge was no longer on the bill. The influenza epidemic is confirmed by another source (*The Theatrical Omnibus*, May 1833, Folger Scrapbook), but The *Omnibus* makes clear that this was not the only reason for the silent cancellation of the remainder of his engagement: 'Mr Aldridge has been the victim of an unmanly, vindictive, and unprincipled persecution'. The journal was referring to some members of the press, whose initially patronizing treatment of Aldridge had given way to hostility. As Marshall and Stock point out, 1833 was the year when slavery was abolished in the British colonies. Reviewers could hardly remain unaware of this current, polarizing issue when they assessed the fitness of an actor of African descent to succeed to the greatest dramatic roles, at a major London theatre, opposite a well-known English actress, Ellen Tree (119, 132). *The Athaeneum*, supposedly the leading publication on theatre and the arts, protested at the idea of 'Wallack's black servant in the character of Othello – Othello, forsooth!' This story about Aldridge's origins had been in circulation for some years. In a letter addressed to the *Theatrical Omnibus* and dated 15 May 1833, Aldridge replied truthfully that he was the son of a clergyman, and had never been a servant, though he was careful to add that he had no contempt for that status. I shall quote a little more of this letter (not in the Marshall and Stock biography), since it gives a good sense of Aldridge's character: 'Need I say more? – I will: – No doubt the sapient and good natured newsmonger who gave this information, presumed that because I am a *man* of *colour,* I must of necessity have been a servant and a slave, and this supposition was of course, in his idea, a sufficient and valid objection to my admission in a Theatre Royal!' (Folger Scrapbook: Aldridge).

The difficulties with which Aldridge had to contend are evident from the fact that even the sympathetic theatre critic of the *Omnibus* writes that he hopes people will support the actor in 'the performance of the limited number of characters to which the colour of skin alone restricts him' – this, after Aldridge had already shown his ability to play characters of all colours.

Moreover, it was obvious that 'the colour of skin' was a restriction only to black actors; the first Jim Crow shows, after their success in the US, came to the Surrey Theatre in 1836, and Aldridge later developed a Jim Crow song himself (Marshall and Stock, 150–1). Yet in 1844 Aldridge played the Duke of Venice in *Othello* at that same theatre while a (white) visiting American actor played the hero (Knight, 209). This was a year after the repeal of the Licensing Act, which ought in principle to have created more opportunities for actors such as Aldridge to have starring careers in London. What Aldridge was doing instead can be guessed from the *Theatrical Times* for 15 April 1848. Drawing, probably, on information supplied by the actor himself, it describes his touring career and the one-man or two-man programmes that he performed when he was unable to act with a repertory company. These were a mixture of lecture; autobiographical narrative ('his grandfather was an African prince of the tribe of Foolah, in Senegal'); speeches by Othello and Shylock; 'Lubbly Rosa', a dialect song accompanied on the guitar 'with a rich gusto and unctuous humour'; and a caricatured black role, 'the marvellous, pompous, and ragged waiter, Mr. Ginger Blue, in the "Virginian Mummy"', in which, the newspaper claims, 'he drew down peals of laughter'.

This description, like so many descriptions of performance, leaves out what one would most like to know: the tone in which Aldridge performed all this. The 1840s were years of Anti-Slavery agitation in both Britain and North America, beginning with the World Anti-Slavery Convention of 1840 in London. In 1845 Frederick Douglass arrived in Britain to speak in public on behalf of the American Negro, chiefly by telling the story of his own life as a former slave. Douglass, who is described by Elizabeth Stanton as looking 'like an African prince' (Douglass, 19), often quotes from *Othello* in his autobiographical works, yet seems not to notice the play's particular relevance to his life. He reports that the abolitionist leaders constantly urged him to 'Tell your story', yet as he became a more experienced speaker his eloquence ironically worked against him: 'People doubted if I had ever been a slave' (Douglass, 217–18). Though Douglass was telling his story at the same time that Aldridge's Othello was telling his, Marshall and Stock have found no evidence that the two men ever met. At such a time, it seems extraordinary that Aldridge should be willing, as he apparently was, to show off his talent for mimicry at the expense of his own race.

And yet, even when he had become a star actor in eastern Europe and could play whatever roles he chose, he invariably followed Othello with the other one for which he was best known, Mungo in Isaac Bickerstaff's *The Padlock*. This extremely popular comic opera was first produced in 1768 with a white actor, Charles Dibdin, as Mungo. Its unremarkable plot involves the elderly Don Diego's intention of marrying his ward Leonora, who is loved by a younger man, Leander. Thinking to keep Leonora safe while he is gone, Diego places a huge padlock on his gate, but his servant and his black slave Mungo help Leander climb over the wall. When Diego returns, he hears the news from Mungo – now extremely drunk and rude – and sensibly decides to let the two young people marry. The story has a slight resemblance to Beaumarchais's *Barber of Seville*, and contemporaries often compare Mungo to Figaro. He is hardly that; nevertheless he was the opera's most popular character, to the point where it was often billed simply as *The Mulatto* (Durylin, 100–1). In the text he comes across as a caricature, sycophantic when sober and threatening when drunk, speaking pidgin English. He sounds uncomfortably like the caricatured black man in nineteenth-century parodies of *Othello* (usually called *Othello Travestie*), where versions of Shakespeare's lines are put into dialect to underline the supposed absurdity of noble emotions among subliterate characters (see MacDonald, 241ff.). A passionate love of music is his one redeeming characteristic. He is sympathetic to the young lovers, but only because they pay him. His opening song, in which he complains of being beaten by his master, apparently sounded poignant in Aldridge's interpretation, but much of the part could only have been meant as comic, and it is clear from contemporary accounts that this is how he played it.

The songs in *The Padlock* were a great part of its attraction, and favourite performers added others of their own choice. When Aldridge played Mungo, one highlight was his rendition of 'Oppossum up a Gum-tree' which a reviewer describes as 'one of the funniest things that can be imagined' (*The Era*, 26 March 1848, quoted Marshall and Stock, 165). The story behind this song is a strange one. The English comedian Charles Mathews Sr was a popular performer of one-man shows – a mixture of narrative, dialogue and recitation; in 'Mr Mathews' Trip to America', first performed in 1824, he gave a brief account of a visit to an all-black theatre in New York, where a Negro actor was reciting

Hamlet's famous soliloquy. At the point where the actor wondered whether to take arms against a sea of troubles 'and by oppossum [opposing] end them', the audience started calling for 'Oppossum'. This turned out to be 'Oppossum up a Gum Tree,' an extremely popular dialect song, and the actor promptly sang it. Mathews seems to have arrived in the middle of the performance; since what survives is only a brief summary of his monologue (Klepac, 106–7), it is difficult to know exactly what was being presented or how spontaneous the audience participation and the actor's response actually were. Aldridge's arrival in England in 1824 naturally led some writers to suggest that he himself was the actor to whom Mathews had referred. The young actor exploited the misunderstanding in his own one-man show, juxtaposing dialect quotations from Mathews with comments in his own 'real' speech, which was as sophisticated as that of any member of his audience. This polite and ironic refutation confirms Aldridge's reputation for good humour; he may have known that Mathews, despite his willingness to exploit them for comic purposes, was sympathetic to the plight of black Americans. 'Opposum up a gum tree' became a regular part of Aldridge's repertoire. According to one writer, 'The ecstasy of his long, shrill note', at the climax of the song, 'can only be equalled by the agony of his cry of despair over the body of Desdemona' (Anon., *Memoir*, 8). Thus, there is no evidence that he felt humiliated at having to perform the comic black characters that constituted perhaps the most popular element in his English repertory.

Nevertheless, it is not surprising that in 1852 he chose to go on a European tour. A letter dated from Leipzig on 25 November, which he asked a newspaper to insert for the benefit of his friends, explained the reason for his venture and indulged in some pardonable gloating: 'From the exclusiveness of the London theatres, and prejudices of certain managers, I saw there was no prospect of exercising my humble talents with any ultimate benefit, and though dissuaded, I embarked in my present undertaking, which has thus far been attended with the most brilliant success' (*Weekly Times*, 5 December 1852, Folger Scrapbook). Later dispatches to the London papers, obviously based on reports from Aldridge himself, tell of enormous receipts, patronage by the aristocracy and royalty of Europe, and such honours as the Prussian Gold Medal for Arts and Sciences. The tour in 1852–54 took him to Belgium, Germany, Switzerland, Hungary and Poland; in 1857 he made a special trip to Stockholm for a royal command performance; in 1858 he played again on the continent, and the Duke of Saxe-Meiningen, whose son would later be famous himself as the leader of a touring company, presented him with the Royal Saxon House Order – the first time an actor had received such a decoration (210).

His most important tour was the one that began later that year, when he visited Russia, a country to which he returned for an extended season each year thereafter until his death on tour in Poland in 1867. His visits, not only to Moscow and St Petersburg but even the remote provinces, seem to have given Russians the same excited sense of discovering the 'real' Shakespeare that the Parisians had experienced during the visit of the English actors in the 1820s. This reality was relative, of course. If his acting texts were more accurate than the translated versions currently being used abroad – some of them still based on Ducis – Aldridge nevertheless remained rooted in the period when his career began: his *King Lear* was based on Tate's adaptation and his *Othello*, like many others in England at this time, omitted IV.iii and V.i. He naturally made his heaviest cuts in the parts of other actors, who in many cases were learning the roles for the first time. Initially, he had brought his own company with him, but he found that it was hard to attract audiences to performances in a language still known to relatively few, and thus, anticipating what Salvini would do in the 1870s, decided to act in English with performers from the local theatres, each playing in his or her own native language. Apparently he indicated the actors' cues either with a special sign or – Marshall and Stock suggest – with broken phrases of German or Russian (235). He eventually learned enough to manage in rehearsals, and sometimes sang Russian folk songs with great success, even acting in a Russian vaudeville (283). Partly on the strength of his overseas reputation, he finally got the opportunity to play at important London theatres: the Lyceum in 1858, the Haymarket in 1865. He was reviewed with respect, though his style seemed rather old-fashioned by now.

It is unfortunate that most of the English reviews of Aldridge are unhelpful and contradictory compared to the European ones. Some English critics praise his diction; others complain of his accent or his weakness in the upper register, accuse him of ranting, or describe him as mannered (MMTC, appendix, 9–10). Attitudes naturally differed according to whether or not his listeners understood English. Two qualities often mentioned, the clarity of his diction and his tendency to repeat words (*Brighton Gazette*, 29 September 1859, quoted Marshall and Stock, 246), may have been accentuated by his need to communicate to non-English-speakers. His Russian biographer thinks that this was also the reason for his tendency to make 'wordless tragic monologues' out of Shylock's groans after Jessica's flight or Othello's laments after Desdemona's death (Durylin, 108). The portrait of him delivering his speech to the senate, which gives some sense of the play in performance (figure 8), suggests a rather restrained delivery.

English critics sometimes found Aldridge reminiscent of Kean. Some details in the Russian accounts confirm this view: when in despair, 'He quietly, slowly, places his hands on his brow and with painful convulsions on his face passes his hands over his head' (Almazov, quoted MMTC, 17). Kean was famous for a similar gesture (Sprague, *Actors*, 195). Aldridge, like Kean, occasionally turned his back on the audience – such an unusual action in this period that it gave the audience the impression that he had forgotten himself (18). From Macready, to whom he is also compared, he may have taken the idea of saying, 'Blood, blood, blood' quietly rather than shouting it (19). Such borrowing of business from other actors was expected and admired. The Russian critics, however, should be treated with caution when they attribute motivation to his actions; for instance, K. Zvantsev describes him gesturing with impatience at the end of Iago's account of the drunken fight ('But men are men', etc.), as if objecting to its 'irrelevant philosophising' (12), when he might simply have been working himself up to his next speech, the rebuke of Cassio. But the fact that Aldridge made them think they could read his mind in this way is the most convincing evidence of his quality as an actor. As Desdemona spoke her last words to Emilia, he buried his face in his hands and 'one was afraid he would take his hands from his face and reveal the expression on it' (Bazhenov, quoted 25); he obviously understood the same principle of tension that later made Salvini hold a long pause after the murder before thrusting his face through the curtains. All accounts agree that he emphasized his love for the murdered woman, to the point where one critic felt that his sobbing 'redeems all the crimes in the tragedy'; for instance, he paid close attention to Emilia's dying whisper and to the servant carrying her body out, as if 'striving once again to enjoy speech of Desdemona' (Zvantsev, quoted 27).

Often, of course, what critics read into his performance was a social message. As Marshall and Stock point out (221), his arrival in 1858 was timely. The emancipation of the serfs, which finally occurred in March 1861, was already in the air; the Czar had published a draft of a liberation document at the end of 1857. Thus, although a few spectators were shocked that he frequently performed Mungo immediately after Othello (Durylin, 36), Russians who knew of American slavery through reading *Uncle Tom's Cabin* found it exciting to see a near-contemporary example of a class in which they took considerable interest. Reports of *The Padlock* are contradictory: some called it hilariously funny and describe Aldridge as 'the personification of good-natured cunning', while others seem to have found it heart-rending. The key to these reactions may be Zvantsev's comment that in the end his interest was neither in Shakespeare nor in Aldridge but in the Negro (Durylin, 35). In other words, Russian spectators who applauded Aldridge were also expressing a coded support for the emancipation of Negroes abroad and serfs at home.

It was in Russia, also, that the question of racial casting first inspired serious discussion. Zvantsev declared that, once he had seen Aldridge as Othello, he felt that he would never want to see any white actor, however famous, play the part (Marshall and Stock, 232). On the other hand, a letter to a newspaper in September 1862 argued that identity of colour between actor and character would be an identity of skin rather than spirit – the antithesis of an aesthetic approach to acting (265–6). Since the letter-writer goes on to say that an Othello black only in his skin would be a source of revulsion, Marshall and Stock are probably right when they conclude that she and her editor were using artistic theory to justify racism (266). But Théophile Gautier, on the same principle, preferred Aldridge's King Lear to his Othello because 'In the former he acted; in Othello he was just himself' (*Voyage en Russie* (Paris, 1895), I: 294–6, quoted 230). Of course it is as absurd to imagine that a black actor need only 'be himself' to play Othello as it would be to assume that any eighty-year-old white actor could 'be himself' as King Lear. But the belief was apparently strong enough that some provincial Desdemonas were frightened to act with him. On one occasion, faced in the final scene with a terrified actress, he is said to have alternated ferocious lines from the play with reassuring whispers in broken Russian. Questioned about his reputation, Aldridge replied, tongue-in-cheek, that he didn't see what the fuss was about, since he had killed only one Iago and two or at most three Desdemonas (269).

No surviving comments from Aldridge indicate to what extent he realized the political role he was playing, apart from a reference to 'my oppressed people' in a letter to Russian actors in 1859 (Marshall and Stock, 244). But Marshall and Stock have found evidence that he gave some of his considerable earnings to the American abolitionist movement (197–8). Since the official censorship of the period actually deleted one Russian historian's comments on the sympathy he felt for Aldridge as Mungo (233–4), Aldridge was probably wise not to put his views on paper. That in later years he was not allowed to play either *Macbeth* or *King Lear* in politically volatile St Petersburg (237) may indicate that his acting was provocative not merely by chance. Yet it would be easy to see him as more like Uncle Tom than a pioneer in the cause of black progress. The long verse speech that he composed and frequently spoke at the conclusion of a performance or a farewell banquet suggests that he had either internalized, or was playing to, his audience's prejudices. He describes himself as a member of the

> swarthy race, late known
> For naught but bloodshed and the murderous groan;
> Mark'd by the God of Havoc and of strife
> To raise the war-whoop, wield the murderous knife,
> To roam unfettered, void of reason's light,
> Lone tribe of mankind in chaotic night.

It was, he explained, 'the Drama's radiance' that had helped 'To drive the clouds of darkness far away' and led him to become 'A wandering son, fired with ambitious flame'. Adapting Zanga's famous lines in *The Revenge* ('Children of the Sun / With whom Revenge is Virtue'), he goes on:

> Though nature to my aspect has denied
> The rose and lily which in you're allied,
> 'Child of the Sun,' with brow of ebon hue
> I stand before you.
>
> (*Era*, 25 November 1860, Folger Scrapbook: Aldridge)

The speech, according to one newspaper account, was frequently interrupted with applause from the audience. It is evident that anyone who admired the characters he played would also admire this self-portrait, since in it Aldridge had astutely created a composite image from the pathetic ignorance of Mungo, the splendid pride of Zanga and the romantic travels of Othello.

Aldridge's willingness to be identified with his roles may explain one of the habits recorded of him as an actor: his 'propensity to alter the text of the author' (*The Morning Post*, 1833, quoted 122), sometimes with 'interpolations' (*The Spectator*, 1833, quoted 125) which the hostile *Athenaeum* reviewer attributed to his inability to remember his original accurately (quoted 127). During Aldridge's London season at the Lyceum in 1858, the press was a little more specific about this practice: the *Illustrated London News* referred to his replacing words and phrases which 'offend his sense of delicacy'; an example, which the reviewer of *The Times* particularly disliked because it was unmetrical, was 'She turn'd to folly and she was false,' in place of 'She turned to folly and she was a whore' (218). It is possible, then, that Aldridge acquiesced less than one might think in the portrayals of black characters that the drama gave him. He evidently played on feelings of tender superiority in his audience while making it clear that he himself needed none of their sympathy. He seems also to have felt that each oppressed group should speak for others; his Shylock was a tragic figure who reacted with horror at the thought of becoming a Christian, and when he played the part in one Russian town a deputation of local Jews presented an address thanking him for his sympathetic portrayal (288). He was twice married – to white women – and it was the opposition of his first wife, who was British, that kept him from returning to the United States during her lifetime. If he had lived to carry out his plan of returning to act there after the American Civil War, American theatrical history might have been very different.

Paul Robeson (1898–1976)

Madge Kendall, who acted with Aldridge, remembered him as having had 'some species of – well, I will not say "genius," because I dislike that word, as used nowadays, but gleams of great intelligence' (Kendall, 29). Whether she would have considered Robeson an example of genius or only of 'great intelligence', there is no doubt that he was an exceptional human being. Unlike Aldridge, he did not aim from the beginning for a theatrical career: he became an actor and singer because he experienced racial prejudice as a lawyer, whereas he was enthusiastically welcomed as a performer. His three *Othellos*, spanning almost thirty years of theatre history, might have been only incidents in a varied life if the part had not become so completely identified with him. In an interview in 1930, Robeson said that he would like to play Hamlet, but no one followed up the idea, nor did anyone ask him to play the other Shakespearean roles identified with Aldridge, such as Aaron, Shylock and King Lear – though in 1958 Stratford director Tony Richardson tried to get him to play Gower, the narrator in Shakespeare's *Pericles*. Even long after he had stopped playing Othello, he frequently ended concert programmes with the hero's final speech, introducing it in a way that left no doubt as to his personal connection with it. The speech, available on some of his recordings, is quoted by nearly everyone who writes about Robeson. In 1967 Edwin P. Hoyt titled his book *Paul Robeson: The American Othello* and on the final page says that the actor's political views were held not wisely but too well. Martin Duberman's magisterial biography uses part of the same speech as its epigraph. In his review of that biography, Eric Bentley noted that 'In the matter of Robeson, all roads lead to *Othello*'. Having seen Robeson play the part, he added, 'If on the stage Robeson did not give us Shakespeare's Othello, in life he did' (Bentley, *TLS*, 12 May 1989).

The 1930 Othello

After the successful London production of *The Emperor Jones* in 1925, and again after the actor's even greater success in 1928 as Joe in *Showboat*, the idea of a Robeson Othello in London was raised almost immediately, by the critic James Agate among others. Robeson agreed, but only on condition that he should first spend several years learning to speak English as pronounced in Britain. He could not choose the production's Iago (the producer, Maurice Browne, cast himself in the role) or its director (Browne's wife, Ellen van Volkenburg), but it was he who chose the young actress who played Desdemona, Peggy Ashcroft. She was eager for the part, because, as she later said, Robeson, aged thirty-two, was already 'a folk-hero, a legendary figure' (Billington, 37). The headlines for the premiere in the *Express* (20 May 1930) capture the sense of an event: 'Vivid Acting as the Terrible Moor. Kissing Scene. Coloured Audience in the Stalls.' This reviewer (H.S.) counted the number of times Robeson kissed Ashcroft, both before and after the murder, but added firmly, 'It was in the part and that was that.' Most reviewers praised Ashcroft and Sybil Thorndike (Emilia) but were divided about Robeson and agreed that the production itself was misconceived ('perfectly terrible' is Ashcroft's description: Billington, 37). Presumably Van Volkenburg was aiming at avant-garde Expressionism; it is hard to see what else could justify the programme's 'Note on the Lighting' which explains that the sets (designed by an eminent artist, James Pryde) were being lit not realistically but from the artist's point of view. These sets were also so heavy to move that the willow scene was almost drowned out on the opening night by 'a veritable bombardment behind the backcloth' (Ivor Brown, *Observer*, 25 May 1930). Other novelties included the retention of the clown and the addition of a singer, along with a good deal of music and dance. It is hard to find more specific information about this important production, since most reviewers thought that their job was to tell the actors what they should have done rather than describe what they actually did. On the evidence of a newspaper photograph (see figure 9), Browne was a physically unimpressive Iago; the prompt-book shows that he had only one costume throughout the play, where Robeson had several, and he cut so many of his own lines that one wonders whether he was deliberately trying to focus attention on Robeson. Reviewers, however, failed to see any such intention behind his performance, which they unanimously loathed. Seen beside the young and charming Ashcroft, Robeson looks gentle and rather bewildered, but his beautiful voice and excellent diction made up for his stiffness; critics loved hearing the lines so well spoken. Agate, who had wanted to see him in the part, was disappointed at his lack of authority: 'he towered above everybody else, but it was a tower which cringed' (19 May 1930). Reviewer Alan Parsons, for all his maddening vagueness, catches something of the uncertainty as to how Robeson should be evaluated: 'it was in its way a great performance, so it is churlish to find fault' (20 May 1930). Margaret Webster, in the audience in 1930, did not think Robeson even a *good* actor, but recognized his greatness (*Daughter*, 106).

Since all three of Robeson's Othellos drew similar comments about the discrepancy between his 'presence' and his acting, it is unfortunate that none of them was filmed. The sound recording of the Margaret Webster production (originally available on records and now on CD) was made in 1944 without Webster's knowledge, after she had left the production. Hastily arranged,

9   Paul Robeson as Othello in the 1930 London production, with
     Maurice Browne as Iago and Peggy Ashcroft as Desdemona

read by a cast of nine with minimal sound effects and no background music, it is a studio recording and sounds like it. The text
was heavily cut, losing for example the opening of the senate
scene and the attempted murder of Cassio, presumably because
the small cast could not make them sound convincing. Much of it
is beautifully read, but in using the recording as evidence one has
to remember that some of the cast agreed with Webster that it
was a very inadequate representation of the production (Spector,
107; Webster, *Daughter*, 117). For the 1959 *Othello* directed by
Tony Richardson, the British Library Sound Archive holds a tape-
recording made during a live performance. The sound quality is
poor and the recording is incomplete, beginning only partway
through I.iii. A huge, unexplained gap extends from Robeson's
exit at IV.i.263 to a point well into the final scene, ending with
Othello's last words (though the promptbook indicates that the
production actually ended with Cassio's two-line tribute). Nevertheless, both recordings, combined with the promptbooks, can
help in evaluating the common claim that all Robeson's directors,
even Webster, somehow failed to exploit his full potential.

[121]

By 1943 Robeson had become much more politically conscious than he was in 1930. In the early part of his career his attitude to his profession was not very different from Aldridge's: that is, he was willing to play roles in which 'typical' Negroes were shown to be lazy, childlike or violent. We have no evidence what black spectators thought of Aldridge's Mungo, if any of them ever saw the performance, but Duberman writes that some who saw Robeson in *Showboat* were offended by his willingness to sing 'Old Man River', with its original opening line, 'Niggerfolk work on the Mississippi', and to play Joe as lazy and politically indifferent, resenting only the fact that if he gets 'a little drunk' he 'lands in jail' (Duberman, 114).

Robeson's travels after *Othello* – to Russia in 1934, via a traumatic glimpse of Nazi Germany; to wartime Spain in 1938 – transformed him into a seriously committed political thinker. Like Aldridge, he came to identify the cause of European Jews and the proletariat with that of black Americans, and felt an immediate love for Russia, where his excellent knowledge of the language added to his popularity. He would have learned from Amanda Aldridge that her father sang Russian folk songs alongside Negro spirituals. Robeson did the same thing in concerts, going on to develop theories about the special musical affinities between Russian and African rhythms. At one point he announced that he would no longer sing French, German or Italian songs because he had nothing in common with the culture that produced them, whereas he felt that Russian, Hebrew and Chinese were languages belonging to oppressed peoples. It was in the 1930s that he first started changing the lyrics of 'Old Man River', replacing 'Get a little drunk' with 'Show a little fight' and 'I'm tired of living and I'm scared of dying' with 'I'll keep on fighting until I'm dying' (Duberman, 214, 604–5) This militant spirit, however, did not seem out of place as the war approached.

The success of the 1943 *Othello* was, as Margaret Webster wrote, in part a matter of timing. Robeson 'matched the part and the hour ... the moment lent it greatness' (Webster, *Daughter*, 107). It was one of those periods when idealism was in fashion, if not so completely institutionalized as in the Soviet Union. The programme notes for the production compared Venice's fighting to protect Christianity in the Eastern Mediterranean with the current situation: 'In our conflict, all races are allied to fight for common ideals. The Negro pilot of the Army Air Corps may fly under the command of Chiang in China; just as soldiers of other races fought with Venice for the preservation of Christianity.' When Robeson used his popularity as a platform from which to attack fascism and express his admiration for the Soviet Union, he was in tune with the times: Russia was an ally against Germany, and each country was eager to emphasize the unity of all racial groups in a common cause. Still, there was considerable nervousness about the production. The Theatre Guild, which was sponsoring it, started quietly, with a trial run in the summer of 1942 in two places where a sympathetic audience could be expected: the Brattle Theatre in Cambridge, Massachusetts, and the McCarter in Princeton, New Jersey. The success was dazzling; a year later, partly recast, the 'Robeson *Othello*' opened in New York and played for 296 performances, always to full houses.

The story of this *Othello*, which still holds the record for the longest run of any Shakespeare play on Broadway, has been told many times. Duberman's biography gives a very full account, drawing on information obtained by Susan Spector for her unpublished PhD dissertation on the early career of Uta Hagen. Another valuable source is the thesis edition of Webster's acting text by Janet Barton Carroll who, in 1977, had the benefit of personal correspondence with many of the surviving actors. There is some disagreement about details – Webster (who played Emilia in addition to directing) said one thing in public pronouncements and another in letters, while Uta Hagen and José Ferrer, the Desdemona and Iago of the production, remembered things differently from her and from each other. Robeson himself seems to have put nothing on paper. Spector's research reveals the close relationship of the three principal actors and their increasing independence from their director and co-actor. Neither Hagen nor Ferrer had the national reputation of Robeson, and both would have been replaced when the play transferred to Broadway if Robeson had not insisted on their remaining (Spector, 102). The long Broadway run was followed by a national tour (by now, Webster had withdrawn from the cast). Conditions were difficult: even though the company refused to play in any cities where theatre audiences were not integrated, there were a number of racial incidents in hotels. Most famous Othellos, notably Salvini and Olivier, have refused to play the part two days in succession

(Olivier told Margaret Webster that he preferred at least four and preferably ten other performances between Othellos: *Daughter*, 87). Robeson had to play it seven times a week – he had no understudy – for a total run of some six hundred performances. It was not only he who found the pace exhausting; Ferrer made the same complaint about playing Iago (Ferrer, 8–9). Ferrer and Hagen were married at the time of the run, but divorced in 1948; Robeson and Hagen had an affair during the run of the play. At times it seems that the actors were taken over by their roles.

Of course, some of the production's excitement was sexual. One reviewer commented on the effect in I.iii when Othello removed the blue cloak Desdemona was wearing: 'This is the first time the Moor touches his bride, and each time this happened, it was as if Othello were touching glass' (Francis Wayne, *The Denver Post*, p. 14, 6 April 1945, quoted Carroll, 229). When he kissed her in II.i there was sometimes 'an audible gasp from the audience' (Carroll, 245). Yet, to anyone accustomed to the sexual explicitness of later productions, it is surprising how innocent the play sounds on the recording. Though Iago and Roderigo are certainly offensive to Brabantio in I.i, neither of them brings out the full meaning of the sexual references; the 'I lay with Cassio lately' speech is spoken without any apparent sexual or homosexual innuendo. Nor does Webster *have* to cut the sexually explicit lines in the 'brothel' scene; Robeson, like many actors before him, simply plays them with infinite sadness, so that the attention is on the intensity of his suffering rather than on what he is actually saying or on Desdemona's response to it. Only Emilia's speaking of 'Alas, what does this gentleman conceive?' – with an ironic edge to the word 'gentleman' – reminds one that such language must have been shocking to the audience. One writer has suggested that the costumes for the 1930 *Othello* placed more emphasis on Robeson's sexuality than those of 1943, when he wore 'flowing robes that wholly conceal the shape of the body, or leave only the arms bare in the murder scene' (Dyer, 111). But most spectators in 1930 felt that the Elizabethan costumes with their padded trunks looked ridiculous and bulky on this actor (Gielgud, 88); Robeson, rather to Webster's annoyance, had his own costumes made when the production transferred to Broadway, so it is likely that he himself, for whatever reason, preferred the 'flowing robes'.

Shortly before the opening of the 1930 *Othello*, Robeson had assured an interviewer, 'The rhythm of Shakespeare has come easily to me, for it is just pure music' (*Times*, 19 May 1930). George Rylands, who directed the Cambridge Marlowe Society recordings of Shakespeare, criticized Robeson on the grounds that 'the rhythm of music is not the same rhythm as that of Shakespeare's blank verse' (Billington, 40). The 'musicality' of Robeson's performance was a constant theme throughout his career; it impressed some and irritated others, including Uta Hagen, whose reaction on first hearing him was that he spoke like a singer rather than a human being (Spector, 98). In the recording, particularly, many passages sound like poems rather than moments from a play. The 'farewell' speech is delivered much as one imagines Kean must have done it, as a heartbreaking lament for past happiness and glory; 'How shall I murder him ...?' is low and brooding rather than vicious. In 1930 Robeson's delivery of 'I would have him *nine years* a-killing' was said to have made the audience 'draw in its breath in terror' (Rupert Hart-Davies, quoted in Billington, 38). In the 1940s it was sorrow rather than anger that he played. The same was true of his hypnotically beautiful reading of 'it is the cause'; in no way does it sound as if the speaker is about to commit murder.

José Ferrer writes that at the first rehearsal he was so overwhelmed by Robeson's vocal superiority that he was ready to give up the part of Iago (Ferrer, 8). Instead, he gave up smoking and sang every day. As a result, his voice on the recording is nearly as beautiful as Robeson's, silky and varied in inflection, though rather mannered by later standards (for instance, he lovingly stresses the sibilants in 'lusts' and the vowels in 'sweet sleep'). A mannerism very noticeable in the recording – though it may have been used less in the theatre – is his frequent prompting of a response through grunted 'um's and 'eh?'s, as when he tells Roderigo that in cuckolding Othello 'thou dost thyself a pleasure and – eh – me a sport, eh?' Since his own background was Puerto Rican, he decided to exploit the character's Latin temperament, using gesture to clarify lines that he thought the audience might not understand (Ferrer, 8). Though Ferrer insisted that newspaper references to his 'light, quick movements round Othello' were 'figments of the critics' imaginations' (Carroll, 132), both promptbook and photographs indicate that in the great scenes of Act III Robeson remained seated while Ferrer circled around him; aware that Robeson's movements could be awkward, Webster deliberately emphasized his monumentality, and the effect may have been to make Ferrer

10　Paul Robeson and José Ferrer as Othello and Iago in
the 1943 *Othello*

seem even more active than he was. Similarly, Robeson's nobility
intensified Ferrer's evil. Emery Battis, a member of the 1942 cast,
remembered that Iago's 'Do not rise yet' could chill the blood
(figure 10 gives some sense of the quiet terror of this moment).
Webster kept the Booth–Irving business in V.i, in which Iago is
about to stab Cassio when he hears the voice of Lodovico.

Uta Hagen gets much less attention from reviewers, and Janet
Carroll found it hard to know 'whether it was Miss Hagen's characterization, or the role itself, which left some critics unimpressed'
(140). Most reviewers felt that Desdemona was inherently a bor-
ing character, although the actress and director both worked to
make her livelier. Physically she looked less young than Peggy
Ashcroft, but on the recording her voice has a distinctive, breathy,
almost boyish sound, as when, in I.iii, she blurts out 'Let me go
with him' after a low-voiced preamble. Daringly, she sings the
willow song with full voice, rather than sobbing or chanting it.
She plays the final scene like someone already resigned to death,
as is clear from the tone of her 'Lord have mercy on me'. The cast

members that Carroll interviewed differed considerably about Webster's playing of Emilia during the New York run. She was, one complained, 'too cultivated'; she played the role as a companion to Desdemona, whereas her 1944 replacement, Edith King, 'played it like somebody's cook, which it should have been' (Carroll, 143). But this was obviously a question of interpretation rather than execution. Webster, like many Emilias since her time, did not play a character too stupid to understand what was going on, but one who was too much in love with her husband to believe the evidence against him or to give him away. Her relationship with Iago was generally affectionate; even when, in IV.iii, he said, 'You are a fool, go to', he followed it with a kiss. Webster may have been the first Emilia to alter the mysterious 'I'll have the work ta'en out' (III.iii.300) to 'I'll have the work copied', thus ensuring that no one will take Emilia for a thief. Like many other directors, she also made the character's silence in III.iv less implausible by keeping her off the stage for much of the time. When Othello threw a purse to her at the end of the 'brothel' scene, she indignantly threw it back at him (Sprague, *Actors*, 205). These were all touches designed to make Emilia less reprehensible.

The 1930 *Othello* had tried to be modern and failed; Webster seems to have succeeded by synthesizing 'the soundest interpretations of the past' (Louis Kronenberger, *PM*, 13 August 1942). Her production style was quick, extremely clear, and lively; at a time when Shakespeare was much less popular in the theatre than he is today, she knew how to make his plays accessible to a large public. She encouraged Ferrer, whose last great success had been in *Charley's Aunt*, to exploit the humour in Iago's role. In the early acts Robeson too was sometimes funny: his line about the 'anthropophagi' was a joke, and the promptbook directs everyone to laugh at it except Brabantio (Carroll, 228). The small parts were carefully thought out; for instance, in II.i, it was made clear that Bianca had come from Venice in the company of a Venetian who was trying to keep her away from the others. She chucked Cassio under the chin as she passed and tried to flirt with Iago until he insulted her with his improvised couplet about the woman who is fair and foolish. The reference to her perfume, on her entrance in IV.i.145–6, was accompanied by a 'Phew!' from Iago. This line, like other apparent ad-libs, was written into the script. Webster left nothing to chance; she also insisted that actors should know, on entering or leaving the stage, precisely where they were coming from and where they were about to go (Carroll, 158). In the interest of speed, she often overlapped speeches that look consecutive on the page, as in the 'lie with her' sequence in IV.i.33–5, where, in the recording, Iago and Othello speak almost in unison. The Iago–Roderigo scenes include many attempts on Roderigo's part to get into the conversation; in IV.ii, as Iago is explaining his plan to have Roderigo kill Cassio, the lights go down; in the dark, the audience hears Roderigo say, 'No, Iago, no!' (Carroll, 315). This exciting atmosphere (Webster insisted that Othello should not 'have time to stop and think': 'Cutting', 33) was meant to help Robeson. From him she sought 'speed above everything; if he slowed down, he was lost' (*Daughter*, 110). Like all the best productions of the play, this one was able to achieve a balance between the two characters because there was no danger that Ferrer's performance would detract from the sheer power and dignity of Robeson's. This essentially old-fashioned, actor-oriented production had most reviewers agreeing that, as Louis Kronenberger put it, it offered, 'more than any Shakespeare I have seen in several years – a real emotional experience' (Kronenberger, *PM*, 13 August 1942).

The 1959 Othello

Robeson's outspoken pro-Russian and pro-Labour views, which he saw as the logical corollary of his hostility to racial oppression, had been in tune with the mood of the country while the United States and Russia were allies; for instance, in 1945 both Ferrer and Webster wrote essays on the *Othello* production for *The American Theatre*, a periodical issued by the Theatre Committee of the National Council of American–Soviet Friendship. But once the war was over, political attitudes were remarkably quick to harden. In 1946 the director and principals of *Othello* were questioned by the House Committee on Un-American Activities. Webster, Hagen and Ferrer were dismissed almost at once, but Robeson was to have years of trouble with the Committee. His opposition to the Korean War, his acceptance of the Stalin Peace Prize in 1952 and his refusal, because of his love for Russia, to denounce any aspect of Stalinism made him unpopular even with many causes he had supported, like the American Labour movement and black political organizations. His passport was withdrawn in 1950, while the loss of concert bookings and opportunities to address an audience created, in effect, an internal exile with damaging consequences for his health, physical and mental. In an attempt to force the lifting of restrictions on his travelling abroad, the Shakespeare Memorial Theatre at Stratford invited him to play there in 1958 as Gower in *Pericles* and in 1959 – immediately after the return of his passport – as Othello. He was able to accept the second invitation; but, because he then became seriously ill with bronchitis, the Stratford *Othello* had to be postponed for a month and had limited rehearsal time.

When the production finally opened, it was an occasion more than an artistic event. Everyone wanted to make up to Robeson for the last ten years, but one biographer called it 'a dismal performance' (Hoyt, 224), while Margaret Webster thought Robeson had become too old and fat and that the production should have been built round him (*Daughter*, 107). The young director, Tony Richardson, had cut and rearranged the text, especially at the end, in ways that might have confused Robeson, given the shortness of the rehearsal period. Richardson was also criticized for what looked like eccentric choices. He seems to have wanted a sick and even decadent Venice, with a feeble, asthmatic Duke (Ian Holm) and an hysterically tearful Brabantio; but this attempt to combine the hero's personal tragedy with an indictment of his society seems simply to have bewildered spectators who were not looking for a reinterpretation of the play.

The Sound Archives tape gives a better impression than the reviews, showing that the production and Robeson himself had at least plenty of *vocal* energy; the promptbook also indicates that the actor was asked for a good deal of movement. Richardson was like Webster in his emphasis on speed (achieved partly through cuts) and in using crowd reactions to underline significant moments: one hears an embarrassed silence after 'the lieutenant is to be saved before the ensign' and gasps of horror at Othello's demotion of Cassio and his later striking of Desdemona. Richardson also sought out the humour in the play, or added to it, as when Cassio speaks of Desdemona as 'our great captain's – uh – captain'. There was plenty of excitement, some of it the result of Loudon Saint-hill's design: once the action got to Cyprus, it was speeded up still further with a single permanent set, though this meant locating Desdemona's bed on a sort of mezzanine so that the dying Emilia had to run up a winding stair in order to reach it (W. A. Darlington, *Daily Telegraph*, 8 April). Critics also noted the pack of Great Danes seeking Desdemona at the end of I.i (*Wolverhampton Express and Star*, 8 April), a highly praised drunken scene in which Albert Finney's Cassio put up a spectacular fight and fireworks at the Cyprus celebrations (W.E.W., *Coventry Evening Telegraph*, 8 April 1959). Did all this detract from the text? This was what some critics suggested; what they probably meant was that Robeson, who no longer found his lines so easy to remember, was swamped by the swirling action around him. But Richardson was clearly sensitive to the actors' vocal qualities, as a few reviewers recognized (J. C. Trewin, *Birmingham Post*, and anonymous critic, *Gloucester Echo*, both 8 April 1959). In particular, he created an effective contrast between Robeson's bass and the high, clear voices of Mary Ure and Sam Wanamaker as Desdemona and Iago. Critical fascination with Robeson naturally overshadowed their performances. The *Times* review, which referred in its headline to miscasting, declared that Mary Ure lacked aristocratic dignity while Wanamaker was a 'slick shyster' whom no one would trust. Though J. C. Trewin liked Ure's clarity and 'crisp edge' (*Birmingham Post*, 8 April 1959), other critics complained about her sharpness of tone. She seemed angry rather than frightened in the scene where Othello demands the handkerchief – an attempt at a modern, spirited woman which most reviewers disliked. Some of the irritation felt towards Sam Wanamaker's playing of Iago (which reviewers insisted on calling Method acting) may have been deliberately provoked by actor and director. He was loud and often funny (his triumphant hitting of the rhymes in his improvised verses got laughs); he openly invited the audience to share his glee at his own cleverness, sometimes prompting them, even more aggressively than Ferrer, with 'hmm?' The cutting also made him look more showy than he was. Part I ended with Iago looking forward to the way in which Desdemona's goodness would become the net that 'shall enmesh them – ALL!' What made this melodramatic was not only that he shouted it out, to thunderous applause, but that Richardson cut Roderigo's entrance, which ought to follow immediately ('How now, Roderigo?' would have deflated the Satanic effect). This Iago had an affectionate if stormy relationship with Emilia (Angela Baddeley); at the end of their scene with the handkerchief, according to the promptbook, he slapped her and she hit him back (to audience laughter). As usual, Emilia was a great success with the audience, though her long speech in IV.iii was cut; the scene ended with 'Beshrew me if I would do such a wrong for the whole world' and the humming of 'Willow, willow'.

And Robeson? His delivery, in the taped performance, sounds slightly more mannered than in 1943: he tends to lift his voice at the end of a line, as drama students are often told to do to avoid dropping into inaudibility. But his gently amused tone in the early scenes with Desdemona is charming and he is surprisingly effective when he turns on her, demanding the handkerchief while she is trying to talk about Cassio. Perhaps on repeated hearings his tone might strike one as that of a schoolteacher rather than a husband (already in 1942 a Boston reviewer noted 'a moralizing, pious quality' in his delivery: C.W.D., *Globe*, 11 August 1942); perhaps his predominant tone is one of reflective melancholy. But he does not sound as old as – judging from the production photographs – he actually looked. On paper, at least, he seems to have been active. Richardson got Robeson on his feet early in the great scene with Iago, on 'Why, what is this?' (III.iii.179), and, for the rest of the scene, references to being emotionally 'moved' were accompanied – literally – by movement. It was a move upstage by Othello that motivated Iago's 'I see this hath a little dashed your spirits' (218); at Iago's first 'I do see you're moved' (221) he himself crossed towards Othello, while his reiteration of the phrase (228) was motivated by Othello's crossing of the stage. After his attack on Iago in the second part of the scene, Othello sat from lines 393 to 447, and Richardson did not ask him for much after this point. The lines leading up to the epileptic fit were more heavily cut than in the Webster production, where he played the entire speech, and the promptbook gives no direction for movement to accompany the lines about Desdemona's ability to 'turn and turn again' in IV.i. The scene with Desdemona in IV.ii was played in their precariously positioned bedroom, which may be why Robeson is directed to sit on the bed at 'false as hell'; on 'O Desdemon, away', she falls into his arms and he takes her into them. Many production choices (such as the omission of Othello's brief entrance in V.i, which is cut in all three versions that Robeson played) are obviously aimed at the enobling of Othello. As Duberman says, a noble Moor was 'the only kind of Othello Robeson had any interest in playing, or could play' (Duberman, 476–7). But most productions of the period would have taken it for granted that this was the right interpretation.

In neither the 1942 nor the 1959 production did Othello, in the final scene, wound Iago. It would be interesting to know whether it was Robeson or Webster who first decided to get rid of this episode; Richardson had also omitted it from his 1956 television production. Though few Othellos and few audiences have worried about it (indeed Salvini's audiences seem to have loved it), the deliberate stabbing of an unarmed man was impossible for such a noble Othello as Robeson's. His line 'If that thou beest a devil, I cannot kill thee' was therefore played to indicate the uselessness of revenge. In order to retain Iago's ambiguous reply, 'I bleed, sir, but not killed', Webster directed that Ferrer should be brought back onstage bleeding on the forehead, presumably as a result of an offstage scuffle (Carroll, 285).

Some of the comments on Robeson in 1959 recall those made in 1930. The old complaint about his lack of authority, already made by Agate in 1930, was heard again from a reviewer who nevertheless thought that 'Whenever he is given the chance he truly dominates the stage' (*Wolverhampton Express and Star*, 8 April 1959). Another said that, while 'occasionally exciting', he 'hardly ever touches the heart' (*The Times*, 8 April 1959). Robert Wraight may have come closest to articulating the general response: 'frequently I had a shameful feeling that, married to any other voice, his acting would have had me talking of under-playing and a certain stiltedness – due perhaps to under-rehearsal' (*Star*, 8 April). But even Robeson's famous voice failed to mesmerize reviewers who still remembered Godfrey Tearle.

The acting of race

The most common response to Robeson's acting is the one that Earle Hyman, another distinguished black Othello, made many years later: Robeson was the greatest of Othellos because 'He did not have to act' (Hyman, 23). Such praise, as Richard Dyer has noted, is double-edged when applied to black actors, since it can imply the absence of intelligence or art (Dyer, 124). Robeson, however, often behaved as if he agreed with his critics. During the run of the Webster *Othello* he insisted that, unlike José Ferrer, he was not an actor (Dyer, 125). But the man who spent so long studying Shakespeare's language before he felt ready to act him in London, and who read the text in a folio facsimile so as to get a better sense of its punctuation and pronunciation, was not simply trying to be himself on the stage; he was trying to *act*. What is interesting is that so many critics wanted to believe the contrary.

Audience response to both Aldridge and Robeson always

focused on their race and read the actor's situation into the characters he played. In Aldridge's case, the nineteenth-century habit of taking Shakespeare's lines personally, whenever the text allowed it, encouraged a reading of *Othello* in the light of controversy over the abolition of the slave trade, the emancipation of the serfs in Russia, and the American Civil War. Robeson was seen as part of the struggle for integration and equality of opportunity, while Othello was identified with the struggle of Robeson himself with the House Committee on Un-American Activities. Though Felix Barker, in one of the most negative reviews of the Stratford *Othello*, objected that Robeson sometimes gave a 'fatal glimpse of a modern American Negro' (*Evening News*, London, 8 April 1959), 'fatal' was the wrong word; the power of Robeson's performance came precisely from the intersection of the Renaissance hero with the twentieth-century black man. In each case, the actor responded to what he felt the audience wanted from him. So Aldridge, when he recited his versified valediction, presented himself not as the thoroughly competent professional that he was but as an amalgam of his most famous theatrical black roles. Robeson, playing Othello seven times a week, acted himself into the role of tragic hero 'perplexed in the extreme.' The songs in Robeson's concerts, both pathetic and defiant, became increasingly personal; when he included Othello's last speech among them, he changed the text, just as Aldridge had, and just as he had changed that of 'Old Man River' long ago: Othello now loved 'wisely but full well' and killed a 'heathen dog', not a 'circumcised' one.

Margaret Webster probably gives the best summary of what contemporaries meant when they said that Robeson was not an actor. He had, she said, 'no concept of "impersonation". He can only do it if he can get a kind of electric motor going inside himself and this has to be started by some feeling – not Othello's feeling, but Robeson's' (*Daughter*, 110). Robeson's problem was not so much lack of formal training as the belief (which some of his admirers shared) that his acting and singing were natural gifts that would be spoiled if he acquired too much technique; in fact, as Duberman points out, he was not really so naive a performer as he sometimes pretended and sometimes used his supposed naturalness as a defence against criticism (Duberman, 269–70). But the issue of 'impersonation', as opposed to 'representation', also indicates how different Robeson's situation was from Aldridge's. Aldridge, in the nineteenth-century actor-manager tradition, largely dictated the nature of his own productions and their acting texts, whereas Robeson was at the mercy of directors and scripts by someone else. While Aldridge's success was often taken as proof that the Negro in general had a capacity for thought and feeling, no one seems to have felt that his playing of roles such as the comic Mungo or the villainous Zanga in *The Revenge* reflected badly either on him or on his race. But Robeson, unlike Aldridge, was playing to two audiences at once. As Ed Guerrero puts it,

> The black celebrity's star potential is largely based on his or her 'crossover' appeal to the vast white spectator/consumer audience held in tenuous balance with the ability to maintain at least the semblance of identification with African Americans ... The black star, while a wealthy, privileged symbol of equality and showcase success for white folks, is at the same time expected to exemplify and speak for the social aspirations of an oppressed racial formation, i.e., black folks. (Guerrero, 282–3)

This need to be acceptable, on different terms, to both black and white audiences explains why, although Aldridge never needed to make a secret of his attraction to white women, Robeson's affairs with Ashcroft and Hagen were, until recently, known only as gossip; because standards of journalism were so different in the 1940s, the episode where Ferrer brought detectives to catch Hagen and Robeson *in flagrante* was never widely reported (Duberman, 311–12). That the actor of Othello should have a sexual relationship with his Desdemona would have provided disturbing proof, to those who wanted it, that mere professionalism is not enough to prevent imitation from becoming reality in such a sexually charged play. (Anxiety on this subject may be one reason why so many husband and wife teams have played the parts.) The racial difference and the fact that both Robeson and Hagen were committing adultery would have confirmed the worst suspicions of white racists while also antagonizing Robeson's black admirers. While Robeson's career may be further evidence that actors are most likely to succeed as Othello if they are already famous *before* playing the part, it also shows what happens when the audience know – or think they know – enough about an actor to create a mental fusion between him and his stage character. It is understandable, after all, that Othello – a character constantly telling his story and admired for doing so – should be the only Shakespearean role Robeson ever played.

CHAPTER VI

The Robeson legacy I:
white Othellos on film, stage
and television

Immediately after Paul Robeson's first American performance of
Othello, one reviewer declared that 'no white man should ever
dare presume to play it again' (Rudolph Elie, *Variety*, 12 August
1942). By the end of the twentieth century the question of whether
black actors should play black roles had become the question of
whether any *except* black actors should play them. The general
acceptance of this view came more quickly in the United States
than in England, but both countries went through a period of
transition in the theatre, with Robeson as a silent, embarrassing,
absent presence in the work of white actors and directors. The
history of white actors in *Othello* after this date is littered with
failures, apart from Olivier's performance, an unashamed *tour de
force* of impersonation; widely praised, it would soon become (on
film and video) a source of embarrassment itself. In 1981 Jonathan
Miller's *Othello*, with its controversial casting of Anthony Hopkins
as an Othello who made no attempt to seem black, brought the
question of race-based casting into the open. Three films made
before the Robeson scandal reached international proportions –
Les Enfants du Paradis, *A Double Life* and Orson Welles's *Othello* –
show white actors playing Othello. The first two of these also
historicize and distance the play by filming it in a theatrical
setting. But they share other concerns that are new; one of these is
the relation of film to theatre.

Carné and Cukor

Near the end of Marcel Carné's *Les Enfants du Paradis* the film
offers a brief glimpse of the historical Fréderick Lemaître playing
Othello in front of a French audience as yet unfamiliar with

Shakespeare. The story is set in the first half of the nineteenth century, a period when Shakespeare was associated with political and artistic freedom; but it was filmed in Nice under the German occupation and first shown in March 1945. Thus it is easy to see Lemaître's defence of the English author against snobbish French aristocrats as part of an allegory about resistance and collaboration. But films about the theatre tend also to be films about film. As Jill Forbes points out, *Les Enfants* sets a mime artist (the historical Debureau) and a mime theatre at the centre of its action to celebrate the silent film tradition (Forbes, 36). Lemaître, who represents the theatre of speech, is naturally drawn to Shakespeare, but what enables him to play Othello is his experience of jealousy, which he immediately transforms into a superb performance. The film shows only two brief extracts from the play: the scene in which Iago arouses Othello's jealousy and the murder, which had been the 'sensation' for Paris audiences in the 1820s. Both are relevant to the plot of the film itself, as is generally the case with theatrical scenes in films. Life becomes art for the great actor, Lemaître, while, for less gifted people, art inspires sordid real-life crime (the murder in the Turkish bath by which Lacenaire probably prevents a double murder by a jealous husband).

Les Enfants was an obvious influence on *A Double Life* (1947), a film by George Cukor with a script by the husband and wife team Ruth Gordon and Garson Kanin. At first, this Hollywood example of *film noir* seems to be simply the best of a number of plays and films on the theme of an actor who, while playing Othello, becomes wildly jealous of his wife, who is playing Desdemona (for others see Hodgdon, 232–8). They appear to be variations on the *Pagliacci* story, which Leoncavallo claimed was based on a real-life incident (music from his opera *Pagliacci* was sometimes played before performances of *Othello* in the early twentieth century). In *A Double Life* a famous actor in late middle age, Anthony (Tony) John, is playing opposite his ex-wife Brita, whom he still loves, in a Broadway production of *Othello*. He has also let himself be picked up by Pat, a waitress in an Italian restaurant. Tony (played by Ronald Colman) is notorious for his tendency to become identified with the characters he plays. The longer the production runs, the more jealous he becomes of Brita. After a performance in which he comes close to killing her during the final scene (figure 11), he seeks out Pat again, apparently identifying her with the 'strumpet' image of Desdemona. When Pat happens to say,

11   Ronald Colman as Tony John playing Othello and Signe Hasso
as his ex-wife Brita playing Desdemona. *A Double Life.* Directed
by George Cukor (Universal Studios, 1947)

'You wanna put out the light?', the cue from the play is too much
for him: he kills her with a kiss, just as, onstage, he has been
pretending to kill Desdemona. His press agent exploits the resemblance between the murder and the play in order to help the run of
the latter. Tony's increasingly disturbed reactions arouse suspicion;
at the next performance, catching sight of a policeman in the
wings, he kills himself in earnest.

   Much more complex than most of the stories about actors who
over-identify with Othello, *A Double Life* is unusual for its emphasis
on the effects of the long run, a uniquely theatrical phenomenon.
Tony and Brita play *Othello* on Broadway for over three hundred
performances. The only remotely comparable event was the 297-
performance run of the Robeson *Othello*, which ended its national
tour only two years before Cukor began making the film. One
critic has noted the possible parallel in the casting of the two
Desdemonas: Brita is played by the Swedish Signe Hasso and
Robeson's Desdemona was the German-born Uta Hagen (Frank,
122). The Kanins always denied any intention of referring to the

[137]

Webster production, but this is not surprising. They may have been protecting Robeson and Hagen, whose love affair was still unknown to the public at large. They may also have been uneasy because Robeson's first interview with the House Un-American Activities Committee had taken place in October 1946.

Though the numerous scenes of *Othello* in rehearsal and performance give the impression that the play is being seen again and again, the film in fact barely shows Iago at all, since Tony needs no Iago to make him jealous. Cukor arranged for the scenes in the theatre to be directed by Walter Hampden, who had starred in the longest-running *Othello* before Robeson's. Hampden, although he did act in film near the end of his life, was the quintessential stage actor; he had begun his career with Frank Benson's company in England and once went on record as saying that he did not think his style of performance suited to film (*Newsweek*, 9 May 1936, 44). He was thus the obvious person to ensure that there would be an unmistakable difference between stage and film acting. Cukor also made the actors perform in a real theatre, not a studio set, with lights beating directly on their theatrical makeup; apart from Hasso, all of them, like Colman, have British accents. The result was to make stage acting in general, and Shakespearean acting in particular, seem irrevocably old-fashioned. Colman's Othello indeed looks rather like the one played by Fréderick Lemaître, on a sumptuously orientalized set. The deliberate cultivation of the archaic in this film suggests that, even for a director who admired the theatre as much as Cukor, the only good Othello was a dead Othello.

Walter Hampden's presence also had the effect of turning back the clock to a period before Robeson, when there was no questioning of the right of white actors to play Othello. And yet anxiety about the impersonation of blackness is subtextually present in the film. Tony, who frequently performs in front of mirrors, does so for the first time in his dressing room, as he murmurs, 'Haply, for I am black ...'. From a white actor, only a few years after the end of Robeson's record-breaking performance, these words are particularly significant: patently untrue, especially since Tony is not even made up for the role, they become the truth for him through sheer force of imagination, just as, later, he looks into a shop window and sees himself reflected as a Moor. It is when he is most eager to make himself believe something that Tony looks into the mirror, as if unable to take any emotion seriously unless he can see someone looking at it. This sense of the actor's 'double life' is reinforced by the film's striking superimposition of scenes from the play with scenes of the spectators watching it.

The idea that an actor can give a great performance only when emotionally identified with a part to the point of insanity seems like the kind of folk belief that would make a serious professional laugh. Yet Shelley Winters, who played the waitress, felt as soon as she read the script that it gave a true picture of 'an occupational disease that many actors suffer from' (Winters, 178). Laurence Olivier, who described Colman's film performance as 'brilliant' (Olivier, *Acting*, 160), also recognized the condition. In his *Confessions of an Actor* he (perhaps disingenuously) attributes the failure of his marriage with Vivien Leigh to the excessive demands made by acting of the highest order:

> I would say that an all-out performance of a part like Titus Andronicus or Othello will teach you all that there is to be known about this drive; high in importance among its components is, of course, sex.
>
> In the first years of Vivien's theatre-acting there was not the passion, the flare, the flame necessary to set the stage alight. It was therefore hard to make her understand, at those times when she was sadly disappointed in the results of my intimate passionate endeavours, that all *that* had gone into my acting, and that you can't be more than one kind of athlete at a time.
>
> (Olivier, *Confessions*, 290)

Whether or not this is a fair explanation of Olivier's private life, it is relevant to the subtext of *A Double Life*, which censorship conditions in the late 1940s did not allow Cukor to make more explicit. Tony is clearly sexually insecure with the sophisticated Brita; his own sophistication is only a veneer concealing both brutality and the fear of impotence. The psychological disturbance triggered by playing Othello is a displacement of anxiety at what must have been suspected if not known about Robeson's immense attractiveness to white women. The interesting aspect of the myths about murderous Othellos over-identifying with their roles is the willingness of audiences to believe in them. It is obviously much more likely that actors in a love scene will fall in love than that one actor in a murder scene will end up murdering the other. The real fear about an actor who becomes over-identified with Othello is not that he will kill Desdemona but that he will make love to her. Racial anxiety is thus another form of sexual anxiety.

[139]

Orson Welles

It is likely that Orson Welles had seen and admired *A Double Life*; possible echoes from it – such as the evocative gauzy curtains flapping in the wind – have been pointed out in his *Othello* of 1952 (Jacobs, *passim*). More generally, the depiction of events through the eyes of a mentally unstable observer links Welles's filmography to the *film noir* tradition. Welles's set designer, Alexandre Trauner, had also designed *Les Enfants du Paradis*, and the two films share a scene depicting murder in a Turkish bath, though the use of this setting for V.i of *Othello* is usually attributed to brilliant improvising on Welles's part while most of the actors were waiting for their costumes to arrive. All three films have a complex relationship to the theatre from which they, in different ways, derive. Just as *Les Enfants* parallels a silent actor with one who loves words, *A Double Life* problematizes the very features that were supposed to make theatre superior to cinema: the 'presence' of the actor and the fact that the performance can change every night. As an American playing Othello opposite a French-Canadian Desdemona and an Irish Iago, Welles was registering his contempt for the view that only British speech was suitable for Shakespeare. But he was under such enormous constraints of both money and time (he even had to dub some of the other characters' voices himself) that it is not always clear how far anything other than these factors is responsible for the difficulty in hearing the film's soundtrack, where, even in the remastered 1992 version, lip movements and sounds do not always go together. It has been suggested that in *Chimes at Midnight*, where Welles seems deliberately to contrast Gielgud's beautiful verse-speaking with his own mumbling, 'perhaps our usual preconceptions about dramatic speech are being deliberately challenged' (McMillin, 90); on this view, remastering Welles's soundtrack may actually falsify his intentions (Anderegg, 117). Since sight normally takes priority over sound in any case, the film's impression is largely a visual one. That Welles replaces words with visual patterning, as the operatic *Otello* replaces words with music, makes it frustrating that the film is hard to see as well as hear. Peter Donaldson's brilliant psychological reading of the tiny reflections that appear in the eyes of the characters and in the water owes much to the sophisticated equipment now available for viewing the film (Donaldson, 98–100). What are lost are two elements that often

12   Orson Welles, Suzanne Cloutier and
Micheál MacLiammóir in Orson Welles's *Othello* (1952)

make the story more bearable in the theatre: its humour and its
verbal beauty. But the endlessly fascinating images of labyrinths,
prison bars and water, though they may well tell the story of
narcissism and bleakness that Donaldson finds in them, provide
visual beauty to counterpoint the claustrophobic reading of the
text. Welles exploits (figure 12) the opportunity to use vertical
contrasts (at this period, especially, characters on a stage tended
to move only in horizontal lines), with a fairly obvious symbolic
difference between the lofty tower of the Cypriot castle in which
Othello and Desdemona consummate their marriage and the

cistern below the castle in which Cassio brawls with Roderigo. Humour is present only in the running gags about Roderigo; instead of picking a fight with Cassio at once, as in the play, he makes several ineffectual attempts to do so in the course of the evening, only to succeed by accident when Cassio is already drunk. The part played by Roderigo's little dog in the scene of his master's murder is a device straight out of *film noir*. So, perhaps, is the emphasis on the disturbing, languorous atmosphere of the fort in the heat, which conveys some sense of Othello's state of mind; Iago appears from time to time, usually behind him and in the distance, and Desdemona wanders around looking beautiful, sad and unattainable. On the stage Lodovico traditionally makes a grand entrance, but the film Othello first sees his menacing ship approach, then wanders into the castle courtyard to find him already seated under a tent, as if he had been enthroned there for ever. This deliberate confusing of temporal and spatial boundaries makes all the characters seem to be moving around in a giant maze.

Thanks to Welles's own willingness to talk about his own work and to Micheál MacLiammóir's enjoyable book about its filming and his playing of Iago (*Put Money in Thy Purse*, 1976), almost too much is known about this *Othello*. We know, for instance, that for Welles the hero was 'the archetype of the simple man' and 'that all-male man whom Shakespeare – who was clearly very feminine in many ways – regarded as a natural-born loser in a tragic situation' (Welles and Bogdanovich, 232). What also emerges, though with hindsight, is the way in which the crucial conflicts of the film were replicated in the world of the film-makers. There was racial tension: MacLiammóir's attitude towards the people of Morocco, where much of the film was made, was a mixture of on-the-record comedy and off-the-record sexual exploitation. There was gender conflict: the happy male-bonding of Welles, MacLiammóir and others, drinking far into the night and making brilliant multi-lingual conversation, contrasts with the fate of Suzanne Cloutier, who was cast as Desdemona entirely on the basis of her looks and sometimes literally deprived of voice and identity by being dubbed and doubled by other women actors. The meaninglessness of the personality of the individual actress is well illustrated by Mac-Liammóir's diary entry on the feat of imagination involved in the early stages of filming, when he had to direct an 'enigmatic glance suggestive of mingled desire and loathing' towards an offscreen

Desdemona who was 'not merely absent but also, so far, non-existent'; at this stage, the part had not even been cast (Mac-Liammóir, 116). MacLiammóir, with no apparent awareness of how a sense of exclusion might create Cloutier's desperate seeking for attention, says that he liked her, yet quotes her only when he can make her look ridiculous. Her apartness carried over, perhaps by design, into the film; the *New York Times* reviewer described her as 'a beautiful, frail and gauzy girl who might be tremendously moving if you could sense her in relation to her man' (Bosley Crowther, 13 September 1955). A British reviewer said, 'I shall always recall her, as a tiny dot at the foot of an immense staircase, gazing adoringly at the monumental bulk of Mr Welles on some upper landing, waiting for the great man to come out of his pose and toss her the cue for a line' (C.A. Lejeune, *Observer*, 26 February 1956). The staircase was a vertical equivalent of the long table that separated husband and wife in the best-remembered scene of *Citizen Kane*. In many ways Cloutier's Desdemona is more in the nineteenth-century tradition than any other, reduced as she is to a haunting symbol of pure beauty; indeed, at one point a tear in her eye actually glitters like the diamond to which a poet would have compared it. At the same time Welles's stress on atmosphere conveys the threat that this beauty implies to a hero who does not know how to make contact with her. As he approaches her in their bedroom in the tower of the citadel on Cyprus, he is given the lines from II.i, 'If it were now to die, 'twere now to be most happy', but they appear to be spoken in voice-over, rather than to Desdemona, and she is given no reply to them. This is true of much of what he says in their scenes together: it seems directed to himself rather than to her.

But the most fruitful tension came from the relationship between the two leading actors. To a tableful of friends and strangers, Welles roared (MacLiammóir's word) that Iago should be played as impotent: 'Impotent ... that's why he hates life so much – they always do.' MacLiammóir, who was homosexual, commented in his journal that at this point Welles's voice was very deep, 'surely somewhat forced' (26), thus revealing both his awareness that Welles was taunting him in public and his suspicion of the reality of the 'all-male male' persona being projected at this point. Nevertheless, the two actors were in essential agreement about Iago: they wanted to avoid the theatrical cliché of the Mephistophelian villain. The cool, business-like figure envisaged by Welles was obviously more suitable for the film medium but, as MacLiammóir recognized, potentially monotonous. The impotence theory provided him with something to bring out in close-up: the 'underlying sickness of the mind, the immemorial hatred of life, the secret isolation of impotence under the soldier's muscles, the flabby solitude gnawing at the groins, the eye's untiring calculation' (27–8). This subtext would replace the self-explanation of the soliloquies, all of which had been cut. MacLiammóir, though much of his dialogue is hard to understand, largely succeeds in the visual projection of this tight-lipped character; Welles, however, makes sure that the only calculating eye is the camera's. The film opens with the terrified Iago being shut into the cage where he will starve to death, and occasional glimpses of the cage from this point on provide a somber reminder of the future that he himself does not know. There is no danger that this Iago will direct the audience's point of view. Though he retains the line about learning the drinking song in England, he does not sing it himself, and one cannot imagine him as the life of any conceivable party. He is constantly seen in motion; not only his famous scene with Othello but his parallel conversation with Roderigo in II.ii take place while both are moving, as if in each case he and his victim were being driven onward by a momentum of which he cannot understand the source.

It is not clear whether Welles ever explained his interpretation of Iago to Fay Compton, who played Emilia. Indeed, he took little interest in Emilia, whom he once described as 'a trollop' (MacLiammóir, 31). As the character does not even appear in the film until the point where she finds the handkerchief, spectators unfamiliar with the play may not have known that she was Iago's wife. When Iago takes the handkerchief from her, the real focus of the scene is not their relationship but the spiral staircase on which they stand, a whirlpool into which she is about to be sucked. She and MacLiammóir, over fifty at the time of filming, are not only a dry and bitter couple but also a distant one. Welles made no attempt, as Trevor Nunn and Oliver Parker would later do, to develop the idea of a sexually frustrated couple envying the happiness of the newly married Othello and Desdemona. In 1947, when Fay Compton had played Emilia in the West End, reviewers had praised her 'flawless elocutionary grace' (*The Times*, 27 March 1947). Her fine English diction may be one reason why Welles minimized her role, which, even so, has struck some critics as belonging 'too much to the stage' (McKernan and Terris, 124); Virginia Vaughan, though she agrees that Compton's performance may be 'jarring in a film based on visual images', recognizes at the same time that it is a welcome contrast to Welles's voyeuristic treatment of the other female characters (Vaughan, *Othello*, 213). In what is left of IV.iii (where Desdemona is barely heard humming a little of the willow song in the distance), she retains much of her famous speech, which is played in the coarse plebian tradition; Desdemona breaks it off by rising abruptly and there is no affection between the women as Emilia goes out, leaving Desdemona to undress herself at the end of the scene.

Though MacLiammóir describes Compton as giving a fine performance in her death scene (155), it is not clear how much of it remains in the edited film. Certainly, in an often muffled soundtrack, Compton's Emilia is strikingly vibrant in such lines as "Tis proper I obey him, *but not now*' and 'Perchance, Iago, I will ne'er go home'. Welles's conception of Iago may not have been Mephistophelean, but when this Emilia says that she will speak in spite of 'heaven and men and devils' (V.ii.219), her inflection on the word 'devils' and her uneasy sideways glance at her husband show that she at least thinks that she is dealing with one. These are among the few moments in the film when the quality of the verse speaking makes an impact in its own right. Meanwhile, however, Welles is working against her with his visual effects. First, in one of his famous depth of field shots, he shows Emilia and Iago together; then Emilia moves (as if on a stage) past Iago into full close-up, and we lose sight of Iago until, too late, we realize that we (and the camera) should have been watching him: as she is telling Othello that she gave the handkerchief to 'my husband', she gasps and the camera cuts to a close-up of a knife, a brief glimpse of Iago's face and his disappearing figure seen from behind. Emilia dies in isolation from Othello and the rest, but the bars behind which Othello has been speaking fall across her, indicating that Iago (soon to be caged himself) has, as he promised, enmeshed them all.

Though the film won the Prix d'Or at Cannes in 1951, its immediate reception in the US was so poor that it was not released in Britain until 1956, at the same time as the 1955 Yutkevich film. Yutkevich's own comment – that Welles's film began with death, while his own began with life – suggests that he may to some extent have been replying to it. There are obvious resemblances between the two, such as the striking images of ships, the use of shadows and reflections, and the ascent of Othello to the awaiting Desdemona on his arrival at Cyprus; but many of the same devices are also present in the early silent film versions and are a natural expansion of the play's Venetian setting. Much of what seemed strange and irritating about Welles in the 1950s – his heavy cutting and transposing of the text and his emphasis on the sexual subtext – is taken for granted now. No one else followed Welles in opening with the funeral of Othello and Desdemona and the punishment of Iago. But his idea of opening the flashback with the wedding of Othello and Desdemona, though not new with him (Oscar Ashe did it in a stage production of 1906), has been followed in nearly every subsequent film version, and many stage ones as well. Though his interpretation of Iago as impotent was no more intelligible to the average viewer than Olivier's attempt in 1938 to play him as homosexual, it was to influence the next generation of directors. Welles himself did not carry the concept into his 1951 stage production, though his stage Iago (Peter Finch) was otherwise not unlike MacLiammóir; Kenneth Tynan described him as 'a clipped starveling, puny and humorless to the bone' (*Evening Standard*, 19 October 1951). This – with the impotence again an important theme – would be the way Frank Finlay played the character in 1964, opposite Laurence Olivier's famous Othello.

Olivier's Othello

The achievement of Olivier and his director John Dexter was to bring to the theatrical *Othello* in Britain the same level of invention that had gone into the film interpretations. Other postwar productions had been conventionally beautiful and noble, apart perhaps from Frederick Valk's powerful Othello, which had first been seen at the Old Vic in 1942; although Valk, a Czech, acted in heavily accented English, he seems to have conveyed the same sense of frightening strangeness as Salvini and is reviewed in much the same terms ('volcanic', 'elemental' and 'monumental' are some of the adjectives used by Audrey Williamson, *Old Vic*, 155). John Neville and Richard Burton alternated the two major roles in 1956 in an effective, simply staged production. Tony Richardson's attempt at a more modern reading of the play in 1959 came into conflict with the effect of Robeson's mere presence, the source of most audience excitement. Just as the stage *Othellos* in *Les Enfants* and *A Double Life* belong to an earlier period, these traditional stage productions anchor the play firmly in the past, making theatre, like opera, seem a natural home for traditionalists.

In 1961 at Stratford John Gielgud, at the peak of his career, played an Othello directed by Franco Zeffirelli. It should have been a triumph; instead, it was a first night of disasters. Some of these were simply accidents, like Othello's beard coming off, but the production as a whole was also seen as disastrous. Zeffirelli is usually blamed for having been too 'operatic', with unwieldy if beautiful sets that usurped valuable rehearsal time. It would seem, however, that the director's concept of the play was more modern than that of his leading actor. Three years later Gielgud saw Laurence Olivier walk on to the stage of the National Theatre at the Old Vic, dressed like an African, barefoot, smiling with half-closed eyes, and radiating complete, self-contained self-satisfaction. 'Staggered', he suddenly remembered that in rehearsals Zeffirelli had tried unsuccessfully to convince him that 'this man is very vain' (Gielgud, 82–3).

Olivier's entrance, which became famous, recalls Stanislavski's conception of the part, as described in 1930. But whereas Stanislavski's Othello was meant to come in carrying armfuls of flowers, giving them to everyone as an expression of his happiness, Olivier, half in a dream, smelled a single red rose (supposedly from Desdemona's bridal bouquet; Dexter and Olivier joked about whether it ought to be white or red); he hummed a little to himself, then used the rose to tickle Iago and remind him not to be over-serious. What he was actually doing in this scene, Dexter wrote later, was not only smelling the rose but trying to 'smell the audience' (Dexter, 17–18). Edward Pechter has pointed out how this smelling of the rose not only prefigures 'I'll smell it on the tree' in Othello's final soliloquy but also establishes the sensuality of the character, often indicated elsewhere in the production by the sense of smell (Pechter, 143). This Othello did not bother to charm either his subordinates or the audience. He gave a powerful and not always sympathetic performance that, James Earl Jones thought, had 'all the paranoia, suspicions and defensiveness of a victim of racism' (Jones and Niven, 165–6). This, as will be clear in the next chapter, is not how Jones thought the part should be played, but it attests to Olivier's power of impersonation. As he explains in detail in his book *On Acting*, he changed his walk, worked to lower his voice, made himself up 'all over' by a special formula, and played a character who was authentically 'other' and very dangerous. His strongly sexual and violent figure may be a reply to Robeson's noble Moor; it also develops the hints in Cukor's *A Double Life* about fear of impotence as a motive for sexual jealousy.

Dexter's production was directed for film by Stuart Burge, and later put on to video. Olivier himself would have preferred to be making a film rather than filming a stage play; he felt that, perhaps for this reason, his own performance was 'tired' and that Frank Finlay as Iago ended up looking better on the screen (Olivier, *Acting*, 198, 200). It is true that Olivier on film suffers from the absence of the 'aura' that always accompanied him in the theatre, and that Finlay's understated playing comes into its own in close-up (figure 13). However, the contrast between the two acting styles becomes part of an exploration of 'otherness' that moves from Othello to include a re-examination of every major character. Thus, the film and video not only preserve a famous example of heroic acting but, because of the all-round excellence of the cast and the production, offer a radically new reading. The most famous influence on John Dexter's interpretation was F. R. Leavis's 1937 essay (reprinted in *The Common Pursuit* in 1952), which argued that the traditional view of Othello's nobility and Iago's intellectuality was sentimental. But the production was also very much a product of the 1960s in its richness of subtext and its emphasis on characters' socio-economic positioning. Class-conflict is visible from the start, as Iago's contemptuous smile in reply to Roderigo's suggestion that he ought not to 'follow' a man he hates reminds the young aristocrat that not everyone has a choice in such matters. The production opened at one of the many times when the possibility of a Turkish invasion of Cyprus was in the news, a fact that gave an extra excitement to the opening of I.iii. Though most of this part of the play was omitted in the final print of the film version, Lodovico (present in this scene, as in most productions) is seen to lay a restraining hand on the Duke's arm when Brabantio's accusations become particularly vehement, perhaps to remind him that the senate cannot afford to antagonize its best military leader at this juncture. Dexter also emphasized the uneasy racial and religious mix on the island: an elderly man in Cypriot costume spits on Bianca, a Cypriot in western dress who is obviously regarded as a traitor to her people.

13   Laurence Olivier as Othello and Frank Finlay as Iago,
National Theatre, London, 1964

A Leavisite concern for moral judgement, which characterized much literary criticism of this period, affected the playing of other characters as well as Othello. Derek Jacobi's Cassio, for example, is a complex figure. He takes a rather smug pleasure, in I.ii, when he asks Iago a question ('Ancient, what makes he here?': line 49) to which he already knows the answer. By the start of II.i he is already more vulnerable, as his lack of military experience makes him twitch every time a gun goes off. It is characteristic of his well-meaning tactlessness that his comment, 'I never knew / A

Florentine more kind and honest' (often spoken after Iago's exit) is directed *to* Iago, whose eyes, as he turns away, flicker with contempt at what he sees as regional snobbery. In the final scene, this Cassio is angry rather than forgiving in his delivery of 'Dear General, I never gave you cause', though after Othello's suicide, somewhat chastened, he admits, 'he *was* great of heart'.

The women, though they are not criticized individually, are presented as products of their social class: Joyce Redman's light-hearted Emilia is sad only when she thinks of her husband's strangeness (in the production's sexual subtext, Iago had been impotent for years, though no reviewer seems to have realized this: Tynan, 8), but has learned not to ask too many questions; Maggie Smith, suppressing her famous comic skills, plays a mature Desdemona whose gentle graciousness and good breeding are finally shown to be limitations in a situation so far beyond her experience. She seems, however, to learn quickly – in IV.ii her initial reaction when Othello falls to the floor weeping is to keep a careful distance from him; but then she kneels beside him in an unsuccessful attempt to comfort him. She is especially touching in IV.iii when, calling again on long-practised social skills, she gracefully curtseys her farewell to the dinner guests who have so recently witnessed her public humiliation.

The excellent National Theatre publication compiled by Kenneth Tynan gives a thorough account of what Dexter and the actors worked out in the early stages of rehearsal, though some of these ideas were intended for the actors' benefit rather than the audience's and may have changed over time (Dexter's autobiography points out that Tynan did not actually record what happened after the first reading: 18). It is unlikely, for instance, that uninformed spectators would realize that Othello, when he re-enters at III.iii.332, is supposed to have tried, and failed, to make love to Desdemona (Tynan, 8), thus colouring the play's crucial scene with a sense of sexual failure that carries through to Act IV, with all its references to 'being a man'. One wonders, too, whether the development of the Othello–Iago scene is fully intelligible as the actors and director understood it. As Tynan explains it, Othello questioned Iago about Cassio on the assumption that he would find some peccadillo like an unpaid mess bill; then, when Iago (at random, and in something of a panic) told him to beware of jealousy, he found himself caught in something he never expected (Tynan, 8). Olivier paraphrased his reactions as

'"Come on, I know you're after Cassio's lieutenancy ... I'll get the truth out of you – come on." ... But,' he added, 'in getting the truth, Othello trips himself up, becomes jealous without being aware of how it began, and goes completely over the edge' (Olivier, *Acting*, 97). Yet the scene, as the video preserves it, shows an Othello aware from the beginning not only of the fact that Iago is trying to manipulate him, but of the form that this manipulation will take. He responds to the initial 'I like not that', with a loud, sharp 'What dost thou say, Iago?'; when Desdemona tells him of Cassio's visit, Othello glances contemptuously at Iago as if to rebuke him for his malicious insinuations; and when, in answer to Iago's question, he says that Cassio 'went between us very oft', his mock-portentous tone seems to be teasing Iago to make what he can of the information.

What seems to startle Othello is the grief-stricken tone with which Iago blurts out, 'beware, my lord, of jealousy'. His response is curious. The words, 'Oh, misery', have always been an interpretative crux in this scene: an 'easily jealous' actor like Kean or Macready already foresaw his own fate at this point; on the other hand, Salvini and Fechter made a point of not taking the words personally, treating them simply as a comment on the jealous state in general. Olivier's Othello seems to think that Iago's rhetorical question or exclamation about the jealous man – 'what damned minutes tells he o'er' – is a genuine question in need of a reply, and he tentatively suggests one: 'O, misery?' He rallies to become indignant at Iago's disloyalty to 'our country disposition'. When Iago says, 'Cassio's *my* trusty friend' (as if to contrast their relationships with the lieutenant), the grief in Othello's face reflects the sense of betrayed friendship of which he has just been reminded. After Iago's 'long live you to think so', confidence can be seen draining out of Othello's face: as he says, 'and yet, how nature erring from itself', he takes hold of the small cross on a chain around his neck. He had crossed himself earlier, when Brabantio accused him of unnatural practices in winning Desdemona. His adopted religion is a defence against something much more frightening, his former belief.

The actors are thus attempting something extremely difficult, showing Iago's success to be largely a result of his hitting on words that trigger already existing feelings in Othello. It is Othello himself who introduces the idea of the unnatural; Iago only takes it up. When Othello re-enters, Olivier's performance becomes bigger as he releases the full power of his brazen higher notes for the 'farewell' speech and the oath, but, paradoxically, it is the sheer momentum of his fury that finally allows Iago to take control. As the two men kneel at the end of the scene, Iago lays his sword on the ground; later, by pushing it a little further into view, he is able to remind Othello to order the death of Cassio.

Though at the time it seemed that Frank Finlay had been ordered to sacrifice his Iago in the interest of a star performance by Olivier, with hindsight it now seems that he belongs, like MacLiammóir, to a new tradition of subdued, ordinary Iagos who succeed because they are taken for granted by everyone else rather than because they inspire any special trust, affection or admiration. The production emphasized the element of improvisation in Iago's plots and his increasing loss of control over them. In Act IV, as Othello's new Lieutenant, he wears the sash that Cassio has forfeited; Lodovico spots this immediately, and his curt response to Iago's greeting, followed by 'How does Lieutenant *Cassio?*', suggests both dislike and suspicion. The suspicion is clearly still present in V.i, when Iago's 'Let's go' and 'Will you go on afore?' (V.i.124, 128) are played as two separate attempts to get the others offstage, after they have shown reluctance to obey him. The couplet of soliloquy with which he ends the scene ('This is the night / That either makes me, or undoes me quite') shows his awareness that time is running out for him. Dexter follows the nineteenth-century practice of having Iago taken off the stage before the end, but not in order to give him an impressive exit. The cue for his departure is 'The object poisons sight; let it be hid', and, like an object, he is dragged away, whimpering with pain.

There was thus no competition for the starring performance that the audience wanted Olivier to give. At the same time, the effectiveness of his impersonation created admiration rather than emotional involvement. Olivier goes all out in the passionate scenes: his fit leaves him rigid with his legs bent and in the air, and its aftermath is felt both in the inarticulate howls with which he responds to some of Iago's lines in the next scene, and in his reaction to the arrival of the Venetian embassy. At first too stunned to reply to Lodovico's greeting, by the end of the scene he is behaving insanely, with a mock-welcome to his guest after which he rushes out screaming.

In so far as Olivier's performance is seen as a *tour de force* of mimicry, it is likely to be offensive, since mimicry is no longer, as it seems to have been in the eighteenth century, an acceptable and even flattering gesture towards a distinctive performer or manner. Olivier and Dexter between them may have wished to show his audiences exactly what it was that they resented in black men (arrogance? sexual potency? mere *difference?*), and then win them to sympathize with such a man in spite of themselves. Even so, only the atmosphere of the early 1960s made such a performance possible. It was a time when Britain still believed itself to be free of race prejudice and a white actor (Peter Sellers) could become famous for his comic Indian accent. In April 1968, when Enoch Powell made his famous 'Rivers of blood' speech urging a halt to immigration to Britain, the extent and bitterness of racial conflict within Britain became clear. This new consciousness about race would change the way in which *Othello* could be played.

The BBC *Othello*

In mainstream British theatre, however, white actors continued to play the title role: Brewster Mason and Donald Sinden for the Royal Shakespeare Company in 1971 and 1979, Paul Scofield for the National Theatre in 1980. Unlike Olivier, these actors were made up lightly, the well-tanned products of an outdoor life rather than of a different ethnicity. As Ian McKellen suggested in 1986, the reason was probably a new embarrassment about racial impersonation: 'Every modern, white actor, taking on Othello, feels obliged to explain why he's not playing him black, which was surely Shakespeare's intention, when the unspoken reason is that to "black up" is as disgusting these days as a "nigger minstrel show".' McKellen went on to add that, precisely for this reason, he had no intention of ever playing the part himself (McKellen, *Acting*, 27). The rejection of impersonation, however, seems to have made Othello even harder for British actors. The directorial solution to the problem was to lower the play's emotional temperature and rely on the 'Chekhovian' realism of the Stratford style at its best. As Julie Hankey notes, in her survey of British productions of this period, it is a style that works beautifully for everyone except Othello, who, reviewers frequently complain, seems to have wandered in from another play. Mason, Scofield and Sinden were all considered irredeemably sane and gentlemanly; thus, when they became passionate, audiences found them simply embarrassing (Hankey, 119–20).

[153]

The turning point in British attitudes to casting came suddenly in 1981, when Anthony Hopkins played Othello for Jonathan Miller in the BBC Shakespeare series. Ironically, Miller's predecessor, Cedric Messina, had wanted to film James Earl Jones in the title role but was prevented by the refusal of the British Actors' Equity Union to let a non-British actor play the part. Faced with protests from all sides, Miller argued that the play was about jealousy, not race, and that casting a black actor would encourage audiences to 'equate the supposed simplicity of the black with the exorbitant jealousy of the character' (Fenwick, 18). It was an argument that would later be used by black actors, but what the director's critics really objected to was not his ideology but its practical result: a white actor was to play the most famous black character in drama, in a televised version likely to become the standard image of the play for a whole generation of school and university students. Miller was, and still is, accused of racism precisely because he did not make race an issue.

Miller explained very clearly what he wanted to do with *Othello*, and most reviewers made it equally clear that they did not agree with his choices. These were: believable 'ordinary' characters; low-key, naturalistic (sometimes barely audible) speech; a production set almost entirely indoors, with largely monochrome costumes which looked unquestionably seventeenth-century but without the gaudiness that suggests theatricality. The anti-theatricality inspired some unusual line-readings: 'Stand, there!' (I.ii.56) became 'Stand there', a calm order to Iago not to advance on Brabantio's approaching party; the speakers at the beginning of II.i were not buffeted by the storm but watching it from a window. A consciously 'made-for-television' version of the play, this *Othello* is aimed at spectators who will be watching from only a few feet away, like visitors to an art gallery. Miller was aware that the average television screen was about the size of a small Dutch painting; he thus treated each frame as a canvas, showing characters, sometimes distractingly, through doors and windows, at the ends of corridors, or in mirrors. At the beginning of the willow scene Desdemona, lit from behind like a figure by Georges de la Tour, sits at her dressing table meditating on a skull. Although the close-ups might make spectators feel like voyeurs, the constant presence of attendants and offstage sounds like the horses' hooves that are audible before Othello's 'farewell' speech are a reminder that few conversations in the Renaissance were really private.

[154]

Despite this concern for an authentic 'period' look, Miller and his cast took a firmly modern view of the story, in which they saw no metaphysical implications. All the protagonists were middle-aged except Desdemona, and even she was surprisingly mature, not a frightened child (Penelope Wilton, who played the part, thought that she must have known Othello for many years while she was acting as a hostess for her father: Fenwick, 24). The production's smallness of scale worked particularly well for Desdemona and Emilia (Rosemary Leach), whose performances allow one to see every shade of thought that goes into, say, Emilia's fatal change of mind that makes her show Iago the handkerchief, or Desdemona's initial attempt to lie about her ability to produce the same handkerchief – 'Why, so I can, sir', followed by a sense of distaste at such unworthy game-playing and a calm 'but I will not now'.

Hopkins offers glimpses of qualities in Othello that would have fascinated others as well as Desdemona: his conjuring tricks over dinner at the beginning of II.iii are a visual equivalent of the stories he once told Desdemona and her father; in poignant contrast, we later see the miserable and silent end of the dinner for Lodovico and Gratiano after Othello's public humiliation of Desdemona. Hopkins's naturalistic performance, by definition, is not grandiose or heroic. But it is not ordinary either; his incessant fiddling, little half-smiles and nervous nodding and murmuring while others speak to him suggest insecurity or absentmindedness, if not neurosis. By contrast, Bob Hoskins's cheerfully psychotic Iago is a man who needs no motive and who refuses to speak at the end because he has nothing to say (the actor thought of him as Rumpelstiltskin, and Miller was inspired by W.H. Auden's famous essay on Iago as 'the joker in the pack': Fenwick, 26). The character laughs, or rather giggles, a lot. When Othello kills himself – quickly and efficiently – Iago responds as if this action were the ultimate practical joke. Miller let the story end with the sound of Iago's laughter ringing down the now-empty corridors.

If this conclusion was disturbing, the production's elimination of the exotic and the unusual was disturbing in other ways. It made the play a 'domestic tragedy' with no meaning beyond itself. Lynda Boose has pointed out some interesting visual patterns in the production, most of them, she thinks, designed to emphasize gender polarization: warm light is associated with Desdemona while Iago is accompanied by 'the preemptive silver light of a masculine world'. Iago at one point is seen extinguishing a candle flame with his fingers, as if determined to 'put out the light' wherever possible. Boose sees the 'masculine world' as one which connives at, or at least does not prevent, the deaths of women, and which probably does not seriously intend to punish Iago (193–5). Such a reading would certainly explain the bleakness of Miller's film, but, to my mind, its absence of 'message' is equally bleak. Unlike Renaissance emblems and symbolic codes, or even the labyrinthine patterns of Orson Welles's film, Miller's patterns are empty of moral significance; their 'curious perspectives' lead not to a true point of view but to a vanishing point. The production is still remembered less for its style than for the outcry over its casting, which brought what is now called identity politics into the public consciousness. It became clear that actors henceforth were going to have to *prove* their right to play Othello.

CHAPTER VII

The Robeson legacy II: casting *Othello*, 1960–97

The last part of the twentieth century saw *Othello* becoming both an opportunity and a site of contention for actors of colour. The questions that most interested the play's critics involved authenticity: who was the authentic voice of Othello? Who could direct the play? Who, in fact, had the right to say anything about it? In this chapter, I shall look at several forms in which the problems of racism were focused in the play, initially through the problem of casting the title role, then through the interpretation of the other roles; the productions discussed in detail will be English, American and South African.

Over most of this chapter, as over the previous one, hangs the shadow of Paul Robeson. Though Robeson played Othello twice in England and only once in the United States, it was among Americans that he had the greatest impact. His record-breaking Othello did not immediately improve the status of black actors in general (Errol Hill, 130), but it did make a difference to productions of *Othello*. Even Robeson's decade of disgrace and internal exile could not undo the desire of audiences to re-experience the impact of hearing a black man speaking, through Othello, about blackness. In fact – perhaps because theatre directors were eager to show that they objected to Robeson's politics, not his colour – the number of productions starring black actors as Othello rose dramatically after 1950. Earle Hyman played the part four times between 1952 and 1958. William Marshall, another Othello of the 1950s, was playing the part for the sixth time when he finally recorded his performance for video in 1985. Black Shakespearean actors were a small enough group to become elaborately intertwined with the figure of Robeson. At least three successful black Othellos – James Earl Jones, Joseph Marcell and Avery Brooks – have also played Robeson in plays or one-man shows. No wonder

Stephen Booth has said that he often seems not to be seeing actors playing Othello, but actors playing Paul Robeson playing Othello (Booth, 333). The Robeson influence may at times seem oppressive, but it has given black actors the sense of professional continuity that white Shakespearean actors have taken for granted.

William Marshall: the Bard production

William Marshall has often sounded almost more like Robeson than Robeson himself: he was 6 feet 5 inches tall, a trained singer, and – though only in high school – a football player. When, in 1955, he played at the Brattle Theatre in Cambridge, Massachusetts, reviewers did not fail to point out that this theatre had been the site of the famous opening night of Robeson's Othello in 1942. In 1959 he came close to playing the part at Stratford, when it looked for a while as if Robeson would be unable to perform. James Earl Jones, who first played Othello in 1956, discovered that his suede boots had been part of Marshall's costume in a New York production of 1953; with a mixture of amusement and reverence, he contemplated the fact that 'I was wearing the boots of the man who almost wore the boots that Robeson wore' (Jones and Niven, 146). Since there is no film or video of a Robeson Othello, the Bard video production starring Marshall, released in 1985, is of particular interest as a link with an earlier tradition.

The early *Othello*s in which Marshall appeared were well received. When the Brattle Theatre production transferred to New York, reviewers found him physically and vocally impressive and one described him as probably 'a more gifted actor' than Robeson (John Chapman, *Daily News*, 8 September 1955). In 1962, after the death of the famous Irish Othello, Anew McMaster, he had a personal triumph in the part at the Dublin Festival, with Micheál McLiammóir as his Iago. Viewers of the Bard *Othello* might have remembered him best for *Blacula*, a 1972 film about a black Dracula in which Marshall – a committed supporter of black rights – agreed to star because he saw it as an attack on the slave trade; his video performance, however, shows no evidence of his political militancy. Earlier reviews of Marshall's various Othellos had sometimes complained that he did not always seem part of the same world as the rest of the cast, and in this video, too, his long experience with the part makes him stand out among a cast which, although professional, had for the most part not spent long with the play. Bard Productions, devised with school and university audiences in mind, was committed to traditional staging and costumes, and Frank Melton, the director, offers an interpretation which gives an idea of what must have happened when a star actor like Aldridge or Booth toured the provinces with a different cast each night. The set is not a recognizable location but a space for acting, with stairs in all directions and a door leading into a small room used to indicate an interior setting; in the eavesdropping scene, where Iago speaks on one side of the door while Othello listens from the other, it is easier than usual to tell what Othello can and can't hear. With complete disdain for subtlety, Iago wears black, while Othello and Desdemona are dressed mainly in white with occasional accents of colour. Asides (Desdemona's 'I am not merry', Iago's 'O, you are well tuned now') are spoken aloud and towards the camera. Each act ends with a freeze-frame: for instance, Part I shows the handkerchief as it falls from Desdemona's hand, frozen against a blood-red background. In other allusions to theatrical tradition, Marshall's first entrance shows him, Stanislavski-like, with a bouquet of flowers (at the start of Act III, Cassio has a bouquet of flowers too). In V.i Melton draws on the famous business associated with Edwin Booth: Iago's murder of Roderigo ('Kill men in the dark! tsk, tsk, tsk,' he says, wiping his blade on his victim's clothes) is followed by his attempt to stab the unconscious Cassio, who is saved only by the approach of Lodovico and Gratiano.

Marshall's Othello, at sixty-one, is probably the oldest Othello on film, but his performance is one of the best arguments for respecting the text's insistence on the age difference between Othello and Desdemona. It justifies the mystery and melancholy underlying his initial air of secret happiness and locates him in a larger world than the other characters. Dark-haired Jenny Agutter gets away from the dumb blonde image of Desdemona and shows her sense of something wrong earlier than most Desdemonas. When Othello tells her about the magic properties of the handkerchief, her responses of 'Is't possible?' and 'is't true?' (III.iv.70, 77) show not awestruck horror but a dawning realization that his 'truth' is of a different kind from hers. Ron Moody's middle-aged, balding Iago – clear, consistent, intelligent and almost entirely external – gives a good idea of how the part may have been played in the eighteenth century. His lines are more heavily cut than those of Othello and Desdemona – though one cut may be a recording mistake: the famous 'I like not that!' is not heard, although Othello later quotes it.

The production features a curious subplot – Melton's invention? – which occasionally resurfaces in other productions: it can usually be recognized by the presence of a character called Lucretia in the cast list. Bianca and a friend (Lucretia) are present among those greeting the new arrivals in II.i; Cassio at once establishes a relationship with them, while Iago and Montano exchange tolerant grins, and the two women are also present in the drinking scene. At the end of Act III (her first appearance in the text) Bianca comes in with Lucretia, and it is the latter, evidently the more suspicious of the two, who whispers to her that the hand-kerchief Cassio gives her 'is some token from a newer friend'. By the time Bianca returns, alone, in the Act IV eavesdropping scene, she is much angrier. The appropriately named Lucretia has evidently poisoned her mind, just as Iago has poisoned Othello's. It is possible that this plot is meant to justify Emilia's description of her husband as 'wayward'. Certainly, the playing of IV.i.161–5 makes it clear that Cassio and Iago are planning to meet at Bianca's house, and that Cassio expects Iago's reason for being there to be the same as his. Perhaps Lucretia has learned her art from a master. In V.i Emilia slaps Bianca, who returns the blow, and both women end up fighting on the ground, with the men standing by in bewilderment. The difficulty with this subplot is not that there is no dialogue to support it – the same could be said of much traditional business – but that it is developed in place of the relationships that Emilia ought to have with the other charac-ters. Because of the cutting of the scene in which Iago gets the handkerchief from her, there is no sense of them as husband and wife. Moreover, when Othello asks Desdemona for the handkerchief, receives the 'wrong' one, and drops it like a poisonous snake, the camera shows Emilia behind the couple, calmly sewing, appar-ently unaware of any responsibility for what is happening.

James Earl Jones and the utopian Othello

The career of James Earl Jones (1931–), still more than Marshall's, is intertwined with the role of Othello, which he has called a 'mountain' and a 'trial by fire' (Jones and Niven, 145). 'You have to start working on the part when you're young,' he told an interviewer (Elin Schoen, *New York Times*, 31 January 1982).

Of his seven performances between 1956 and 1982 he himself preferred the 1964 one in Central Park, New York, directed by Gladys Vaughan. During rehearsals for this production, which took place at the height of the American Civil Rights movement, Jones found that the producer, Joe Papp, kept urging him to display 'black rage', while Vaughan suggested that he think of himself as a sun god, so far above the other characters that he has no need to resent them (158). This latter view was the one Jones preferred, but he seems to have reached a compromise between Vaughan and Papp: as he said, 'It is the cause', he placed Desdemona's white hand next to his brown one, 'making the line a comment on race prejudice' (Edith Oliver, *New Yorker*, 24 October 1964, 93–5). On the other hand, he was perhaps too cultured for most reviewers – 'more like a benign college president', said Tom Prideaux in *Life*, adding that Jones needed to pull out all the stops, as Laurence Olivier was currently doing at the National Theatre in London (11 December 1964). Jones's own view was that Othello 'was revered in his own world where there was no racism. He has no sense of inferiority as the Western black man sometimes has' (Jones and Niven, 165–6) – and therefore should behave calmly, like someone who expects to get his own way. Though he has played in modern-dress *Othellos*, Jones prefers those with a historical setting which allow him to make the hero the product of a rich Muslim culture: 'Was Othello a savage? All I had to do was go to the Alhambra in Spain to know that it could not be so' (Jones and Niven, 161).

Jones has always insisted, recalling Margaret Webster's direction of Robeson (and forgetting Ellen van Volkenberg's), that women make the best directors of *Othello* because they are less likely than men to undervalue Desdemona and the romantic relationship which for him is the heart of the play (Jones and Niven, 159). In his autobiography he admits that he has 'a way of falling in love' with his leading lady; though he jokes that 'It is not true that I marry all my Desdemonas', he did indeed marry two of them (Jones and Niven, 171). The fact that he is able to be so frank about his attraction to (mainly blonde) white women is a sign of his immense distance from Robeson, whose affairs with Ashcroft and Hagen were a closely guarded secret until long after his death. Reviews and personal recollections suggest that the most effective moments in Jones's performances came in scenes with Desdemona rather than Iago. There was no doubt of his love for her, though in later performances it took on an almost fatherly tone. Spectators remembered his laugh in the playful scene at the beginning of Act III before madness descended.

Jones's most famous Othello was also his last, under Peter Coe's direction in 1981 for the American Shakespeare Festival in Stratford, Connecticut. When the partly recast production transferred to Broadway in 1982, it received further directorial attention from Zoe Caldwell; Jones welcomed her alterations, not least because she had played Bianca in the 1959 Stratford production with Paul Robeson. When she told Jones about the 'wonderful fragrance' that came from Robeson's robes as he swept by, Jones scented his own robes with musk as an experiment (Elin Schoen, *New York Times*, 31 January 1982). However, as the reviews and his own autobiography make clear, the Robeson magic had definitely faded by 1982. While most reviewers who saw *Othello* in Connecticut thought that there was a good balance between Jones's Othello and Christopher Plummer's Iago (figure 14), by the time the play reached New York Charles Michener in *Newsweek* said it should be retitled *Iago* and Walter Kerr described Plummer as giving 'quite possibly the single best Shakespearean performance to have originated on this continent in our time' (*New York Times*, 14 February 1982). Both Kerr in 1981 and Frank Rich in 1982 (*New York Times*, 4 February) felt that the production made one 'ache' (both use the word) for 'this too clever man' (Kerr, 30 August 1981) even more than for Othello. The burned-out, despairing quality – the sense that his success always turned to ashes as soon as he achieved it – might have spoken with particular immediacy to the world of tired businessmen. Even allowing for the inevitable bias in Jones's autobiographical account of the production, it is clear that its problems were not simply those of an ordinary competition between two star actors. Peter Coe's direction seems to have focused on Iago, and the festival's historian notes that Plummer had 'an unusual amount of input even into details of the production' (Cooper, 252). The reviewers, for the most part, shared this focus. They simply did not care very much about Othello. Even when Brendan Gill in *The New Yorker* praised Jones, he described Othello's qualities almost with contempt as his 'simple-minded acceptance of adulation ("She loved me for the dangers I had passed") and his masculine pride'. Gill's comments on Desdemona were even more negative: she 'knows nothing of the world, Othello, or her own body'. On

14   James Earl Jones as Othello and Christopher Plummer as Iago,
Stratford, Connecticut, 1981

the other hand, he admired not only Plummer but Iago himself,
and particularly the fact that he *succeeded*: 'I hope nobody will
think the worse of me when I confess that I felt a grudging admiration for his having outwitted the carnage that closes the play. We
are promised that Iago will be taken away and tortured, but I
suspect that he escaped his jailers and passed a contented old age
on Cyprus, pulling wings off flies' (*New Yorker*, 15 February 1982).
At Stratford, apparently, the audience's last glimpse had been a

spotlit Iago rising from the floor to wave his sash in the air and laugh in triumph (Cooper, 253). Like the end of Jonathan Miller's BBC *Othello* (also 1981), Coe's intention is difficult to interpret: was it, for instance, a comment on the indestructibility of evil or a sardonic gesture towards the tough-minded, success-orientated ethos of the early 1980s? If there was any irony, it was lost on audiences, and Zoe Caldwell had deleted that bit of business before the New York run. Even so, Plummer's fascinating performance succeeded in establishing amoral amusement as the tone of the play. Jones himself said later that it was easier to play Othello when Robeson played it, since 1943 was a time of war and national idealism. By contrast, 'In a time of national cynicism our play worked, but sadly enough, it worked like theater of the absurd works' (Jones and Niven, 305).

Blackness in Britain and Ben Kingsley

The earliest black Othellos in Britain tended to be American or West Indian. Gordon Heath, an American, played the part on stage in a touring production in 1951 and in a BBC TV version, directed by Tony Richardson, that was broadcast on 15 December 1955. His Othello, on the archived broadcast tape, is a young and appealing figure in the romantic tradition, an effect created in part by filming Othello against more highly decorated backgrounds than those of the other characters (Elwyn Jones, 5). Despite a few fluffs in the Cyprus scenes (recorded live), it is well worth seeing and suggests that Richardson's much-maligned Stratford production might have worked well with a younger and more flexible actor than Robeson. On the other hand, when the West Indian actor-dramatist Errol John played Othello at the Old Vic in 1963, many reviewers disliked his performance so much that they took the opportunity to attack what they took to be race-based casting, even though he had in fact been a last-minute substitute for a white actor. James Earl Jones felt that this actor, a friend of his, was too 'uptight' and 'defensive' an Othello (Jones and Niven, 165–6). There would not be another black actor as Othello at a London theatre until 1984.

Thus, when it was announced that Terry Hands would direct Ben Kingsley in the next RSC production (1985–86), the decision was carefully validated by emphasis on the actor's background: his real name was Krishna Bhanji; his father had come to Britain from East Africa; he had recently played the title role in the film *Gandhi*. In Britain (though not America) Asians, like other non-Caucasians, are often called black. Despite Kingsley's exotic appearance (his multicoloured, braided wig was copied from one he had seen in Morocco), the advance publicity emphasized the symbiotic relationship between him and the Iago of David Suchet – 'two faces of the same disturbed spirit' as Kingsley called them (Jackson and Smallwood 2, 171). They had both grown beards for the production, and in one newspaper photograph they are shown from the same angle to bring out their physical resemblance (*Sunday Observer Magazine*, 22 September 1986), something that would have been difficult in a production focused on racial difference. The way in which the actors spoke about their relationship recalls MacLiammóir's comment on the relationship he thought was developed in the Orson Welles film, with 'the growing dependence of Othello on Iago's presence, the merging of the two men into one murderous image like a pattern of loving shadows welded' (MacLiammóir, 28).

Both men took a psychological approach to the play, as actors generally do, but at the same time were reluctant to pin it down. Most reviewers, however, were convinced that the production was offering a homosexual interpretation of Iago. It is evident that when reviewers are primarily interested in whether Iago and Othello love each other, there will not be much room either for Desdemona or for a political appraisal of the play. Niamh Cusack was not asked for her views on playing Desdemona, and Kingsley and Suchet hardly mention her in the essays they contributed to the *Players of Shakespeare* series, in which Stratford actors talk about their experience of a particular Shakespearean role. Unlike most British directors of the period, notably John Barton in his famous 'Victorian' *Othello* of 1971–72, Hands did not set his production in a recognizable social milieu. Ralph Koltai's black set indicated the spaces of action with rectangles of light created by fluorescent tubing (Othello crawled into the front rectangle to eavesdrop on Iago and Cassio, who occupied the rectangle at the rear). Costumes were mainly white or off-white. At times the contrast of bright and dark was hard on the eyes, just as the screaming of the actors at moments of high tension was painful to hear (listening to the tape in the British Library sound archive confirmed what I remembered from my own experience). The characters' suffering was shared, not observed.

15   Janet Dale as Emilia, Naimh Cusack as Desdemona, Ben
Kingsley as Othello and David Suchet as Iago. Directed by Terry
Hands, RSC, Stratford-upon-Avon, 1985

Hands, whose productions often exploit a play's metatheatrical
moments, showed the characters experimenting with playing, or
becoming, each other. Niamh Cusack's Desdemona was a young
woman with both an appetite for new experiences and a taste for
mimicry: on Cyprus, she changed into Asian dress for her
wedding night; she parodied Cassio's flowery, emotional style in
her little scene with him, and later (figure 15) imitated Othello
himself in the mock-pomposity of 'It shall be full of poise and
difficult weight' (III.iii.82). There were other moments when the
characters appeared to make an extra-dramatic appeal to the
audience. It was of course Iago who did this most frequently: in
II.i, at the front of the stage, he turned the silent conversation
between Desdemona and Cassio into a dumb-show with himself
as the interpreter, and his 'How now, Roderigo?' (IV.ii.174) became
a joke about the number of times he had already said the same
thing, thanks to the character's propensity for turning up out of
nowhere. Even Othello took part in this game, pointing at Iago
and mimicking him to the audience on 'By heaven, he echoes me'.
   The lack of social context made reviewers uncertain how to
describe Kingsley. Some call him a 'dilettante' and 'intellectual'

[166]

(Milton Shulman, *London Standard*, 8 January 1986) or 'a proud articulate Arab mystic' (Jack Tinker, *Daily Mail*, 8 January 1986); others complain of his strident voice; two refer to him simply as 'a curiosity' (John Barber, *Daily Telegraph*, 9 January 1986; Christopher Edwards, *Spectator*, 18 January 1986). In some ways, this Othello, despite his Asian-African ancestry, was simply invisible. Only a few years later, newspapers were claiming that Willard White (at The Other Place in 1989) was the first black actor to play Othello at Stratford since Robeson. Thus Kingsley's otherness was a movable quality, relevant or irrelevant depending on the needs of the writer.

Angry Othellos and rewriting the script

Who, then, had the right to play Othello? Was it enough to be partly non-Caucasian? What about actors such as Earle Hyman, whom one reviewer described as ethnically black but 'actually lighter than many of his white colleagues in stage makeup' (Edith Oliver, *New Yorker*, 13 February 1978)? Would actors have to submit a DNA test or family tree before being allowed to play the part? When the Puerto Rican Raul Julia (1940–92) played Othello in Central Park in 1979, one reviewer, presumably wishing to defend this casting, suggested that Julia's background gave him special insight into the psychology of a jealous husband (Gerald Rabkin, *Soho Weekly News*, 16 August 1979, 55). This rather naive remark suggests that the excitement originally generated by the 'Robeson effect' could be repeated any time the audience found itself responding to the play as if the actors were representing themselves rather than simply impersonating, however well, the characters created by Shakespeare. Black and Hispanic actors could be conflated as acceptably 'other', so long as the theatre could be seen to be addressing the economic issue that was really at the heart of the problem – the need to employ a fair proportion of non-Caucasian actors.

But simply performing *Othello* with a black actor in the title role did not satisfy the needs of the post-civil-rights era in America. Recovering the lost or ignored history of African-Americans meant recognizing their diversity and complexity – exploring both Islam and African tribal religions; advocating militant, political and religious alternatives to the dominant culture. Olivier himself had been the first to incorporate some of these new conflicts and interests into *Othello* when, abandoning his love for Desdemona, he threw away the conspicuous cross he had been wearing and returned to what was presumably meant to be his original tribal practice. Acting *Othello* at the Atlanta Alliance Theater in 1979 (directed by Wallace Chappell), Paul Winfield made the same gesture, discarding both Christianity and European values as he discarded Desdemona. But Winfield, a black actor, went further. In Act IV, he refused to play the 'trance', which he regarded as demeaning to Othello. Instead, he began the scene alone on the stage: 'Attired in ritual robes of native Africa, he chanted over a pile of time-whitened bones, squatting to beat the stage floor rhythmically, eventually collapsing from the very intensity of the ceremony. Counter to the text, only then did Iago enter' (Lower, 220). Winfield also cut all the asides in which Othello comments on the overheard dialogue between Cassio and Iago. As Charles Lower points out, Winfield was making the same choices that most nineteenth-century actors had made, but where they were protecting their own sense of what a hero should be, he was protecting an entire race.

He was protecting it, above all, from any suspicion of stupidity. When Orson Welles described the Othello he played as 'elemental' and a 'simple man', he could be sure that no one would think that these adjectives applied to him. But in the context of the controversial history of affirmative action in the United States, the depiction of any black man as intellectually inferior or full of primitive emotions was obviously inflammatory. Awareness of this possibility could be inhibiting: Errol Hill writes that, when he played Othello at Dartmouth College in 1969, he was described as 'too intellectual in the early scenes', precisely because he was making 'a conscious effort ... to avoid the conventional image of the noble savage' (Hill, xxv). On the other hand, when an actor did attempt to give the role its full emotional range, he might find himself identified with the part in the wrong way. At the Young Vic in 1984, David Thacker directed the first major British production to star a black Othello, the West Indian Rudolph Walker. Though both the production and Walker himself were generally well received, at least two reviewers expressed uneasiness: Brian Masters frankly stated that 'this Othello appears more stupid than good, suggesting the very prejudices which the production overtly wishes to condemn. As he is played by a black actor, ... the irony is even more uncomfortable' (Brian Masters, *Standard*, 14

May 1984). Another writer worried about his own reactions at the point when the character went berserk: 'Does this, as is meant to happen, show how prejudices are made, or does it *repeat* the prejudice, and confirm the stereotype?' (Barney Bardsley, *Tribune*, 18 May 1984).

Hollywood's first really successful black actor, Sidney Poitier, told James Earl Jones that he had refused to play Othello, because 'I cannot go on stage and give audiences a black man who is a dupe' (Jones and Niven, 298). Poitier's sense of having to speak for his race reached its logical conclusion in what is now called identity politics. In 1998 the distinguished black British actor Hugh Quarshie articulated for an audience at the University of Alabama the same view that had caused so much controversy when expressed by the white director Jonathan Miller in 1981:

> When a black actor plays a role written for a white actor in black make-up and for a predominantly white audience, does he not encourage the white way, or rather the wrong way, of looking at black men, namely that black men, or 'Moors', are over-emotional, excitable and unstable, thereby vindicating Iago's statement, 'These Moors are changeable in their wills' (1.3.346)? Of all the parts in the canon, perhaps Othello is the one which should most definitely not be played by a black actor. (Quarshie, 5)

Quarshie finally decided 'that black actors should continue to play the role', but only if they showed that Othello 'behaves as he does because he is a black man responding to racism, not giving a pretext for it' (20–1). Almost incidentally, he added that if black actors didn't have to play Othello they would be free to play Iago (20).

This last point was important. As I have shown earlier, the nineteenth-century practice by which two well-known actors alternated the roles of Othello and Iago had not only provided audiences with a competitive sport but also enabled each actor to see the play from both sides. When Othello became a role exclusively for black actors, the practice naturally stopped; the last important alternation was that of John Neville and Richard Burton at the Old Vic in 1956. Yet many Othellos have felt that they were incomplete without this opportunity: Earle Hyman has written, 'During all the years I played Othello, I often thought that I could have played a better Othello if I had had the opportunity to play Iago' (Hyman, 28). James Earl Jones, who first encountered

Othello by reading the part of Iago to his father's Othello, has always insisted on the importance of seeing the play through Iago's eyes as well as Othello's. Naturally, the casting of a black actor as Iago creates problems, especially in the early scenes where he joins Roderigo in making racist remarks, and also contradicts the play's emphasis on Othello's isolation. But the desire to extend the number of roles for black actors was already working against the traditional image of Othello as the only black man in a white world. In 1964, when Gladys Vaughan's production transferred to Broadway and she needed an understudy for James Earl Jones, she invented the non-speaking part of a black orderly who accompanied Othello everywhere and who finally handed him the sword with which he kills himself (Jones and Niven, 164). This character reappeared in a few other productions in which Jones acted; in some productions Othello is now provided with black servants as well. But the idea of a black Iago has appealed to many, for an obvious, if depressing, reason: nobody accuses villains of being stupid.

Two plays by American authors use a black Iago to take out some of their anger at Othello as well as at the other characters in the play. James Earl Jones was convinced that Othello's pre-play life must have included a period in Spain before the expulsion of the Moors. On this assumption, C. Bernard Jackson wrote *Iago* for a multiracial theatre group at the Inner City Cultural Center theatre in Los Angeles (1979). The play presents itself as a rewriting, and a 'righting', of the Othello story by Emilia, who is determined to clear her dead husband's name from the slanders of Cinthio and Shakespeare. Both she and Iago, like Othello, are Africans who lived in Spain until the final expulsion of the Moors drove them to the service of Venice. Shakespeare's words are transposed (or rather awkwardly combined with pseudo-Shakespearean dialogue) to give the 'true' version of the story: it is Cassio who speaks salaciously about Desdemona in II.iii and sings a drinking song, while Iago, as a Muslim, is scrupulously sober and respectful. Since Iago and Emilia are the heroes of the play, Othello can be shown as the dupe he is so often accused of being. When he shows reluctance to lead his people back to Africa and combat the new Portuguese practice of sending slaves to the Americas, Iago and Emilia rightly suspect that Desdemona is being used as a bribe to keep him in the Venetians' service. Othello's choice of the incompetent and treacherous Cassio as his lieutenant is a stupid decision, based on the desire to show his gratitude to his wife's country. His murder of Desdemona seems almost a minor matter, since her thoughtless intervention on behalf of Cassio (which extends to writing to Venice behind Othello's back) leads to the lieutenant's military takeover of the island, his torturing of Iago to death, and a mutiny in which nearly everyone is killed. In the play's framing device, Emilia and other performers re-enact the story for an 'author' who, after being forced to act several parts in turn, is finally killed; since his name is William, the play can be seen as revenge on Shakespeare himself.

An earlier reworking of the Othello plot by Charles Marowitz, *An Othello* (1972), widely performed both in England and the US, has been more lasting in its effect. It omits Emilia and gives Iago (who, again, is black) no personal relationships. All the characters are politicized: Desdemona is a feather-headed white liberal who loves Othello because she has a romantic fixation on African culture and is longing 'to be pummeled into submission' (Marowitz, 292). As the other characters perform a version of the play in Marowitz's collage style, Iago keeps up a stream of sarcastic and obscene comments on Othello's sexuality and his willingness to play the white man's game. At first ignored and apparently un-heard by the other actors, he eventually provokes them into trying to order him out of the play; Othello, speaking as an actor rather than a Venetian general, reminds him how hard it has been to get this far. Iago's aims are not purely destructive, however; he can see that Othello has no hope of success in the white world and, as the play moves into its final scene, he warns that suicide will simply play into the hands of the others. As Othello hesitates, the white cast members turn on him and cut his throat, leaving Iago to drag out the body 'with a curious kind of love' (Marowitz, 310).

In 1989 Hugh Quarshie himself co-directed (with Sue Dunder-dale) a black Othello (Clarke Peters) and a light brown Iago (Paul Barber) in Greenwich, England. The production aimed not only to avoid a too-simple image of 'otherness' but also to exhibit an overlooked aspect of racism, the snobbery of the light-skinned towards the dark-skinned. ('Black' is black only by contrast with white; skin colour has always been as important as ethnicity for African-Americans. James Earl Jones writes of the protests when he was cast, in *The Great White Hope*, as a character who in real life was much blacker than he is (Jones and Niven, 188). The Liz White *Othello* of 1960 contrasted an African Othello with a cast otherwise consisting of lighter-skinned African-Americans, so that, as Peter Donaldson puts it, Brabantio's rejection of Othello was the black American's rejection of his own racial past (Donaldson, 139).)

White reviewers of the Quarshie production in England were apparently not sensitized to this preoccupation: at least one critic described the two actors as being the same colour (D. A. N. Jones, *Sunday Telegraph*, 19 March 1989), while another could not understand why 'The "café au lait" Iago (Quarshie's adjective) cannot accept a black general, but the "olive-skinned" Cypriots apparently can' (Paul Taylor, *The Independent*, 16 March 1989). Quarshie's militantly anti-colonialist reading was substantially the same as that of Stanislavski, who had recommended that the Cypriots be played as dark-skinned (Stanslavski, *Produces*, 81–6). But even a sympathetic reviewer called the Greenwich production both under-cast and 'under-resourced' (Jim Hiley, *The Listener*, 30 March 1989). It would certainly have been more successful if Quarshie himself had played either of the two major roles (the Iago in particular was universally condemned). Many reviewers felt that the American Clarke Peters was potentially a fine Othello, though still too young, but that he had been handicapped by a production which gave him no context for the great speeches.

The *Othello* directed by Hal Scott in Washington, DC, with Avery Brooks as Othello, Andre Braugher as Iago and Franchelle Stewart-Dorn, another African-American, as Emilia, was a more successful execution of the same concept. First given in June and July 1990 at Rutgers University (Robeson's alma mater, where both Brooks and Scott taught), the production moved in November to the Folger Shakespeare Theatre. This theatre is modelled on the Elizabethan Fortune Playhouse, and John Ezell's sets were designed to merge with its architecture; they emphasized wood, especially in the Cyprus settings, with lacy carved windows and interlocking spiral staircases, which to one reviewer suggested M.C. Escher's drawings (Johnson-Haddad, 477). The production celebrated the richness of African and Islamic culture as much as the familiar Venetian splendour. Scott, after doing some research, decided that Othello came from a Tuareg tribe in Mauretania (a view that Salvini, incidentally, also held: *Leaves*, 140). The costumes (by Daniel L. Lawson) were exceptionally rich and colourful, especially the African fabrics worn by Othello and Emilia, with long trains that displayed them to the full extent. Iago, unlike his wife, had discarded ethnic dress for that of the Venetian military, but sometimes, like Othello, wore the traditional Tuareg headgear, thus indicating his ambivalent status between Venice and Cyprus. Drawing perhaps on Robeson's own theories about the underlying relationships among cultures, Brooks declared that Shakespeare's language 'feels very comfortable' within the essentially oral African tradition (*Washington View*, December/January 1991).

Although it is not unusual for late twentieth-century productions to open with the marriage of Othello and Desdemona, Scott emphasized its sexual consummation by showing them naked in bed together, thus making Iago's jeers in I.i 'even more disturbing than they usually are' (Johnson-Haddad, 477). Jordan Baker's Desdemona, more isolated than Othello in this context, but at the same time singled out as ethnically privileged, played an unusually assertive character, beating Othello's chest with her fists in IV.i (Johnson-Haddad, 479), *snarling* the line "Tis meet I should be used so, very meet', and aggressively responding to Othello's accusations in the murder scene (Timpane, 36). This interpretation was part of a production that was fast and high-pitched throughout; some of the small-part actors were accused of screaming their lines. No one could accuse this black Othello of being too tame. In Washington, DC, Brooks's emotional temperature seemed too high for most reviewers, and several commented on audience laughter when he was 'writhing on the floor and flinging himself about' (Johnson-Haddad, 479). Bob Mondello, who wondered whether Brooks wanted 'to be remembered as the best Othello of 1878', described the actor's over-the-top style:

> Nostrils flaring he rolls his head, slumps his shoulders, and begins breathing irregularly. A scene later, he's recoiling with each word of betrayal Iago hisses. Should three such words fall in a single sentence, he flinches three times. Another scene, and he's begun flailing and writhing as if afflicted by ravenous insects ... All this before intermission, for heaven's sake. (Bob Mondello, 'Grand Othel', *City Paper*, 12 December 1990)

André Braugher's Iago got better notices. Reviewers agreed that the end of III.iii, which (as often) immediately preceded the interval, was an emotional highpoint: 'Othello has vaulted to the upper level and Iago to center stage: one shouts, "Now art thou my lieutenant," and the other responds, "I am your own for ever" at the same mad volume. The lights fall and we are left breathless'

(Timpane, 36). Since each man at that point raised his arm, with his fist clenched, the audience would surely have recognized the Black Power salute. Braugher's Iago is also described as holding Othello in his arms during his fit and caressing him, then breaking down and crying: 'I love this man,' he said to journalists, 'but I have to kill him' (*Washington Entertainment Magazine*, December 1990/January 1991). It sounds almost like the end of the Marowitz play. Yet it also recalls the RSC *Othello* of 1985, when, after Othello's suicide, David Suchet's Iago threw himself on the body and had to be dragged away. In the context of that production, the moment was interpreted as confirmation of Iago's homosexuality. As played by two black actors, this love–hate relationship became an allegory of self-destruction.

Reviewers of Scott's production divided, as one might expect, into those who thought the casting made no difference to the play and those who found meaning in it. Several thought that Othello's willingness to trust Iago becomes much easier to believe when the latter is the only other black man in the play, and one claimed that the production made him rediscover such lines as Iago's 'In following him, I follow but myself' (Mondello, *City Paper*, 14 December 1990). But, as with the Greenwich theatre production, another reviewer found that the casting made Iago's behaviour unintelligible: why should he react with indignation to Brabantio's racist remarks, while Othello, imperturbable, signalled to him to calm down, yet utter such remarks himself in I.i and listen without emotion when Roderigo made them? But when Brooks visited a predominantly black school in the city, the schoolchildren had no difficulty in understanding the interpretation: 'It was one black man undercutting another,' one of them said. Brooks himself stated what he saw as the moral: 'When you betray your brother, you plot your own death, the death of your people and the death of your culture' (Courtland Milloy, *Washington Post*, 11 December 1990).

Othello and apartheid: Johannesburg, 1990

Because, historically, the United States was a country that allowed the slavery of black Africans, and because Britain was involved in the slave trade, American and British productions of *Othello*, once the question of race became paramount, were always more tinged with unease than those in the rest of the world. By contrast, in

Japan, though the play was popular as a love tragedy, a director insisted as late as 1960 that the play was difficult for Japanese audiences to understand because there was no race prejudice in Japan (Ray Falk, *New York Times*, 11 September 1960). Yet a *Kabuki Othello* written by Karen Sunde and directed in 1986 by Shozo Sato, a Japanese director in the United States, created a version in which Othello was an Ainu, one of the indigenous people of Hokkaido who are physically different from other Japanese. A notorious production by Peter Zadek in Hamburg in 1976 deliberately caricatured racial and gender stereotypes, making Ulrich Wildgrüber play the title role much like the prewar animal-like Othellos, in a King Kong costume, with obviously phoney black makeup that rubbed off on Desdemona (Kennedy, 269). In photographs and descriptions his work is indistinguishable from the crudest racist propaganda, but he was of course playing to a self-consciously liberal and tolerant audience for whom this was precisely the most shocking kind of spectacle. It was aimed, Dennis Kennedy argues, at racism, not race – 'underscoring the cliché and thereby deconstructing it' (Kennedy, 269). It has been suggested that the remarkable number of *Othellos* in Germany in 1992–93 was a consequence of collective guilt over a recent arson attack on a shelter for homeless immigrants (Hütter et al., 160). Like Zadek's production, and like George Tabori's in Vienna, 1991 (see Carlson), many directors in countries lacking black actors have used the messiness of black makeup as a way of commenting on the racist implications of their own casting. Yet one black critic, the Nigerian S. E. Ogude, has declared that, since the character of Othello is a caricature, 'A black Othello is an obscenity. The element of the grotesque is best achieved when a white man plays the role. As the play wears on, and under the heat of lights and action the makeup begins to wear off, Othello becomes a monstrosity of colors: the wine-red lips and snow-white eyes against a background of messy blackness' (Ogude, 163).

The question of speaking for, speaking as and speaking to members of an oppressed group took on a different meaning in 1987 when Janet Suzman, a white South African who had spent much of her working life in Great Britain, directed *Othello* at the Market Theatre in Johannesburg, South Africa – in the last years of apartheid, when no one suspected how quickly the system would be brought to an end. The play had been acted in Cape Town by the country's first civilian theatre company as early as

1829 (D. Johnson, 36), probably with as little sense of its relevance as in the American South at the same period; in 1987, when Martin Orkin published his *Shakespeare Against Apartheid*, *Othello* was rarely taught in South African schools, probably because its relevance had become too obvious (Orkin, 107–8). Suzman's project can of course be criticized as 'inauthentic' or presumptuous, terms often used when people attempt to speak for an oppressed group to which they do not themselves belong. But the production, coming as it did three years before the end of apartheid, took considerable courage and determination from all concerned; it was an immensely successful theatrical and political event, and one that attracted an unusually large number of black African spectators. Casting a distinguished black South African actor, John Kani, in the title role would not have been unusual elsewhere, but, as the Market Theatre's artistic director, Barney Simon, said, 'in this country, it becomes a political decision as well as an artistic one' (www.onlineclassics.net/plays/main.html: Othello Documentary). If the 'white, liberal audience' found it a tragedy, the black audience, according to Kani, took it to be 'a topical, pungent and appallingly relevant social drama about the eternal fraudulent deceptiveness of the white liar' (Billington, 28). As Suzman recognized, it was, like Margaret Webster's production in 1943, an example of a play finding its historical moment.

The stage production was Suzman's first experience of directing; she went on to tape it for television in only six days (Suzman, 'South Africa', 40). Though there are occasional problems with the production (the actors were allowed greater freedom with the text than usual, and the cutting is sometimes surprising), this is a powerful and at times almost unbearably harrowing version of the play. The video (1988) gives several full views of the stage set, as if to make clear that it is showing a theatre production, but at the same time makes use of cinematic devices such as the freeze-frame and slow motion (as when Iago tosses the handkerchief into the air and it floats there). An almost cinematic soundtrack accompanies the action. Barking dogs create the atmosphere of Venice at night; the lush lyrical rhythms of the willow song underline several of Desdemona's appearances and recur in the final moments of the play.

In a reversal of the usual hero–villain polarization, small, frail-looking John Kani (plate 1) confronts an Iago (Richard Haddon Haines) who towers over everyone else in the play, especially his embittered but helpless wife. The Venetian part of the play is riddled with racism: when Brabantio refers to Othello as 'such a thing as thou', Roderigo spits; even the line 'Here comes Brabantio, and the valiant Moor' becomes a snarled, disgusted 'Here comes the Moor'. Some of Brabantio's lines are given to Gratiano, so that the two brothers form a united front against Othello; when Brabantio seems on the point of collapse, even Iago joins the sympathetic crowd around him. The fact that Suzman saw all the characters in terms of their attitudes to racial difference gave Haines's Iago a particular intensity of viciousness; she modelled him on Eugene Terreblanche, a racist demagogue, and her video documentary about the making of the production juxtaposes him with Haines at one of the latter's most hideous moments. This Iago constantly stresses the animality of the Moor, usually by poking his fingers into places where they should not be. As he mimics the phrase 'I have already chose my officer', he picks his nose; when he compares Othello to an ass he heehaws and jerks up and down, waving an imaginary phallus, then sticks fingers in both his nostrils; after Othello's 'Goats and monkeys', when he is left alone on stage, he repeats the phrase in a gorilla posture, scratching himself under his armpits.

Kani, in contrast, is quiet and rather sad. Even at the beginning, when Iago asks, 'Are you fast married?', he seems melancholy, then suddenly gives a radiant smile. His manner and costume are different from anyone else's; his vowel sounds are different; more than any other performance of Othello, this one is genuinely *other*. His instant twitching reaction to Iago's use of the word 'cuckold' (III.iii.169) suggests a culture in which the word still has a profoundly humiliating meaning. It is his sense of helplessness in a world where other people make all the rules that explains both his willingness to believe Iago and his numb, miserable passivity in the final scene; even so, it is difficult to understand his trust in someone who spits after telling him that Desdemona's love is only the sign of 'a will most rank, / Foul disproportion, thoughts unnatural' (III.iii.236–7). The story seems loaded against him from the start. Like the cage that waits for Iago in Welles's film, his fate is visible throughout: the most prominent feature of his costume is a collar of bone from which hangs the small curved weapon with which he will eventually cut his throat. Because the contrast between good and evil is politically polarized, it is sharpened to the point where viewers in a calmer world might find only melodrama in Iago, with his loud, stage-villain laugh and his shifting eyes, and Othello, a pathetic victim about to be turned out into the night. But in the context of the late 1980s, when interracial sex was a crime and the opposition to apartheid seemed to be helpless against a monolithic state apparatus, this polarization was reality for many people.

Suzman's treatment of Emilia is more nuanced than her depiction of the other characters. Initially, the production makes the character rather more guilty than usual. When Desdemona drops the handkerchief on her way out with Othello, the camera shows Emilia lurking in the shadows, then cuts to a close-up of her hand on the handkerchief, as if she has pounced on it. Sitting on the floor, breathing in the scent of the handkerchief, she leaves no doubt that she knows she is doing something wrong, especially since, instead of saying that she will have the work 'copied', she says she will 'give it to Iago'. At the same time, Iago's treatment of her explains why, despite a show of defiance, she feels she has no choice. The camera accentuates his mixture of jeering and menace as he suddenly looms behind her, visible only from the crotch down, as he asks, 'What make you here alone?' and then holds a knife to her face. It is not clear whether Emilia is speaking as a racist or simply as an abused woman when she tells Desdemona, 'Would you had never seen him!' (IV.iii.16), or when she spits at Othello while snarling that Desdemona had been 'too fond of her most filthy bargain' (V.ii.153). But the extent to which she shares Iago's venom, and his habit of spitting, makes her role in the final scene even more crucial than usual. When she understands her husband's role in what had happened she is faced with a choice: to let a black man take the blame for a murder which has roused an almost primitive hatred in her, or to identify herself with Othello who, like her, has been a victim of her husband's lies. Iago openly threatens her with a knife. Her ensuing desperation gives an all-or-nothing quality to Dorothy Gould's performance, which is at full volume throughout, regardless of the demands of the small screen. The result is – deliberately? – almost intolerable. More important for Suzman, I think, is the fact that Emilia reaches out her hand toward Othello as she dies, and that he himself closes her eyes. In such a race-dominated society, this brief moment of physical contact between the two characters is obviously weighted with significance, as is the hand that Lodovico gently lays on Othello's arm when telling him that

Plate 1   John Kani and Joanna Weinberg in the final scene of the
play. Directed by Janet Suzman, Market Theatre, Johannesburg
(Focus/Portobello Video Productions, 1988)

Plate 2   Patrice Johnson as Desdemona and Patrick Stewart as
Othello in *Othello*, directed by Jude Kelly, Shakespeare Theatre at
the Lansburgh, Washington, DC, 1997

he is a prisoner. This is the only screened version of the play in which anyone pays any attention to Emilia at her death. Iago's two victims are able, though only in their last moments, to transcend racial difference and Emilia shows that it is possible to fight one's way out of racism, though only at great cost.

Patrick Stewart and the 'photo-negative' *Othello*

It was probably inevitable that the notion of race-based casting would reach its logical conclusion in a production of *Othello* where the hero was white and all the other characters black. The idea for what he called a 'photo-negative' production came from Patrick Stewart, who, though he realized that the role of Othello was no longer available to a white actor, had wanted to play it for years. In 1997 Michael Kahn of The Shakespeare Theatre in Washington, DC, was the first to take up the idea. Washington was an obvious place to try an experiment of this kind. The majority of the city's resident population is black, though it draws most of its audience from people who live outside the district: academics, government workers, political and military leaders and a large international contingent. Another possible reason for Kahn's decision may have been topical. The murder of O. J. Simpson's blonde wife in June 1994, followed by the protracted, highly publicized trial of the popular African-American sports hero and television star, made the plot of *Othello* relevant to the point of explosiveness. It is understandable that 1997 might have seemed the right time for a production showing something other than a black man murdering a white woman (Russo, 4–6). As might have been expected, the production sold out as soon as booking opened; Stewart's performance, the main reason for the excitement, was generally praised.

The style of this *Othello* was a complete contrast with Hal Scott's of 1990 (see above, pp. 172–4). In 1992 The Shakespeare Theatre had moved from the Folger to a new purpose-built auditorium, the Lansburgh. Simple and classical in design, it no longer seemed to demand an 'Elizabethan-style' production and often used either multi-purpose scaffolding or Expressionistic settings. Many of its greatest successes had resulted from the mixture of British directors and American actors. Jude Kelly of the West Yorkshire Playhouse was invited to direct *Othello*; she opted for modern dress and a military setting, though not one evoking a particular period. At the beginning of rehearsals there had been talk of altering some of the lines to reflect the casting, but in the end the language of colour was left unchanged, though references to swords and other weapons were modernized.

Although the production concept was based on the contrast between Othello and the rest of the cast (figure 16), in practice the most important contrast was between Venice and Cyprus, whose inhabitants evidently loathed each other. In Venice social status and race went together. Its rulers and army were entirely black, apart from Othello, while Brabantio's servants were white. The Cypriots, though many reviewers took them to be white, were played by actors who were either Hispanic or of mixed race, while Bianca was white and blonde, for once justifying her name. It was the crowd scenes that displayed the most obvious reversal of racial roles: the Cypriots were on the receiving end of a good many silent or unscripted insults from the dominant Venetians, and one was heard to shout back, 'We fight your wars for you!' This cultural antagonism seemed based less on race than on what race symbolized, a difference in emotional temperature, indicated by the colour-coding of the costumes. Venice was always dark (it was raining as the play began) and its soldiers wore purple jackets and berets, changing to khaki on Cyprus, while Brabantio was a clergyman in black. The soldiers of sunny Cyprus, island of Venus, wore orange. Red, the warmest point on the passion spectrum, was used very sparingly – for the rose petals that Desdemona scattered over Othello when they first appeared in I.ii, and for the blood that finally stained the bed sheets. Only the costumes of Othello and Desdemona suggested that they might be capable of reconciling the two worlds. Stewart's Othello was dressed like the Venetians but distinguished from them by the strange tattoo on his bald head and the bright multicoloured sash on his uniform; the very young-looking Desdemona, Patrice Johnson (plate 2), also dressed in light, warm colours that linked her with the Cypriots, though as the play went on her clothes became darker, making her look older and recalling the atmosphere of Venice.

A 'star performance' requires delicate negotiation between what the actor wants to do and what his audience will accept from someone it 'knows' in a different context. Since at least some of Stewart's television fans knew that he was also a Shakespearean actor (the *Star Trek* scripts sometimes exploit this fact), the casting did not create much of a problem, but the actor's television image

16 Franchelle Stewart-Dorn as Emilia, Ron Canada as Iago,
Patrice Johnson as Desdemona and Patrick Stewart as Othello.
Directed by Jude Kelly, Shakespeare Theatre at the Lansburgh,
Washington, DC, 1997

may have encouraged an emphasis on the comic as well as the
heroic aspects of Othello's character. His honeymoon relationship
with Desdemona was presented as charming and rather funny,
particularly because of the age difference which both of them
seemed to enjoy. When he arrived at Cyprus in Act II, he
completely ignored the welcome party, made a dash for his wife
and started to carry her off to the nearest bedroom. Then, belatedly
noticing the ranks of saluting soldiers drawn up to greet him, he
put her down and told the army, as an afterthought, 'News,
friends, our wars are done, the Turks are drowned.' It was evident
that Othello had been mistaken when he assured the senate that
his private life would not interfere with his military duties.

This was only one of the moments at which the production's
undercutting of Othello seemed to anticipate, or perhaps forestall,
what the play itself was going to do to him. For instance, Kelly
stressed the parallels between Othello and Roderigo. The latter
was first seen carrying a bouquet of flowers when he rushed on in
I.i (presumably Iago had intercepted him on the way to visit
Desdemona). In I.iii Roderigo crouched miserably on the floor of
the senate, sobbing over the loss of Desdemona; in IV.i Othello
crouched in the same position. Stewart himself displayed some

nice comic self-deprecation, as when, having told the audience that he was declined into the vale of years, he seemed to anticipate their agreement by protesting, 'Yet that's not *much*!' (III.iii.270). Even in the final scene, rather than trying to avoid the potential laughs on dangerous lines, like 'every puny whipster gets my sword' (V.ii.242), he invited them. This was possible because Stewart's popularity gave him almost unlimited capital on which to draw. He was also able to suggest a mysterious and tragic past history. Like Jones, who got the idea from his drama coach Ted Danielewski (Jones and Niven, 148), he said of Desdemona, 'when I love thee not, chaos is come [*pause*] again.' It was not clear exactly what had rescued him from chaos, Desdemona or his military career and its saving qualities of discipline and routine; what mattered was that the possibility of a return to chaos had been opened before Iago even began to speak.

Stewart, with his beautiful deep voice and perfect diction, is for American audiences the quintessence of Englishness: sophisticated, restrained, light, humorous. Kelly balanced this unusual Othello by casting as Iago Ron Canada, a bulky middle-aged black actor who seemed the archetypal non-commissioned officer, frequently writing things down in a notebook and obsessively saluting his superiors. Iago was also an abusive husband (an all-too topical subject, in the wake of the Simpson trial), as was obvious from Emilia's cowed behaviour. He was openly rude to her in II.i: one was presumably meant to wonder why this did not arouse any-one's suspicions of him, and then to realize that this was a society that took such behaviour for granted. Franchelle Stewart-Dorn, who had already played a very different Emilia for Hal Scott in 1990, was praised because, as Bob Mondello wrote, 'she tells you more about Iago through her body language than you learn from the man himself in all his soliloquies' (*City Paper*, 21 November 1997). Her short scene with Iago over the handkerchief was the keynote: when he seized on her word 'thing' and replied 'It is a common thing / To have a foolish wife' (an obscene joke that normally goes uncomprehended), her 'is that all?' was a gasp of relief that he had not after all decided to say something much more obscene. The willow scene was important for her recognition that the general's wife had something in common with her after all. Even so, when, among the hypothetical justifications for infidelity, she offered, 'Or say they strike us', the air was heavy with the silence of the two abused wives, each too ashamed to confide in the other. Against this background, her outburst in the last act was like a discovery of the power of her own speech.

In the most generally disliked stage business of the production, Iago, in IV.i, used a blackboard to give Othello ocular proof of his wife's adultery by listing 'kissing', 'naked in bed', and 'handkerchief', then writing Desdemona's name and underlining the 'demon' in it (when Othello used the abbreviation 'Desdemon' in IV.ii he deliberately stressed the last two syllables so as to bring out the pun). For a moment each character looked like an academic giving a lecture on the play's major themes. In the final scene the academic approach took over completely. The production retained – as few productions do – nearly all the dialogue that follows the murder of Desdemona. During rehearsals, Stewart himself commented in an interview on the difficulty of keeping up the momentum: 'I'm pretty sure I can get through the killing of Desdemona eight times a week ... But then, you see, I have another 25 minutes of stage time after she's dead' (*Washington Post*, 12 November). In dwelling on the elaborate unraveling that follows, as the characters analyse the events with no apparent concern for the feelings of the man at the centre of them, Kelly was, I think, showing how completely the Venetian view of life had prevailed. In rehearsals, apparently, Cassio gave Othello the weapon with which he killed himself and the other actors tacitly colluded in letting him have an 'honourable' death. But the ending as finally played left the hero isolated in his final moments. As the lights went down over the bodies on the bed, the rain started again, the final obliteration of everything Othello and Desdemona had represented.

This photo-negative *Othello* did not do for the play what Hugh Quarshie had asked for, or what some spectators had thought would happen. In so far as it explained Othello's susceptibility to jealousy, it did so by hinting at some nameless horror in his past and a corresponding obsession with happiness in the present, not by making his behaviour a response to racism. It did not make white audiences imagine themselves in the situation of oppressed black people. It provided a large number of good roles for black actors in a high-profile production, but most reviewers emphasized the superiority of Stewart to everyone else in the cast. Although it seemed to be shaking up racial stereotypes, the visual coding of intellectual difference had been reversed only for the characters, not the actors: the white Othello was lean, cerebral and humorous, while the black Iago was heavy-set, obsessed with rules and a wife-abuser. Racial issues frequently arose in the post-show discussions, but, as one actor pointed out, white spectators would have been made genuinely uncomfortable about race only if the majority of spectators had been black, which was never the case. When the words of the play contradicted what was visible on the stage, it was easy to ignore what was being said and read the play in terms of its visual images. Some reviewers thought that it would have made more sense to rewrite the text, or at least to create a context in which a white general would be a genuine outsider and a black society would be credibly powerful. But in any case audiences who saw not Othello but Patrick Stewart of *Star Trek* might have recognized in him an example of the world beyond the world no less Utopian than James Earl Jones's notion of Othello's homeland where racism is unknown: the starship, with its multiracial crew, over which the actor presided in the famous television series. Perhaps there are no circumstances in which the play can disturb white audiences' complacency about race, whatever its emotional effect may be otherwise; this seems to be the conclusion that Thomas Cartelli draws, quoting the despairing comments of Nigerian writer Ben Okri (Cartelli, 123–4). The really disturbing element in Kelly's production was not its depiction of race but its emphasis on the military world and its treatment of the female characters. These were the two most important aspects of productions of the 1990s, and they will be the subject of the next chapter.

CHAPTER VIII

Othello at the end of the century: sex and soldiers

In 1989 Michael Billington wrote in *The Guardian*, '*Othello* is currently the least revived of all Shakespeare's tragedies and the reasons are not far to seek: casting problems and racial guilt' (16 March 1989). During the next ten years all this was to change. Two major stage productions (by Suzman and Nunn) became available on video, as did Oliver Parker's film, the first since Welles's to be made for the commercial market; the Welles film itself reappeared on video with a re-mastered soundtrack, disappeared again, then reappeared as a DVD. *Othello* seemed to have become, as Edward Pechter put it, 'the Shakespearean tragedy of choice for the present generation'. Pechter saw this phenomenon as a consequence of the transformation of literary criticism 'by feminist, African American and postcolonialist studies' (Pechter, 2). These interests had been reflected, and even anticipated, by some theatre practitioners: Helen Faucit, writing from Desdemona's point of view, had been unusually critical of Othello; Stanislavski had pointed out the irony in Othello's role as a black general serving a colonial power; Robeson's whole relationship with the play is itself a document in African-American culture. In the late twentieth century, however, critics were not only focusing on issues of race, class and gender but attempting to negotiate their competing demands for attention. Feminist approaches in particular tended to stress the parallels between the two different kinds of oppression from which Othello and Desdemona suffer. Putting the parallel in theatrical terms, Dympna Callaghan points out that the Jacobean Othello and Desdemona would have created their race and gender through makeup (Callaghan, esp. 84–5), while, more cynically, Sheila Rose Bland argues that this staging practice should be the model for modern directors: since the play caricatures both black and female characters, Othello should be played by a white actor in blackface and all the women in the play should be played by men (Bland, 31). Anxious not to 'subsume under the aegis of white/ European feminism the historical particularity of heterogenous race and ethnic struggle', Imtiaz Habib argues that sexual jealousy is a natural consequence of Othello's feminized status as a colonized subject. 'Material dispossession produces a reconstructive grasping for an exaggerated sexual control.' (Habib, 147)

Feminism has strongly affected many late twentieth-century productions of the play, notably by bringing Desdemona onstage for more of the time. It has become commonplace to open the play with the heroine's elopement rather than Iago and Roderigo's reaction to it, or to have her present during at least part of Othello's conversation with Iago at the beginning of I.ii. Most directors also place more emphasis on the marriage of Iago and Emilia and many are now taking Bianca seriously as a character rather than a comic floozie. Though publicity for the Suzman and Kelly productions focused on their treatment of race and racism, both were feminist as well, not only in giving a strong role to Desdemona but also in making all three of the play's women victims of male abuse: Iago was clearly abusive toward Emilia, while the story of Bianca – sympathetically depicted by both directors – was given a horrific closure: rejected even by Emilia, her one possible ally, she was left at the end of V.i to be attacked, raped and – in the Suzman production – possibly killed by Iago-trained soldiers. There were some mitigating touches: Suzman made Emilia hesitate before leaving, as if suspecting what might follow; Kelly had Cassio, before he fainted, try to exonerate Bianca from Iago's accusations. But the image of soldiers attacking the most socially powerless of the play's three women was indicative of something that has been part of many productions of the play: its hostile perspective on the military world.

Military *Othellos*

In a pre-production talk during the run of his National Theatre *Othello* (1997), Sam Mendes distinguished what he saw as the two main production styles for the play: the 'operatic', with exotic costumes and long flowing robes, and (his own choice) the 'military' one. Generally, film and made-for-television productions have used Renaissance settings, while theatre directors have put the actors into military dress of the nineteenth or twentieth centuries. One reason for the popularity of this style in the 1990s was that many directors wanted to avoid the look of a 'costume production', which might aestheticize and therefore distance the characters' pain. Khaki or navy-blue uniforms avoid what Mendes meant by 'flowing robes' – the 'Orientalism' that, after Edward Said's influential book of that name (1978), made it as reprehensible to glamorize Othello's cultural background as to make it the reason for his degeneration into murder. One exception to the usual theatrical practice was Suzman's Renaissance setting: she argued that modern dress would make the submissiveness of Desdemona and Emilia unbelievable, while to set the play in any other period would suggest an arbitrary link with South African political history (Suzman, 32–3). Iago and his followers were more like paramilitary thugs than members of a regular army, because the English Renaissance did not have standing armies, uniforms capable of denoting more than the most basic distinctions or an elaborate code of discipline affecting behaviour both off and on the battlefield.

Although Restoration productions dressed the central characters in contemporary uniform, with Othello in the red coat of a British general, the reversion to Moorish dress in the late eighteenth century and to historical costume in the nineteenth made it easy to ignore the military setting. Some early productions in modern dress had experimented with uniforms, as in 1929 at the Birmingham Repertory Theatre (directed by H.K. Ayliff), where Iago is listed in the programme as a 'Staff Sergeant Major'. But it was John Barton's 'Victorian' production for the Royal Shakespeare Company in 1971 that had the greatest influence. As reviewers discovered, uniforms clarified the characters' rank and class, as well as the distinction between soldiers and civilians in the Venetian senate and the scene of Lodovico's arrival in Cyprus; they also made it easier to see, as Ronald Bryden put it, 'why Othello should trust his senior NCO more than his new bride from home' and why characters were obsessed about their reputations: 'Where else, today, but in the Army could we accept a drunken fight spelling disgrace for Cassio or a man regarding his wife's infidelity as the ruin of his career?' (*Observer*, 12 September 1971). The setting helped the rather stolid British Othello (Brewster Mason, an actor with a military background), who looked more at home in a context in which senior officers were supposed to repress rather than shout their feelings. Small-part actors who had to stand on stage for long periods without speaking found it easier to do so when they were regimented. The crinolined figures of Desdemona and Emilia (Lisa Harrow and Elizabeth Spriggs) looked appropriately out of place among all the uniformed men in the outpost of Cyprus. Where the more traditional type of production often included Cypriots of both sexes among its extras, military *Othello*s since Barton's have been more likely to draw attention to the largely male world of the play and the unease created by the presence of women.

In the United States, particularly, where the armed forces have a large proportion of 'minority' soldiers and where a military career sometimes enables African-Americans to escape from poverty and social exclusion, the military setting has obvious contemporary relevance. When *Othello* was given at the Canadian Stratford Festival of 1994, the theatre programme included a chronology of significant dates in US race relations as they had affected the American military, from the US Supreme Court decision of 1896 ordering 'separate but equal' status for different races, through the appointment in 1940 of the first black US Army general, to the end of segregation in the Army in 1948. The programme did not mention what must have been in the minds of most of the audience: the attempts, after the 1991 Gulf War, to persuade Major-General Colin Powell, an African-American, to run for president in the 1992 election. In the 1990s, during the highly publicized controversies over young women's attempts to enter military academies and sexual harassment in the armed services, productions emphasized the negative side of the profession. Of a Georgia Shakespeare Festival *Othello* in 1999, which focused on the brutal treatment of Desdemona in a misogynistic military environment, one reviewer wrote, 'brutality is part of the culture and casualties are inevitable. All we can do is watch' (Worrall, 24).

The Trevor Nunn *Othello*

Though Trevor Nunn strongly emphasized the military setting of the play and the psychology of the men who choose a military career, his treatment of their world was relatively sympathetic, perhaps because his famous production (The Other Place, Stratford-upon-Avon, 1989), filmed for television in 1990, predated most of the negative publicity about the military. His is an almost loving recreation of a military camp, from the barracks in which the drinking scene takes place, to the sound of reveille that prompts Iago's 'By the mass, 'tis morning', to the badly played chapel organ at the start of the second half. (Nunn had realized that III.iii takes place on Sunday, a fact deducible from Desdemona's insistence that Othello should see Cassio 'tomorrow night, or Tuesday morn': III.iii.60.) The military atmosphere was also softened by its setting in a past which variously suggested the American Civil War or the Edwardian era. The most obvious analogy, reinforced by the women's costumes in particular, was with Chekhov's *The Three Sisters*, a play about officers and men stationed in a remote place. Willard White's Othello is a credible career officer who has struggled to get where he is and rages terrifyingly when he can see it all vanishing before his eyes. Cassio (Sean Baker) is no glamorous Florentine but a hard-working, self-made man caught between his original social class and that of the officers. The movement from Venice to Cyprus at the beginning of II.i is also a movement from the rather stuffy civilian world to the freer military one. Nunn establishes the basic decency of the army officers and men through their reactions to the news that Othello is about to arrive 'in full commission here for Cyprus' (II.i.29). The soldiers react with consternation to the announcement that Othello is about to supersede Montano, obviously a popular officer; but Montano himself (Philip Scully), with his unhesitating and generous 'I am glad of it', immediately defuses the situation. When Cassio barges in with his luggage, nearly knocking one of the soldiers over, he becomes an interloper in a happy and loyal garrison. Iago, on the other hand, makes himself welcome at once, showing concern for the seasick Emilia, offering drinks and tobacco where they are needed, and including the women in his rough but apparently affectionate teasing.

Another memorable moment comes a few minutes later, as the laughter at Iago's jokes dies down. Still nervously waiting for news of Othello, the group falls into tense silence, broken only by the sound of somebody whistling. On video, Nunn has the camera imitate the spectator's gaze, panning across the group in search of the source of the whistling and eventually reaching the expressionless Emilia (Zoe Wanamaker), whose importance is thus established early. The whistling is another reminder of Chekhov, as is Emilia's pipe-smoking in a later scene; in fact, the best comment on Wanamaker's interpretation is a comparison with the two Mashas (in *The Seagull* and *The Three Sisters*) who express their boredom and marital unhappiness by whistling and smoking, rather than making any attempt to avert the tragedies around them. Emilia likewise remains indifferent even when, a moment later, Desdemona's attempted cheerfulness breaks down; she begins to sob, and Cassio comforts her. There does not seem much danger that this quietly prim and embittered woman, who gives Iago the handkerchief as indifferently as she asks him to give it back, will take any trouble for the sake of this much younger woman, with whom she has so little in common.

When Othello arrives in Cyprus, he lifts Desdemona (Imogen Stubbs) on to a box and circles delightedly around her, but she, rejecting the pedestal on which he has placed her, leaps recklessly into his arms (figure 17). Emilia's expression, when they kiss, may be read either as racist disapproval or envy at their happiness. Nunn and Stubbs agreed that Desdemona should not act as if she knew that she was going to be killed in Act V, and the sheer vitality of her performance is one reason why the final scene is so harrowing. Desdemona's very eagerness to understand her husband's world created a parallel between her story and Othello's that is latent in the play but not usually brought out in production: what Othello learns from Iago about the immorality of Venetian women is similar to what Desdemona learns from Emilia about men in general. Thus, instead of questioning the cause of her husband's unexpected brutality, Stubbs's Desdemona, trying to convince herself that she has just had a valuable learning experience, declares brightly, 'Nay, we must think men are not gods' (III.iv.149). The delicately nuanced relationship between the two women reaches its turning point in IV.iii. In the previous scene, Othello has searched Desdemona's dressing table with a key taken from Emilia. Now, for Emilia's benefit, Desdemona unlocks a secret drawer in the same table, but, instead of the incriminating letters for which Othello had been looking, she takes out a little box of sweets that Cassio had given her in III.iii; the two women, giggling like schoolgirls, share their illicit late-night feast. Emilia has resisted Desdemona's attempts at intimacy until now; but, at the end of the scene, when Desdemona says 'Good night', Emilia impulsively seizes and embraces her. It is this brief moment of friendship that explains why, contrary to all the indications she had given earlier, Emilia cannot let the death of Desdemona remain unexamined. While spectators of *Othello* are

17   Imogen Stubbs as Desdemona jumping into Othello's arms.
Willard White as Othello, Sean Baker as Cassio, and Ian McKellen,
far right, as Iago. Directed by Trevor Nunn, RSC at the Other Place,
Stratford-upon-Avon, 1989

used to seeing Desdemona's dead hand feebly seized by another
dying hand that has been groping for it, in Nunn's version that
hand is Emilia's rather than Othello's, and the gesture is high-
lighted on the video by a close-up that emphasizes the 'wife for
wife' pairing: 'the camera allows audiences to see the wedding
ring each woman wears' (McGuire, 80).

In a radio interview during Trevor Nunn's 1989 *Othello*, Ian
McKellen insisted that Iago was not 'evil incarnate ... He's part of
the soldierly world ... and it's from that that his strengths and
weaknesses come' (*Kaleidoscope*, BBC radio). Two years after
playing Iago, Ian McKellen starred in Richard Eyre's *Richard III*
at the National Theatre (1991), a production which showed how
an impoverished emotional and erotic life makes a society
vulnerable to cheap substitutes like the fascist cult of ceremony
and death. Though Nunn's society was warmer than Eyre's,
McKellen's Iago can also be seen as perverting and exploiting the
human need for love; Vaughan perceptively notices the number of
times that the promptbook specifies that he is to 'cuddle' people
(224). Yet the warmth is fake, as his costume shows: everything
that can be buttoned is buttoned, in contrast with the relaxed look

of the other characters' uniforms. The iconography of repressed sexuality is as obvious as the red cloak that associated Booth and Irving with Mephistopheles. In III.iii, when the enraged Othello sweeps everything off his desk, Iago's obsession with order becomes almost comic; horrified, he starts picking up the papers and, even when Othello is threatening to kill him, uses one hand to ward him off with a chair while with the other he continues to clutch the precious documents. Yet it is Iago's apparent capacity for emotion that finally wins Othello. Following the implicit direction for the two men to kneel side by side for the end of the oath-taking that ends III.iii, Nunn emphasized the extent to which this moment is like a marriage. Seeing Iago's bowed head and his hand over eyes apparently brimming with tears, Othello says, 'I greet thy love', in a way that reminds one that he had loved Desdemona for pitying him. Iago goes on to offer an exchange of sacrifices to their new friendship: after 'my friend is dead' he adds 'but let her live', in tones which ensure that Othello will vow Desdemona's death as a balance to Cassio's.

Few productions of *Othello* have been more concerned than Nunn's to give full weight to the Othello–Desdemona relationship. Yet there was some justification for the complaint that the result, especially on the video, ended up being Iago-centred. In a production full of props and detail, the close-ups favour Iago: he enjoys doing several things at once, as when he, talking rapidly, makes the punch for the barracks party, spikes it with hard liquor, finds a place to put it and so on. Virtually every line is decorated with some bit of business, each one flowing so smoothly into the next that it is hard to tell whether the superb technique is McKellen's or Iago's. Othello, by definition, cannot play tricks of this sort, however much the production emphasizes his strength and presence. Willard White's relatively subdued manner is small-scale like the production: his 'fit' is rather muted, and, although he is able to speak such almost unspeakable lines as 'Blow me about in winds, roast me in sulphur, / Wash me in steep-down gulfs of liquid fire!' (V.ii.277–8), he does so by making them a prayer rather than a scream of agony. On camera with McKellen he suffers from the contrast between his broad expansive face, which seems to have nothing to hide, and the mysterious folds and lines of McKellen's, which invite the spectator to watch for the revelation of dark secrets in his not fully understood feelings.

Sexual suspects: the Oliver Parker film

The fact that the Oliver Parker film was released during 1994, a year dominated by the O. J. Simpson case, reinforced something already present in the film, the theme of wife-abuse. At the time of filming, the actor playing Othello, Laurence Fishburne, was best known to the general public for *What's Love Got to Do with It?*, the story of Ike Turner's abuse of his wife, the rock singer Tina Turner. This of course lent a special intensity to Othello's relationship with Desdemona, while Iago (Kenneth Branagh) was also played as a wife-abuser. Casting a popular black American actor as Othello and a well-known British Shakespearean actor as Iago, with a Swiss Desdemona, seems like a return to Welles's international cast with its non-standard Shakespearean speech and was probably a calculated attempt to make the film commercially viable for an international audience. Irène Jacob, the brunette Desdemona, was movingly intelligent, frank and trusting (figure 18). But the fact that she, her father and the Duke of Venice all spoke English as a second language meant that, instead of being the social norm against which Othello is set, they were themselves outside it. Isolated on Cyprus, both Desdemona and Emilia were natural victims.

Parker cut nearly fifty per cent of the text and provided plenty of visual excitement to accompany what remained: the Cyprus crowd, delighted at the arrival of the Venetians, burns a turbaned Turk in effigy and embarks on a celebration of operatic proportions; Iago illustrates his plans for Othello, Desdemona and Cassio with chess pieces, which he finally drowns; Othello and Iago are seen fencing; Othello nearly drowns Iago in the sea; Iago, trying to escape at the end, finds himself in the same room as the dying Roderigo, loses his nerve and runs out into the arms of his pursuers. The gorgeous sets and historical costumes are traditional. Fishburne's slow, quiet, rather frightening strength recalls Welles's interpretation, and the gauzy curtains of Welles's film reappear in Parker's. The film was not well reviewed initially, but its critical reception improved after it appeared on video, probably because, as with Welles's film, its visual patterns are easier to appreciate with repeated viewing.

Some of these patterns are obvious and rather predictable, like the visual flashbacks that illustrate, or replace, verbal effects. As Othello tells the Senators about his wooing of Desdemona we see

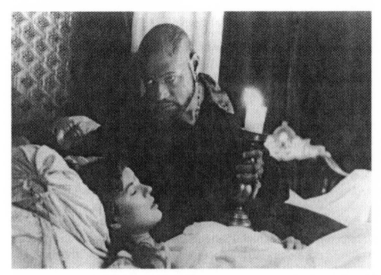

18   Laurence Fishburne as Othello prepares to murder Irène Jacob's Desdemona in the Castle Rock film. Directed by Oliver Parker

it happen. After Iago has poisoned Othello's mind, we again see Brabantio warning Othello to 'look to her'. But sometimes Parker's film language is, if anything, still more difficult to read than Welles's. The difficulties begin at the start: Desdemona is seen running though the streets of Venice, and anyone familiar with the story will realize that she is eloping; but a moment later she is seen in a gondola with a black man in a white mask, who is *not* Othello (viewers have argued about what is going on here, and H. R. Coursen even wondered whether her companion might be 'an allegorical "Tragedy"': 175). Unlike other films that try to show Othello's jealous fantasies, this one gives no indication that they *are* fantasies. Othello parts the curtains of his bed and sees Desdemona engaged in sex play with Cassio. He draws back, as if waking from a nightmare, but when he looks at the bed again the couple are still there. Parker takes the fragmented shot even further than Welles: in the sequence leading up to Othello's fit, the camera gives us rapid glimpses of different parts of the naked flesh of Cassio and Desdemona, creating a counterpart to Othello's 'Pish! Noses, ears and lips' (IV.i.42). In some of the dialogues the choice of close-up is puzzling: it may make sense to focus mainly on Othello's face during most of Iago's description of Cassio's dream, but it is hard to see why the camera shows mainly Iago's face during Othello's 'Now, forever farewell'. The final shot of the bed shows it loaded with the bodies of all four protagonists, leaving it uncertain whether Iago has died, or is about to die, like the others. The final image is of two bodies being lowered overboard from Lodovico's ship – a contrast to the Yutkevich film, in which Lodovico is apparently taking them back to Venice for a state funeral. Who are those dead people: Othello and Desdemona, Othello and Iago, or (a further suggestion of McGuire's, 86) Desdemona and Emilia? Are they considered fit only for burial at sea, or are they undergoing a ritual of purification and forgiveness? This was in fact a revised ending; Michael Maloney, who played Roderigo, said that the film originally ended with Iago maintaining complete silence under torture, but that Parker finally decided that this would seem a glorification of evil (Starks, 86).

These examples show not only the power of visual images but also the difficulty of interpreting them when they are not accompanied by words. One of the film's most puzzling, if memorable, visual effects is the plotting of Iago and Roderigo as they lie under a cart on which a (heterosexual) couple is having sex, an image that seems meant to raise questions about their relationship. At least one critic had no doubt that Iago was 'a gay man who loves Othello but cannot admit it and so destroys him and his wife' (Burt, 241). It is at any rate evident that Parker, like Welles, imagined Iago as impotent. Branagh's expression is bland and unrevealing, but, even though the heavy cutting in II.i removes all textual indication of Emilia's relationship to Iago, Anna Patrick leaves no doubt as to the character's sexual frustration when she invades her husband's bed, bringing the handkerchief with her as a bribe. Iago seems to be about to give her what she wants, then brutally turns her over and mimes sodomizing her, at which point the camera cuts to his soliloquy in close-up, while Emilia, though no longer on camera, is still presumably the object of his sexual mistreatment. Yet she cannot be meant to hear him tell the camera that 'I will in Cassio's lodging lose this napkin' (III.iii.324). Either we are meant to accept the convention that characters cease being present when the camera stops looking at them, or Iago is impudently creating this convention himself; at the end of another soliloquy, he blocks the camera lens just after he has put out a candle with his fingers (a counterpart of stage productions where Iago seems to control the lighting and sound effects). In each case, the metafilmic gesture follows a moment that is clearly 'sensational' – playing, that is, to a hypothetical mass audience that is assumed to like watching sex and pain. Parker may imply that this essentially ordinary man is a projection of our fantasies or a dramatic device, doing his best to give us the kind of movie we 'really' wanted.

Anna Patrick, an attractive and graceful woman with no touch of shrewishness (most of the lines suggesting this quality were cut) is a companion rather than servant to Desdemona and plays Emilia as very much in love with her 'wayward husband'; this is a marriage that she still hopes can be rescued. The two women are seen together more than in most other versions, as if to emphasize the parallelism in their stories. Cutting the text avoids the problem of why Emilia does not speak up earlier about the handkerchief, and one could imagine that she had forgotten all about it. At the end of IV.ii, when Iago has comforted Desdemona, Emilia impulsively seizes his hand as if to thank him for being the man she always knew he was. The pay-off of this interpretation comes at the end. Othello names the handkerchief as the chief justification for his actions and, in the most exciting moment of the film, the camera rapidly cuts between the faces of Emilia (who realizes what this means) and Iago (who realizes, for the first time, what her knowledge means for him); Iago's lines to her are quiet but emphatic asides, prolonging the suspense as to whether she will indeed choose to 'be wise and get you home'. When she chooses instead to 'speak', Iago seizes her, uses her as a human shield on his way to the door, then stabs her and throws her body at his pursuers to slow them down. Although this western/gangster film cliché is an example of the film at its most obvious, the poignant and sympathetic treatment of Emilia shows what it is at its best.

'Tragic bureaucrat': Sam Mendes' staging

Sam Mendes's *Othello* at the Royal National Theatre, London, and on tour in 1997–98 reminded many spectators of Nunn's 1989 production. Both were designed for small theatres (The Other Place and the Cottesloe auditorium); Anthony Ward's set for Mendes recalled Bob Crowley's earlier one in its use of slatted screens – opaque or airy, depending on the lighting – behind which other characters could sometimes be seen. The intimate theatre spaces lent themselves to small-scale effects: at the start of II.i, for instance, instead of rushing around in the wind and rain, Montano and the Gentlemen were taking tea indoors, letting others bring them weather and war reports. Like Nunn, Mendes divided the play at the point where Othello and Desdemona go off, leaving the handkerchief behind – 'like an unexploded bomb' (Michael Owen, *Evening Standard*, 9 March 1998). But, if a description of Trevor Nunn's Chekhovian *Othello* inevitably sounds like a novel, the Mendes version, much more heavily cut, seems more like a film. Whereas early films often imitated theatrical effects, late twentieth-century theatre directors who grew up with film sometimes use its techniques in their stage productions. Rejecting the quick, fluid Renaissance staging, where characters are constantly exiting and entering an unlocalized space, Mendes got rid as far as possible of entrances and exits, in favour of blackouts after which characters were 'discovered' in a set. This style was also appropriate to the period in which he had set the play. Mendes chose the 1930s because he wanted a recognizable social and military hierarchy, but the characters' uniforms could not be linked to either World War. The characters had guns, but the only gunshot in the play was heard when Iago killed Emilia. There were no strong climaxes. In keeping with their twentieth-century setting, the characters did not create their music and poetry but bought it. Iago's rhyming couplets in II.i, up to the verses about Desdemona, came out of a book ('my Muse', he called it), which he produced from a suitcase; Desdemona played the willow song on a gramophone record.

The tone was cooler than Nunn's, with perhaps less subtext and more desire to link the scenes in a chain of cause and effect. In III.i–ii (which were conflated and heavily cut) the clown and other soldiers treated Cassio with contempt; when Othello and others set off to see the fortification, they walked past him as if he were invisible. This episode confirmed Iago's advice about the need to approach Othello indirectly, through Desdemona, and also explained why Cassio left her so hastily when he saw Othello approaching. Another sequence involved the sheets on Othello's bed. At the beginning of IV.ii Othello examined them in search of clues, an idea that probably goes back to Ronald Eyre's 1979 production in which Donald Sinden actually *sniffed* them (Hankey, 281). At the end of the scene Desdemona gave one of the sheets to Emilia, asking her to put it on the bed that night. Mendes is one of the few directors to wonder whether Emilia's crescendo on 'the Moor's abused', ending with her reminder that Iago once suspected her

[197]

with Othello, might be heard by Desdemona. Maureen Beattie's Emilia ended her speech with a gasp of horror, fearing what she might have let out, but Desdemona appeared too lost in misery to hear anything. Even so, in the willow scene Emilia seemed overwrought when speaking about women's infidelity, as if trying to justify her past behaviour.

Mendes wanted Othello and Desdemona to convey a powerful sexual relationship, so he chose a young actor (David Harewood, the first black actor to play the part at the National Theatre) and cut the lines about Othello's 'young affects' being 'defunct'. Desdemona (Clare Skinner) was also very young, startlingly slight and isolated when she first appeared in the door to the senate chamber. Mendes gave her an active role – it was she, for instance, who helped the wounded Montano offstage in II.iii; and in IV.ii, when Othello was at his most virulently insulting, she began fighting back, ineffectually beating at his chest with her fists. Because of their youth, both she and David Harewood's Othello were sympathetic figures but also seemed inevitable victims of an older and more experienced Iago (Simon Russell Beale: figure 19). Like McKellen in Nunn's military *Othello*, Beale, a superb actor, was helped by a production which gave him plenty of props, like the soldiers' playing cards from II.ii with which he illustrated 'this honest fool', 'the Moor' and Desdemona. He was both violent and compulsively tidy: at one moment sweeping everything on to the floor in a fit of rage on 'I hate the Moor', then picking it all up again. At the end of III.iii, left alone on stage, he retched, either from nerves or self-loathing. In the final scene all emotion seemed to have drained from him, and he remained totally expressionless even when Othello made a perfunctory, almost experimental, thrust at him.

Mendes felt that both Cassio and Iago were recognizable and ordinary military types, responding in different ways to their overseas posting. But Iago's ordinariness was also his motive. As Beale himself put it, Iago is not 'a great military mind' but a rather dull person compared with 'golden boy Cassio' (Interview with Matt Wolf, *New York Times*, 5 April 1998). In practice, the contrast between Iago and the other characters was perceived largely in sexual terms. The villain was an unattractive, overweight man of 'utter emptiness', 'emotionally crippled', who 'hated being touched' (Jackson and Smallwood, 254, 255); the hero and heroine were young, attractive, and radiantly fulfilled. The problem with such

19   Simon Russell Beale as Iago and David Harewood as Othello.
Directed by Sam Mendes, National Theatre, London, 1997–98

casting is not only that it contradicts what the text says about the respective ages of these characters; as Robert Smallwood points out, it also becomes particularly hard to see why Roderigo believes Iago's assurances that Desdemona will soon be tired of Othello (Smallwood, 254).

In 1987 Julie Hankey put the 'banality of evil' Iagos into a political context: 'Only the post-Hitlerian world could imagine such a thing' (118). David Harewood insisted in interviews that his own experience of racism gave him an understanding of Othello's career – no white actor could know what it was like, 'coming from so little, to have risen so high and then to be destroyed' (Andrew G. Marshall, *Independent*, 12 May 1998). But Mendes's production came across as personal rather than political. Though Beale's interpretation was described as 'Evil Made Ordinary' (Ben Brantley, *New York Times*, 11 April 1998), its sheer power paradoxically worked against its ordinariness, to the point where several reviewers suggested that the play had become the story of a 'Tragic Bureaucrat' (Charles McNulty, *The Village Voice*, New York, 21 April 1998).

Post-Cold-War productions: Prague and Santa Cruz

If the political approach to *Othello* is rare in Anglo-American practice, central and eastern Europe share a long tradition of interpreting Shakespeare's plays politically. When modern plays were subject to severe censorship, this author's classic status allowed directors to put on productions that were readily recognized as comments on the current situation. A production was a subversive text to be decoded in a collective act by actors and audience who were unable to express their resentment in more open forms. As I have already noted, the dominant Marxist approach for much of the century treated the tragedy as one of betrayed trust. The widespread awareness of American racism, by contrast with the Soviet ideal of multiculturalism, made the play implicitly political. In Germany, as Wilhelm Hortmann points out, the aftermath of the Second World War, combined with the influence of Brecht, saw a desire to debunk the harmonizing and reconciling interpretations of classical drama in favour of an emphasis on what was taken to be the reality behind them: 'glaring oppositions and negations, disruptive egoisms, murderous passions in the grip of an incomprehensible, absurd disorder' (Hortmann, 'Changing Modes', 221). The end of the Cold War required yet another rethinking. *Othello* became a political allegory in a production at Schwerin, Germany, directed by Michael Jurgons, which treated Othello as the South (or the Third World) and Desdemona as the West (the pleasure-loving First World, looking for excitement). Iago's grey uniform recalled those of the National People's Army. He stood for the East (the newly discredited Second World of Socialism) and his motive was hatred of those who knew how to enjoy themselves: the lazy, self-dramatizing Moor and the fun-seeking Miss Desdemona (Hütter, 163).

The three *Othello*s at the National Theatre in Prague in the second half of the twentieth century show a parallel development in the communist world from official idealism to widespread cynicism, particularly after the Russian invasion of Czecho-slovakia in 1968. The 1951 *Othello* (directed by Jan Skoda) took the traditional view of the noble Moor and depicted his destruction by a treacherous careerist whose machiavellianism was an early manifestation of capitalism. When Emilia wished that heaven would

> put in every honest hand a whip
> To lash those rascals naked through the world
> Even from the east to the west

(IV.ii.144–6)

it was clear that the east was East and west was West (Stříbrný, 'Perestroika', 7–8). But in 1972, only four years after the Soviet invasion, a production by Václav Hudeček reflected the cynicism of what can now be seen as the last phase of communism in eastern Europe. In place of the heroic and idealistic Othello, Radovan Lukavský played a hero who was a tough mercenary and a murderer, not an innocent victim of intrigue, facing an Iago (Rudolf Hrušinský) who was undemonic and pudgy. The director cut much of the poetry, now seen as an obfuscation of the reality of society (Kudláčková, 86). Perhaps as a result, this once-popular tragedy had to wait twenty-six years for its next production.

The 1998 production by Ivan Rajmont at Prague's Estates Theatre took a rather similar view to Hudeček's, juxtaposing its bleak and unromantic vision of the play with the lovely eighteenth-century theatre (the original venue for the premiere of Mozart's *Don Giovanni*) in which it was performed. Shakespeare is more contemporary for Europeans than for English-speaking audiences, since his plays are usually performed in modern translations. It is common for each new director to commission a new translation, thus ensuring that the language harmonizes with the production style. Rajmont had worked with Martin Hilský, his translator, on previous occasions, and each knew what the other wanted: a modern and colloquial translation that did not soften the sexual language. No music was used, though in the Cyprus scenes the sound of waves could sometimes be heard. Heavily cut for performance, the play moved quickly, helped by Josef Ciller's ingenious set. After the first act, played in front of curtains as if to suggest that it was only a prologue, the curtains opened on a revolving stage which represented both the whole and the separate sections of the Cyprus scenes, so that characters could walk from one section into another, dispensing with conventional entrance and exit lines and allowing Rajmont, like Mendes, to open scenes *in medias res*. Some crucial entrances remained, and these were often made via the auditorium, as if deliberately playing against the baroque architecture and its gold leaf decoration.

One space was the men's, a sort of officers' recreation room with a piano, chairs and a billiard table; another was the women's, consisting of Desdemona's trunks, one used as a wardrobe and one as a seat.

This was a production in a country where there are effectively no black actors. If there is an Other in central Europe to whom Othello might be compared, it is the gypsy, but this kind of interpretation did not appear to be an option for Rajmont. In some respects his production recalls the 'military' versions of the west. Othello was a credible nineteenth-century officer. Never exotically dressed, he wore a version of the same rather drab uniform as everyone else; it was clearly not his strangeness that had attracted Desdemona to him. In his first appearance, with a bouquet of roses and a cross on a chain about his neck, Othello (Boris Rösner) recalled Olivier to western spectators, Stanislavski to those who knew the Russian tradition. Characteristically, he dropped the roses almost at once, forgetting about them as he went into the house to get ready for the senate. In a gesture towards the Yutkevich film, Rajmont had Desdemona drop her handkerchief on her way out of the senate; Iago picked it up and returned it to her. Even before Othello's mind was poisoned by Iago, he was already brutal in the early scenes toward the soldiers and even towards Iago. The drunken fight was also nasty: Cassio, who was played unpleasantly throughout, attacked the others with a broken bottle and hit Iago for saying that he hoped to be saved. The absence of the pride, pomp and circumstance of glorious war made Othello not only drab but unsympathetic.

Another reason why Othello's tragedy was comparatively unaffecting was that Iago was played by a popular actor (Oldřich Kaiser) whose long trenchcoat and battered good looks were reminiscent of Peter Falk as Colombo. The other characters liked him; he plied them with drink and cigarettes and accompanied one of his drinking songs on the piano; the audience continued to find him funny for a good part of the play. He got laughs on 'Put money in thy purse' (apparently because Hilský's translation was particularly colloquial at this point), when he damned Cassio with faint praise, and when, narrating Cassio's supposed dream, he kept glancing at Othello to see how far he could go in gross suggestiveness. Figure 20 shows Othello and Iago at the moment of their joint swearing of vengeance. Like Olivier, Rösner discarded his cross when he renounced Desdemona and love; he then began to beat on a water drum (with which he had earlier threatened to crush Iago). His loud, impressive rhythm was followed by Iago's

20   Boris Rösner as Othello and Oldřich Kaiser as Iago.
Directed by Ivan Rajmont, National Theatre, Prague, 1998

lighter, perhaps parodic, one, as the latter joined his vow to
Othello's, the one rhythm attempting to dominate the other.

A great deal of Zuzana Stivínová's characterization of Desdemona depended on costume. As in the Yutkevich film, she arrived
on Cyrpus dressed in men's clothes. In the scenes in 'her' space on
Cyprus, the audience could see two dresses hanging in her wardrobe trunk, a white and a red one, as if offering Othello alternative
views of his wife. The red dress, worn by Desdemona in her little
after-dinner scene with Lodovico and Othello, was the same colour
as the one in which Bianca was briefly glimpsed parting from
Cassio in V.i. Desdemona could in fact be read either way, since she
was both sexy and innocent. Rajmont had wanted the combination
of the two, pointing out that Iago envies her because, despite her
limited experience, she in some ways knows more than he does.

The production often seemed to take Iago's own view of the play, if not of the women, and this was particularly true in the final act. In V.i, after Cassio had killed Roderigo, Iago stabbed Cassio and grabbed the handkerchief from his pocket. Othello leaped down from an upper level in the auditorium and ran on to the stage; Iago gave him the handkerchief and Othello rushed off. Iago also ran off, obviously convinced that Cassio was dead, but Cassio had seen him and, as the scene darkened, could be heard calling for help. There was thus no need to explain how the other characters learned of Iago's villainy. When Emilia cried murder in V.ii, only Iago entered, and only Othello learned the truth about the handkerchief; shortly after Emilia's death, the other characters came in and briefly ended the play. There was thus no opportunity for Othello's actions to be even partially explained to the other characters. Iago was brought on in handcuffs, but Othello did not wound him and there was no talk of torturing him. The outraged Cassio had no hesitation about repeating the gesture with which Othello had demoted him in Act II, stripping off the general's symbols of rank and curtly ordering him to be taken away. Othello held everyone at bay with a knife during his final speech; Cassio reached out for it and Othello, after pretending to hand it over, turned it on himself. It would have been possible to see this bleak ending as Iago's triumph, except that any satisfaction he might have felt had been destroyed by Othello's assertion that it was 'happiness to die'.

The audience did not appear to respond to this production on a political level; for instance, the exchange in I.i between Brabantio and Iago ('You are a villain.' 'You are a senator') got no laughs at all, even though the Czech Republic had only recently acquired an upper house of senators who had been the target of considerable ridicule. Rajmont claimed in the programme that the tragedy was based not only on race and jealousy but also on problems of communication. Only a few years after the revolution, he was already conscious of the difficulty of distinguishing between free speech and irresponsible speech, and of the misuse of language in a world where the word 'democracy' was as all-purpose, and hence as meaningless, as 'honest'. For this reason, he described the play as consisting of three successive tragedies: Brabantio's, Cassio's and Othello's. In an otherwise heavily cut text, Rajmont retained the rhymed exchange of sententiae in I.iii because of Brabantio's 'But words are words' (I.iii.219), which he took to be the first statement of the play's nihilism. The cuts at the end of the play left only the lines that could be taken as a comment on the misuse of language. After Othello's suicide, Cassio's 'O bloody period' got laughter because the preciosity of the phrase came across so clearly in translation. Lodovico replied with the last line, a translation of 'All that's spoke is marred', which, in this version, actually meant something more like, 'No more of words; it's all useless.'

The cynicism of this interpretation results partly from the Czech distrust of all military figures, especially after the Russian occupation, partly from the association of the romantic and heroic view of Othello with Russian tradition and Soviet ideology and partly from suspicion of the rapidity with which post-Cold-War Czechs were following Iago's advice to put money in their purses. The absence of meaning, the distrust of words and those who use them – politicians, governments and indeed everyone – ended by offering an Iago's-eye-view of the play. Perhaps post-Soviet productions, for the time being, have nowhere else to go.

In one of the few recent western productions to take a political view of the play, in 1998 at the Shakespeare Festival in Santa Cruz, California, Australian director Michael Donald Edwards identified Venetian imperialism with British imperialism. Othello and his officers wore the dazzling red coats that once represented the British army, and Iago's promotion to lieutenant was more obviously visible than usual. Venice was indicated by a giant Lion of St Mark on a sliding screen at the back which also served as one of the main entrances (figure 21 shows the predatory appearance of the Lion, though the fact that it appears to be sinking its claws into Iago is only an effect of photography). In the Senate scene, three gold chairs with red brocade seats faced three identical ones. When the action moved to Cyprus, the six red and gold chairs were replaced by six rattan chairs in precisely the same position, a symbol of the colonizer's imposition of imperial form on local matter.

The opening tableau, a tableau of the marriage of Othello and Desdemona, offered the one successful mixture of two cultures, as the accompanying music (compiled and composed by Robby MacLean) began as an Arab prayer, then merged into a Brahms melody. But once the Venetians arrived in Cyprus, they were isolated from their surroundings rather than a part of them. No Cypriots were visible except Bianca, played by a black actress to

21   The Lion of Venice and Iago (Paul Whitworth), Santa Cruz,
     California. Directed by Michael Edwards, 1997

emphasize the fact that Othello was helping to repress his own
people. Othello, played by a young actor (Robert Jason Jackson),
showed the division of his loyalties by wearing uniform in the
play's first half and African robes in the second, where he was
thus more closely identified with the splendidly dressed Bianca.
The off-the-shoulder yellow dress of Desdemona (Lise Bruneau),
with its frills and artificial flowers, could hardly have been more
inappropriate to the Cyprus setting, and her white gloves further
insulated her from her surroundings.

   The production was not unsympathetic to the couple, despite
their imperialistic context; in this respect, it was like the post-
Stanislavski tradition. But neither Othello nor Desdemona was
strong enough to prevent the play from being dominated, still
more than the Prague production, by its Iago, Paul Whitworth.
Whitworth carried vulgarity farther than any other Iago except
perhaps Haines in the Suzman film: as he sang of King Stephen's
breeches, he presented his backside as illustration; Roderigo
almost gagged with revulsion at the explicit comments on Othello's
'weak function' and the 'villainous thoughts' that Iago's pelvic
contortions were miming to him. Whitworth's was a performance

worked out in every detail, from the strangulated sergeant-major cockney voice to the awkward movements: torso at an angle, hands on hips, arms suddenly flung out in gestures suggesting a caricature of Richard Nixon. The Nixon effect suggests the connection between the production's political theme and its treatment of Iago, who might otherwise seem only a criminal psychopath. Whitworth saw him as 'perversely creative', a 'virus' that improvises and adapts to different circumstances, and showed the character not only thinking but remembering, as he underlined moments that depended on audience recollection of earlier ones. For instance, having ridiculed Roderigo's choice of the word 'blest' to describe Desdemona ('blest fig's end'), he showed how Iago appropriated it himself when he told Cassio that she was 'of so free, so generous, so – [pause] blest a disposition'. This ability to improvise, to appropriate other people's language and thought-processes for his own ends, recalls Stephen Greenblatt's famous contention that the capacity for empathy is often only the way in which the powerful exploit the less powerful without seeming to do so (Greenblatt, 224–9). Most of the time, however, the performance – quite deliberately – gave little sense of an inner life. At the end of the 'brothel scene', briefly alone on stage after Desdemona's departure, this Iago sniffed Desdemona's hairbrush and looked at himself in her mirror, hastily putting it down again when he heard Roderigo coming. This was as close as we got to a sense of his feelings after the curious intimacy with Desdemona to which his new rank had gained him access. Whitworth had heard from a criminal lawyer that murderers often display nothing but blankness when confronted with the people they have wronged, and at the end he was both vicious and empty.

The military environment of the Santa Cruz *Othello* suggested the ruthless efficiency of long-established nineteenth-century imperialism; the army outpost of the Prague production, on the other hand, was a makeshift organization – perhaps the reality behind that imperialism, as seen from a post-Soviet perspective. The difficulty with both *Othello*s, well thought out as they were, was that, in making the characters reflect a negative view of society, they projected negative reactions not only on to Iago but on to all the other characters as well.

Stratford-upon-Avon and Ashland

Two productions in 1999 – at Stratford-upon-Avon, England, and the Oregon Shakespeare Festival in Ashland, Oregon – offered what might be called a return to the romantic and tragic *Othello*. In common with most of the other *Othello*s discussed in this chapter, they contrasted the sexual excitement between hero and heroine with the sexual frustration of Iago and Emilia. They also emphasized the military atmosphere of the garrison on Cyprus. Since, however, they were given in larger theatres than most of the productions I have been describing, they also had larger casts and placed a greater emphasis on spectacle. It was largely through visual rather than verbal means (indeed, both productions did some modernizing and rearranging of the text) that they achieved the poetic quality that was their most striking, even surprising, feature. The Stratford *Othello*, which opened on 21 April 1999, was directed by Michael Attenborough, and the Othello and Desdemona were Ray Fearon and Zoe Waites, who had previously played Romeo and Juliet with the same director in 1998. The Ashland Othello, Derrick Lee Weedon, had played Coriolanus at the festival some years earlier with the same director, Tony Taccone. This contrast had much to do with the differences between these two *Othello*s.

Some critics placed Attenborough's production among Stratford's finest revivals (e.g., John Peter, *Sunday Times*, 25 April 1999); those who disagreed with this assessment (e.g., Michael Billington, *Guardian*, 22 April 1999; Robert Butler, *Independent on Sunday*, 25 April 1999) felt that the lack of a significant age difference between hero and heroine resulted in a lack of 'weight'. Fearon had grown a long pointed beard for the role; even so, this was another production in which the lines referring to Othello's advancing years had to be cut, while Iago described himself as having looked upon the world for *five* times seven years. Iago was played by Richard McCabe, a comic actor with a dark side; in this production he looked like Malvolio, a portly figure with the beginning of a double chin, clearly dangerous, certainly jealous of the desolate and unhappy Emilia (Rachel Joyce), and probably (as a result?) impotent. But, if the production, complete with quotations in the programme about the problems of married men on military service, sounds much like the standard 1990s *Othello*, it gained much from the sense of marital intimacy that Fearon

[208]

and Waites projected from the start. Attenborough made the most of their youth by setting them against an elderly Venetian senate, where only the Duke seemed to feel any sympathy for them; there was a sense of complete shared understanding in the couple's quick exchange of glances when they realized, as the meeting broke up, that only one of the senators had shaken hands with them.

Robert Jones's simple but effective decor, along with Peter Mumford's lighting design, emphasized the couple's growing sense of imprisonment in the scenes that followed. The streets of Venice were created entirely from lighted lattices and shutters projected on to an otherwise black background. As if playing with the idea of Iago as a devil, Attenborough had him spin the globe at the end of the senate scene, thereby plunging the stage into darkness; to the sound of thunder, the floorcloth was removed to show bare boards, and the elegant furniture of Venice gave way to primitive chairs and tables. The light, airy atmosphere of II.i offered the false hope that Othello and Desdemona had reached a place of freedom, an appropriate background for the ecstatic poetry of their reunion. But when they moved into the 'camp' (the word they consistently used instead of 'castle'), the stage's open vista was broken by posts forming a colonnade, with a canopy of plain canvas descending half-way down. When, in their presence, the herald read out the proclamation of a holiday to celebrate their wedding night and all the troops saluted them, the young couple again exchanged glances. Their new world, they realized, was one in which there would be no private life. The men's drinking rituals immediately after the herald's announcement were the first evidence of how constricting even off-duty fun could be. Supervised by Iago, who announced, 'Gentlemen! Canniken!' the officers played the first of a series of highly regimented drinking games. These were also sexually threatening, involving not only pulling down the trousers of various victims (as also happened in the Nunn production) but a mimed rape with a bottle.

As the action proceeded, the set closed in more and more: the descending canvas concealed the colonnade behind a series of doors, each containing the small flapped window of a prison cell, then the doors themselves gradually disappeared, apart from the one into Desdemona's bedchamber. The tension between public and private roles came out most forcibly at the beginning of IV.iii, as Desdemona, facing upstage, graciously waved goodnight to her

Venetian guests; turning toward the audience as she entered her room, she showed that she was on the point of collapse. The room would be a sanctuary only during her scene with Emilia; after that it too would become a trap.

All three protagonists acted with passion, as indeed they needed to in a production given in Stratford's large and difficult main house (plate 3 shows both hero and villain sweating under the pressure of their encounter); the balance between the social and the personal interpretation of the tragedy was clear, and there was real freshness in the Othello–Desdemona relationship. McCabe's Iago, like Emrys James in 1971, played the accordion in II.iii; he showed his revulsion at what he was inventing in the 'I lay with Cassio' speech, and initiated a mingling of bloods in the oath-taking at the end of III.iii. In the crucial scene at the end of IV.ii, when Desdemona made it obvious how much she needed someone to hold and comfort her, he visibly panicked, nervously gesturing to Emilia to look after her mistress. On receiving an equally strong gesture of refusal from Emilia, he then allowed himself a reluctant and awkward embrace that clearly disturbed him.

McCabe, like Ron Canada and Simon Russell Beale, had the sweaty, overweight appearance that Kitty Malony's friend recommended for Iago in the late 1880s. Probably a joke at the time, it has become almost as characteristic of modern productions as the darkly satanic figure of the nineteenth century. Though Cinthio's story introduces its nameless ensign as 'of handsome presence but the most scoundrelly nature in the world' (Honigmann, Introduction, 373), the late twentieth century, like the seventeenth and eighteenth centuries, for the most part tried to avoid making the character physically attractive. At present, it seems that the problem of finding a visual coding for evil – one that that will allow the actor to be a convincing deceiver of other characters but not of the audience – has been solved entirely in sexual terms. The new polarization has some advantages: unlike most of the other groups with which Iago's villainy has previously been associated, impotent wife-abusers are unlikely to complain publicly about being stereotyped as villains. It does however involve some cutting of the text, clearly written with a different balance in mind. More seriously, it destroys what may have been the intention behind Shakespeare's choice of an ageing black hero and a youngish villain: to question received ideas of goodness and attraction. Even so, the Iagos of Beale and McCabe in many ways did what

Plate 3   Ray Fearon as Othello and Richard McCabe as Iago.
Directed by Michael Attenborough, RSC, Stratford-upon-Avon, 1998

Plate 4 Derrick Lee Weeden as Othello and Amy Cronise as Desdemona. Directed by Tony Taccone, Oregon Shakespeare Festival, 1999

Othello was supposed to do: they won the audience's sympathy, despite their appearance, by the sheer power of acting. Being older and more experienced than their Othellos probably gave them an advantage in this respect.

The Ashland *Othello* was recognized by many reviewers as having succeeded in doing something on a larger scale than usual. As one reviewer put it, it not only conveyed 'the play's true grandeur' but made one understand 'why the play is called *Othello* instead of *Iago*' (Robert Harwitt, *San Francisco Examiner*, 1 March 1999). The two things – grandeur and an emphasis on Othello – tend to go together. Derrick Lee Weeden is an impressive actor and, though still too young to be declined into the vale of years, could truthfully say, as he did, that he was 'declining ... yet that's not much'. He is tall and powerful-looking, with a voice that has a remarkably varied range, and (perhaps because he comes from a family with a long tradition of military service dating back to the American Civil War) can present a convincing image of the kind of military leader who actually takes his men into battle. Since many people attend the Ashland Festival regularly, and Weeden had played there many times, he was already known and respected by his audience.

Though many Shakespeare plays at Ashland are given in the large outdoor Elizabethan theatre, where Taccone had previously directed *Coriolanus*, this *Othello* required the carefully controlled sound and lighting (mainly nocturnal) of the smaller Angus Bowmer Theatre. Costumes were eclectic – suggesting the Renaissance, but with modern suits under the red senatorial robes in I.iii. There were occasional suggestions of something more exotic. For the ten minutes before the play began, Othello and Desdemona, robed in rich, predominantly golden colours, held a pose which suggested the Emperor and Empress on a set of Japanese court dolls. In the background was Todd Barton's synthesized music, a rhythmic low boom like a heartbeat punctuated by unsettlingly sharp, ominous sounds (similar sounds were heard later after Brabantio's 'She hath deceived her father, and may thee'). As the house lights went down, the couple rose and faced each other; Othello's gorgeous robe fell back, revealing his bare chest marked with deep scars. Desdemona gently caressed the scars, and the actors held a long pause before turning and running upstage, followed by other figures in moving spotlights.

Thus, by contrast with most of the productions I have

described, this one made Othello, not Iago, the focus of mystery and speculation. The scarred body has recently become a focus of critical interest and the Parker film had already shown Desdemona touching the scars on Othello's face and neck. At Ashland the scars became thematic. In the Venetian scenes Othello's body was almost completely covered. On Cyprus, where he went barearmed, other scars were visible. At two points in the play his hand unconsciously went to them, as if he were returning to his past: once on 'chaos is come ... again' (which had the same apocalyptic meaning for him that it had had for James Earl Jones and Patrick Stewart), and again on 'And yet, how nature, erring from itself'. Desdemona (Amy Cronise), while presenting the traditional blonde appearance, was tall and clear-voiced, not childlike, and her most noticeable characteristic was straightforwardness. Being intelligent, she could see the unattractive side of Iago and showed that she did. In II.i, she asked Iago, 'There's one gone to the harbour?' as a way of telling him that he ought to be doing something useful instead of making negative remarks about his wife in public, and she was equally peremptory with the foolery of the clown later on. This was not a shy Desdemona: Othello said (as in the Folio) that she had given him 'a world of kisses' and one could believe it from her frank delivery, never inhibited by fear even during the horrors of Act IV; her singing of the willow song was an attempt to cheer herself up rather than to identify herself with its pathos. Even her last words were lucid. She clearly intended to exonerate Othello by claiming to have committed suicide, but not to say that everything was her fault.

In the opening moments of the play Iago (Anthony Heald) watched Othello and Desdemona from the front, his back to the audience from which he seemed to have emerged. The production on several occasions placed him in this position, as if to underline and question the audience's relationship to the character. The few negative comments that I heard on this production suggested that it had achieved its elevation of Othello by a deliberate subordination of Iago. Certainly, Heald was denied any of the usual means of winning audience sympathy. A gaunt figure with shaved head and bare arms under a leather cuirass, as if to show that he had nothing to conceal, he was not particularly attractive or funny or charming; he barely sang at all in the abbreviated drunken scene; and Othello was clearly superior to him when they engaged in fencing practice during their crucial dialogue in Act III. But

Heald's performance was strong and convincing, and audiences during the intervals were still talking more about his motives than about any other aspect of the play. Only the end, when he was dragged offstage to torture screaming, 'No, no!', might be seen as a rather cheap way of avoiding the other extreme of glorification of evil.

The production's focus on Othello was helped by its lack of realistic detail – which, as I have noted, nearly always encourages an Iago's-eye-view of the story. Taccone used the barest minimum of props and settings – no maps or globes in the senate scene, no procession of luggage at Cyprus, no desks for Othello and Iago to sign papers in III.iii; no dressing table for the willow scene. The drunken scene was played around a vat of wine on a cart; there was a single chair for the 'brothel scene' and at the end a bed was moved in on a platform, where it was seen against a background of lighted candles which reminded spectators of Baz Luhrmann's film of *Romeo and Juliet*. The only significant element of William Bloodgood's spare set was a rectangular pond near the front of the stage. Opinions differed about its effectiveness, and particularly the fact that it was covered with glass in some scenes so that characters could walk over it, which caused some amusement when it first happened in I.iii. The water served various practical functions: Othello pushed someone backwards into it in the street scuffle of I.ii; Iago dipped a cloth in it and pressed it at the back of Cassio's neck after the drunken scene; Othello held Iago's head under water at the climax of his anger in III.iii; Desdemona washed her legs and feet in it in IV.iii. These utilitarian uses may sometimes have had a symbolic value, since fire also seemed important in the background of several scenes, and the contrast that is made overt in the exchange between Othello and Emilia – 'She was false as water'; 'Thou art rash as fire' (V.ii.132) – is part of that sense of the 'elemental' which Orson Welles and James Earl Jones had seen as crucial to the play. The religious significance of the water became more explicit at the end of the first act. Unusually, the play had two intervals. Just prior to the first, Cassio, on the upper level with other soldiers, read the herald's lines from II.ii about the celebration of Othello's nuptials. As he spoke, Othello and Desdemona entered below, dressed in white, and knelt behind the water (plate 4). They dipped their hands in it and anointed each other's foreheads, then rose and moved upstage, while, as Iago watched from the front, a white sheet with red petals on it was made to float above their heads like a canopy. The same sheet was used at the end of the play to cover the corpses of Othello and Desdemona.

The play's second interval relied for some of its effect on another feature of the set, somewhat reminiscent of the design for the Nunn and Mendes productions: slatted screens that could be raised and lowered, seem opaque, or show figures moving behind them. Characters who spoke from behind the screen – as Othello did in the eavesdropping scene – were miked so that their words seemed to come from different points in the auditorium. At the end of IV.i, after Othello had struck Desdemona, Lodovico's lines ('Is this the noble Moor' etc.) were divided among the rest of the cast, who were seen only in silhouette as they moved behind the screens. Because the light behind them was broken up by the slats, it was almost as if they were moving against a strobe. Othello stood, legs wide apart, with his back to the audience, while Iago, in a spotlight near the front of the stage, answered the choric questions, which were probably audible only in Othello's mind. The last speaker was a woman, perhaps Desdemona, who said, 'I am sorry that I am thus deceived in him', to which Iago replied, 'He is that he is', his arms raised in a noncommittal gesture. The lights came up for the interval, but Othello did not leave the stage: stage hands and extras walked past him as if he were invisible, while he sometimes muttered to himself and some-times walked in a circle. Breaking the frame of the play unsettled the audience: some went out; some found themselves unable to leave the theatre and even wanted to tell others to sit down.

Other overlappings drew attention to parallels in the play's design, such as the one between Desdemona and Bianca. At the point where most directors end the first half, the oath-taking between Othello and Iago, Desdemona appeared on the upper level just as Othello said, 'Damn her, lewd minx!' and searched for the lost handkerchief while the two men, below, plotted her death. Between III.iv and IV.i, Cassio left Bianca on stage alone. As Othello and Iago came on, each in a spotlight, Bianca moved around them, also in the light, sombrely waving the handkerchief. Standing in front of Othello as he finally broke down, she seemed at that moment to embody everything he imagined of Desdemona. Bianca again appeared in the willow scene, now on the upper level, just as Emilia was asking, 'What is it that they do / When they change us for others?' (IV.iii.95–6).

The absence of realistic detail (Venice and Cyprus were indistinguishable), along with the expressionistic lighting and sound effects, emphasized the extent to which the play was happening in Othello's mind. When Emilia knocked at the bedroom door in V.ii, for example, the sound was deafening: it was what Othello heard, not what she had the strength to do. His suicide was helped, perhaps excessively, by expressionistic devices which overcame the usual questions about where he gets the weapon and why no one stops him: fixed in a spotlight while the other characters froze, he stabbed himself in slow motion. As soon as he had kissed Desdemona, spoken his last line and fallen dead, the lights came up again and the entire cast shrieked in horror. The remaining lines were cut (some of Lodovico's had been transposed to an earlier point). As often, the effect of the ending was mediated by its effect on the other characters. Cassio, a slightly built man with glasses, who had been shown to be seriously pious, even puritanical, at the beginning, now dragged himself to the foot of the bed, then looked up to heaven as if to ask whether it was still there.

An important factor in the success of both the Stratford and the Ashland productions was their distinct emphasis on a strong and sympathetic Othello and Desdemona whose marriage seemed, even more than most marriages, an act of courage. The stage setting at Stratford and the expressionistic techniques used at Ashland also created a sense of an inner life – even a poetic one – for both characters, thus avoiding the tendency of modern productions to focus attention mainly on Iago and his hidden motives. If the contrast between hero and villain was largely worked out in terms of their sexuality, the aspect of the play that most closely touches on the lives of its spectators, neither production over-simplified that contrast into 'sex – good; no sex – bad'. Sexuality, in Attenborough's production, was the most intimate manifestation of that need for an inner life that the play seemed constantly to deny its characters; in Taccone's production it was part of a quasi-religious sense of involvement with elemental forces. In both cases the contrast between Othello and Iago returned to a redefinition of what it means to be a hero or a villain. Arguably, both could be seen as returning to the classical view that a heroic role is one of great emotional range, while the villain is essentially a limited character.

Epilogue

I am glad to be able to end this book with evidence that *Othello* still has the power to move audiences. This is all the more gratifying in that many turn-of-the-century conditions make this effect more difficult to achieve. Most people are likely to make their first acquaintance with the play not on the stage but on video, where the rewind button and freeze-frame allow them to remain in control, deconstructing their experience before they have it. Or they come to it full of distrust of its racial and sexual politics. Once actors refused to play Iago because they did not want to be thought of as villains; now we are more likely to find black actors refusing to play Othello because they do not want to be considered stupid or animal-like, or women wanting to cut lines that make Desdemona seem too submissive and weak. The desire to make the characters behave as we want, and the reluctance to believe that actors are 'only' acting, has clearly been a motive behind the various adaptations of the play charted in this book.

Anti-racist activists are understandably afraid to recognize any positive developments that might be seized on as an excuse for complacency about social injustice. Nevertheless, the movement from silence about racism to its foregrounding is already taking the discussion in new directions, some of which may yet find their way into mainstream productions of *Othello*. One of these is the recognition of common ground among historical victims of racial discrimination. It is often forgotten, for instance, that the expulsion of the Moors from Spain was closely followed by that of the Jews. Marowitz's *Othello* adaptation turned Brabantio into a comic Jewish father with a Brooklyn accent, who asks the audience, 'Would you like your daughter to marry one?' The old man agrees to work with Lodovico and the Duke for Othello's ruin, after which they sadly admit that 'red tape' is still holding up his admission to their country club. Peter Sellars, in a production of *The Merchant of Venice* at Chicago's Goodman Theatre in 1994, cast the play with African-American actors as the Jews, Asian-Americans as the Belmont household, and Latinos as the Venetians; as he put it, 'the reality of anti-Semitism is extended to include parallel struggles and their related issues' (quoted Worthen, 77). Other late twentieth-century productions of *Merchant* (Royal Shakespeare Company, 1998; Shakespeare Theatre at the Lansburgh, 1999) have drawn attention to the fact that the racism of the play's white characters is directed not only at Shylock but also at the Prince of Morocco, the Moorish slave made pregnant by Launcelot, and other black slaves who were silent members of the cast. Fiction has likewise attempted to show the complex interrelatedness of racial victimization. *The Nature of Blood* (1997), by the West Indian novelist Caryl Phillips, moves between Othello's first-person narrative and Jewish experience in the twentieth century: Othello, seeking a scribe to write a letter for him to Desdemona, goes into the Venetian ghetto and employs an old man who will later be burned in a vicious pogrom; at the end of the book an elderly doctor in Israel, the brother of a Holocaust victim, has a brief sexual encounter with a new immigrant from Africa who has suffered from the prejudice of Israelis against blacks. The Jewish-American novelist Philip Roth, in *I Married a Communist* (1998), takes as his hero a Jewish actor/activist who knows Robeson and is in many ways his mirror image, as much concerned with injustice towards blacks as Aldridge and Robeson were concerned with injustice towards the Jews. Paul Gilroy recently argued for a study of the concept of *diaspora* in relation to both blacks and Jews, provided that it avoids 'a pointless and utterly immoral wrangle about which communities have experienced the most ineffable forms of degradation' (Gilroy, 212). The theatre world has already, it seems, been reaching in practice what Gilroy suggests in theory. This global perspective has further implications for the casting of *Othello* and may make possible a more balanced and varied relationship between pleasure in acting and pleasure in identification.

APPENDIX

Major actors and staff for the twentieth-century productions discussed

Stage productions

Savoy Theatre, London, 1930
Director: Ellen van Volkenberg   Designer: James Pryde
Othello Paul Robeson   *Emilia* Sybil Thorndike
Iago Maurice Browne   *Cassio* Ralph Richardson
Desdemona Peggy Ashcroft

Old Vic Theatre, London, 1938
Director: Tyrone Guthrie   Designer: Roger Furse
Othello Ralph Richardson   *Emilia* Martita Hunt
Iago Laurence Olivier   *Cassio* Anthony Quayle
Desdemona Curigwen Lewis   *Roderigo* Stephen Murray

Brattle Theatre, Cambridge, Mass., 1942
Director: Margaret Webster   Designer: Robert Edmond Jones
Othello Paul Robeson   *Desdemona* Uta Hagen
Iago José Ferrer   *Emilia* Margaret Webster

Shakespeare Memorial Theatre, Stratford-upon-Avon, 1959
Director: Tony Richardson   Designer: Loudon Sainthill
Othello Paul Robeson   *Emilia* Angela Baddeley
Iago Sam Wanamaker   *Cassio* Albert Finney
Desdemona Mary Ure   *Bianca* Zoe Caldwell

Old Vic Theatre, London, 1964
Director: John Dexter   Designer: Jocelyn Herbert
Othello Laurence Olivier   *Emilia* Joyce Redman
Iago Frank Finlay   *Cassio* Derek Jacobi
Desdemona Maggie Smith

Royal Shakespeare Theatre, Stratford-upon-Avon, London, 1971–72
Director: John Barton   Designer: Julia Trevelyan Oman
Othello Brewster Mason   *Emilia* Elizabeth Spriggs
Iago Emrys James   *Cassio* David Calder
Desdemona Lisa Harrow

Royal Shakespeare Theatre, Stratford-upon-Avon, 1979
Director: Ronald Eyre   Designer: Pamela Howard
Othello Donald Sinden   *Emilia* Susan Tracy
Iago Bob Peck   *Cassio* Gareth Thomas
Desdemona Suzanne Bertish

American Shakespeare Festival, Stratford, Conn., 1981–82
Director: Peter Coe   Designer: Robert Fletcher
Othello James Earl Jones   *Emilia* Aldeen O'Kelly
Iago Christopher Plummer   *Cassio* Kelsey Grammer
Desdemona Shannon John

Royal Shakespeare Theatre, Stratford-upon-Avon, 1985
Director: Terry Hands   Designer: Ralph Koltai
Othello Ben Kingsley   *Emilia* Janet Dale
Iago David Suchet   *Cassio* Tom Mannion
Desdemona Niamh Cusack

The Other Place, Stratford-upon-Avon, 1989
See below under Video productions

The Shakespeare Theater, Washington, DC, 1997
Director: Jude Kelly   Designer: Robert Innes Hopkins
Othello Patrick Stewart   *Emilia* Franchelle Stewart-Dorn
Iago Ron Canada   *Cassio* Teagle F. Bougere
Desdemona Patrice Johnson

The National Theatre, Prague, 1997
Director: Ivan Rajmont   Designer: Jozef Ciller
Othello Boris Rösner   *Emilia* Miluše Splechtová
Iago Oldřich Kaiser   *Cassio* Ondřej Pavelka
Desdemona Zuzana Stivínová

Old Vic Theatre, London, 1998
Director: Sam Mendes   Designer: Anthony Ward
Othello David Harewood   *Emilia* Maureen Beattie
Iago Simon Russell Beale   *Cassio* Colin Tierney
Desdemona Clare Skinner

Santa Cruz Shakespeare Festival, Santa Cruz, Ca., 1998
Director: Michael Donald Edwards   Designer: Dipu Gupta
Othello Robert Jason Jackson   *Emilia* Ursula Meyer
Iago Paul Whitworth   *Cassio* William Hulings
Desdemona Lise Bruneau

Royal Shakespeare Company, Stratford-upon-Avon, 1999
Director: Michael Attenborough Designer: Robert Jones

Othello Ray Fearon *Emilia* Rachel Joyce
Iago Richard McCabe *Cassio* Henry Ian Cusick
Desdemona Zoe Waites

Oregon Shakespeare Festival, Bowmer Theatre, Ashland, Oregon, 1999
Director: Tony Taccone Designer: William Bloodgood

Othello Derrick Lee Weeden *Emilia* Robynn Rodriguez
Iago Anthony Heald *Cassio* Andrew Borba
Desdemona Amy Cronise

Film productions

Director: Dmitri Buchowetski, 1922

Othello Emil Jannings *Cassio* Theodor Loos
Iago Werner Krauss *Brabantio* Friedrich Kühne
Desdemona Ica Lenkeffy *Roderigo* Ferdinand von Alten
Emilia Lya de Putti

Director: Orson Welles, 1952

Othello Orson Welles *Cassio* Michael Lawrence
Iago Micheál MacLiammóir *Roderigo* Robert Coote
Desdemona Suzanne Cloutier *Bianca* Doris Dowling
Emilia Fay Compton *Brabantio*: Hilton Edwards

Director: Sergei Yutkevich, 1955

Othello Sergei Bondarchuk *Emilia* A. Maximova
Iago Andrei Popov *Cassio* Vladimir Soshalsky
Desdemona Irina Skobtseva *Roderigo* E. Vesnik

Available commercially with dubbed English soundtrack. The National Film
Archive in London has a copy with the original Russian soundtrack.

Director: Oliver Parker, 1995

Othello Laurence Fishburne *Cassio* Nathaniel Parker
Iago Kenneth Branagh *Roderigo* Michael Maloney
Desdemona Irène Jacob *Bianca* Indra Ove
Emilia Anna Patrick *Brabantio* Pierre Vaneck

Video productions

British Home Entertainment, GB, 1965
Director: Stuart Burge
(a film of the 1964 National Theatre production—Dir: John Dexter)

Othello Laurence Olivier — *Cassio* Derek Jacobi
Iago Frank Finlay — *Roderigo* Robert Lang
Desdemona Maggie Smith — *Bianca* Sheila Reid
Emilia Joyce Redman — *Brabantio* Anthony Nicholls

BBC/Time-Life Films, GB, 1981
Director: Jonathan Miller

Othello Anthony Hopkins — *Cassio* David Yelland
Iago Bob Hoskins — *Roderigo* Anthony Pedley
Desdemona Penelope Wilton — *Bianca* Wendy Morgan
Emilia Rosemary Leach — *Brabantio* Geoffrey Chater

Bard Video, GB, 1985
Director: Franklin Melton

Othello William Marshall — *Cassio* Deveren Bookwalter
Iago Ron Moody — *Roderigo* Joel Asher
Desdemona Jenny Agutter — *Bianca* Eugenia Wright
Emilia Leslie Paxton — *Brabantio* Peter MacLean

Focus/Portobello, GB, 1988
Director: Janet Suzman
(the production at the Market Theatre, Johannesburg)

Othello John Kani — *Emilia* Dorothy Gould
Iago Richard Haddon Haines — *Cassio* Neil McCarthy
Desdemona Joanna Weinberg — *Roderigo* Frantz Dobrowsky

Primetime, GB, 1990
Director: Trevor Nunn

Othello Willard White — *Emilia* Zoe Wanamaker
Iago Ian McKellen — *Cassio* Sean Baker
Desdemona Imogen Stubbs

BBC TV, GB, 1995
Director: Tony Richardson

Othello Gordon Heath — *Cassio* Robert Hardy
Iago Paul Rogers — *Roderigo* James Maxwell
Desdemona Rosemary Harris — *Bianca* Billie Whitelaw
Emilia Daphne Anderson — *Brabantio* Edmund Willard

BIBLIOGRAPHY

Abel, C. Douglas. '"Alexander the Little": The Question of Stature in Edmund Kean's Othello', *Theatre History Studies* 9 (1989), 92–105.

Alger, William Rounseville, *Life of Edwin Forrest, the American Tragedian*, 2 vols, Philadelphia, 1877.

Allen, Shirley S., *Samuel Phelps and Sadler's Wells Theatre*, Middletown, Conn., 1971.

Anderegg, Michael, *Orson Welles, Shakespeare and Popular Culture*, New York, 1999.

Anon., *A Brief Memoir of the Theatrical Career of Ira Aldridge, the African Tragedian*, London, n.d.

Anon., *The Wonderful Secrets of Stage Trick; or A Peep behind the Curtain*, London, printed for the author, 1794.

Archer, Frank, *An Actor's Notebooks*, London, n.d. [c. 1900].

Ashwell, Lena, *Reflections from Shakespeare, a Series of Lectures*, ed. Roger Pocock, London, n.d.

Auerbach, Nina, *Ellen Terry: Player in Her Time*, New York, 1987.

Austin, Gilbert, *Chironomia, or, A Treatise on Rhetorical Delivery*, ed. Mary Margaret Robb and Lester Thonssen, Carbondale, Ill., 1966.

Ayers, Alfred, *Acting and Actors, Elocution and Elocutionists, a Book about Theater Folk and Theater Art*, New York, 1900.

Ball, Robert Hamilton, *Shakespeare on Silent Film: A Strange Eventful History*, London, 1968.

Bate, Jonathan, *Shakespearean Constitutions: Politics, Theatre, Criticism 1730–1830*, Oxford, 1989.

Bell's Edition of Shakespeare's Plays, vol. 1, London, 1774, Facsim. ed. London, 1969. 148–232.

Bennett, Jill, and Suzanne Goodwin, *Godfrey: A Special Time Remembered*, London, etc., 1983.

Bentley, Eric, 'Torments of a Superman': Review of Martin Bauml Duberman, *Paul Robeson*, *TLS*, 12 May 1989, p. 507.

Bertrand, Édouard, *Shakespeare et Voltaire: Étude sur l'expression de la jalousie dans 'Othello' et 'Zaïre'*, Grenoble, 1896.

Billington, Michael, *Peggy Ashcroft*, London, 1988.

Bland, Sheila Rose, 'How I Would Direct *Othello*', in Mythili Kaul, ed., *Othello, New Essays from Black Writers*, Washington, D.C., 1997.

Boaden, James, *Memoirs of the Life of John Philip Kemble*, 2 vols, London, 1825, repr. New York and London, 1969.

——, *Memoirs of Mrs. Siddons, Interspersed with Anecdotes of Authors and Actors*, London and Philadelphia, 1827.

Boose, Lynda, 'Grossly Gaping Viewers and Jonathan Miller's *Othello*', in L. Boose and R. Burt, eds, *Shakespeare the Movie: Popularizing the Plays on Film, TV, and Video*, London, 1997, pp. 186–97.

Booth, Edwin, *Shakespeare's Tragedy of Othello as Presented by Edwin Booth*, ed. William Winter, Philadelphia, 1920.

Booth, Stephen, 'The Best Othello I Ever Saw', *Shakespeare Quarterly* 40 (1989), 332–6.

Bowdler, Thomas, ed., *The Family Shakespeare*, 10 vols, London, 1818.

Bradley, A. C., *Shakespearean Tragedy*, London, 1965.

Budden, Julian, *The Operas of Verdi: Vol. 3, From 'Don Carlos' to 'Falstaff'* (rev. edn), Oxford, 1992.

Burt, Richard, 'The Love that Dare not Speak Shakespeare's Name: New Shakesqueer Cinema', in L. Boose and R. Burt, eds, *Shakespeare the Movie: Popularizing the Plays on Film, TV, and Video*, London, 1997, pp. 240–8.

Bushnell, Howard, *Maria Malibran, a Biography of the Singer*, University Park, Penn., 1979.

Busi, Anna, *Otello in Italia, 1777–1972*, Bari, 1973.

Callaghan, Dympna, *Shakespeare without Women: Representing Gender and Race on the Renaissance Stage*, London and New York, 2000.

Campenon, F.-V. *Essais de mémoires, ou lettres sur la vie, le caractère, et les écrits de J.-F. Ducis*, Paris, 1824.

Carlisle, Carol Jones, *Shakespeare from the Greenroom: Actors' Criticisms of Four Major Tragedies*, Chapel Hill, N.C., 1969.

Carlson, Marvin, '*Othello* in Vienna, 1991', *Shakespeare Quarterly* 44 (1993), 228–30.

Carroll, Janet Barton, *A Promptbook Study of Margaret Webster's Production of* Othello, PhD dissertation, Louisiana State University, 1977.

Cartelli, Thomas, *Repositioning Shakespeare: National Formations, Postcolonial Appropriations*, London, 1999.

Chatenet, Jean, *Shakespeare sur la scène française depuis 1940*, Paris, 1962.

Cibber, Colley, *An Apology for the Life of Colley Cibber*, ed. B. R. S. Fone, Ann Arbor, Mich., 1968.

Clairmont, Claire, *The Journals of Claire Clairmont*, ed. Marion Kingston Stocking, with David Mackenzie Stocking, Cambridge, Mass., 1968.

Clarke, Charles Cowden, *Shakespeare-Characters: Chiefly Those Subordinate*, London and Edinburgh, 1863.

Coghill, Nevil, *Shakespeare's Professional Skills*, Cambridge, 1964.

[Cole, John], *A Critique on the Performance of Othello by F.W. Keene Aldridge, the African Roscius*, Scarborough, 1831.

Coleman, John, *Players and Playwrights I Have Known*, 2 vols, London, 1888.

Conrad, Peter, *A Song of Love and Death: The Meaning of Opera*, New York, 1987.

Cook, Dutton, *Nights at the Play: A View of the English Stage*, London, 1883.

Cooke, William, *Memoirs of Charles Macklin, Comedian*, London, 1806.

Cooper, Roberta Krensky, *The American Shakespeare Theatre: Stratford, 1955–1985*, Washington, London and Toronto, 1986.

Coursen, H. R., *Shakespeare: The Two Traditions*, Madison, N.J., and London, 1999.

D'Alfonso, N. R., *Otello Delinquente, lettura fatta nell'università di Roma per la fine del corso di psicologia criminale nell'anno 1909–10*, Rome, 1910.

Dalmonte, Rossana, '"Une écriture corporelle": la musica e la danza', in Ezio Raimondi, ed., *Il sogno del coreodramma: Salvatore Viganò, poeta muto*. Reggio Emilia, 1984, pp. 145–239.

Dechmann, George, *Histrions and the Histrionic Art*, London, 1899.

Dexter, John, *The Honourable Beast: A Posthumous Autobiography*, New York, 1993.

Dickins, Richard, *Forty Years of Shakespeare on the English Stage: August 1867 to August 1907: A Student's Memories*, n.d., no publisher or place.

Donaldson, Peter S., *Shakespearean Films / Shakespearean Directors*, Boston, 1990.

Dorval, Patricia, 'Shakespeare on Screen: Threshold Aesthetics in Oliver Parker's *Othello*', *Early Modern Literary Studies* 6.2 (May 2000), 1.1–15 (http://purl.oclc.org/emls/06–1/dorvothe.htm).

Douglass, Frederick, *Life and Times of Frederick Douglass*, New York and London, 1962.

Duberman, Martin Bauml, *Paul Robeson*, New York, 1988.

Ducis, Jean-François, *Othello*, ed. Christopher Smith, Exeter, 1991.

Durylin, S[ergei], *Ira Aldridge*, Moscow and Leningrad, 1940 (in Russian).

Dyce, Alexander, *The Reminiscences of Alexander Dyce*, ed. Richard J. Schrader, Columbus, Ohio, 1972.

Dyer, Richard, *Heavenly Bodies: Film Stars and Society*, New York, 1986.

An Egley [sic] upon the Most Execrable Murther of Mr. Clun, On of the Comedeans of the Theator Royal, London: Edward Crouch, n.d. Repr., G. Thorn-Drury, ed., *A Little Ark Containing Sundry Pieces of Seventeenth-century Verse*, London, 1921, pp. 30–1.

Eliot, T. S., *Elizabethan Essays*, London, 1937.

Empson, William, *The Structure of Complex Words*, Cambridge, Mass., 1989.

Estève, Edmond, 'De Shakespeare à Musset: variations sur la romance du Saule', *Revue d'Histoire Littéraire de la France* 29 (1922), 288–315.

Evans, G. Blakemore, ed., *Shakespearean Prompt-books of the Seventeenth Century*, vol. 6 [*Smock Alley Othello*], Charlottesville, Va., 1980.

Faucit, Helena, *On Some of Shakespeare's Female Characters*, Edinburgh and London, 1885.

Fechter, Charles, *Othello* (acting edition), London, 1861.

Fenner, Theodore, *Opera in London: Views of the Press 1785–1830*, Carbondale, Ill., 1994.

Fenwick, Henry, 'The Production', introduction to *The BBC TV Shakespeare: Othello*, London, 1981.

Ferrer, José, 'The Role of Iago in Shakespeare's *Othello*', *The American Theatre* 1 (August 1945), 7–9.

Ffrench, Yvonne, *Mrs Siddons, Tragic Actress*, London, 1954.

Fielding, Henry, 'A Journey from this World to the Next', in *Miscellanies*, vol. 2, ed. Hugh Amory, Oxford, 1993.

Fisher, Jay, *Théodore Chassériau, Illustrations for Othello*, catalogue of Baltimore Museum of Art exhibition, 11 November 1979–6 January 1980.

Folger Promptbooks (listed by number in text).

Folger Scrapbooks: Ira Aldridge, Edwin Booth, J. B. Booth, 'Othello'.

Fontane, Theodor, *Shakespeare in the London Theatre 1855–58*, translated and edited by Russell Jackson, London, 1999.

Foote, Samuel, *A Treatise on the Passions, so far as they regard the Stage; with a critical enquiry into the theatrical merit of Mr. G—k, Mr. Q—n, and Mr. B—y. The first considered in the Part of Lear, the two last opposed in Othello*, London, n.d. (printed for C. Corbett).

Forbes, Jill, *Les Enfants du Paradis*, London, 1997.

Forrest, Edwin, *Othello: The Edwin Forrest Edition of Shakspearian and Other Plays*, ed. James M. Nixon, New York [1860].

Frank, Sam, *Ronald Colman, a Bio-Bibliography*, Westport, Conn., and London, 1997.

Full Report of The Trial of Cox versus Kean, London, n.d. [1825?].

Furness, Horace Howard, *The Letters of Horace Howard Furness*, ed. H.H.F.J. [Horace Howard Furness Jayne], 2 vols, Boston, 1922.

Furness, Horace Howard, *Othello: A New Variorum Edition of Shakespeare*, Philadelphia, 1886, repr. 1963.

Garcia, Gustave, *The Actor's Art*, London, 1882.

[Gentleman, Francis], *The Dramatic Censor, or, Critical Companion*, London and York, 1770.

Gielgud, John, *Shakespeare: Hit or Miss* (with John Miller), London, 1991.

Gilman, Margaret, *Othello in French*, Paris, 1925.

Gilroy, Paul, *The Black Atlantic: Modernity and Double Consciousness*, London and New York, 1993.

Golder, John, '"Mon Sans-culotte Africain": A French Revolutionary Stage *Othello*', in Heather Kerr, Robin Eaden and Madge Mitton, eds, *Shakespeare: World Views*, Newark, Del., and London, 1996, pp. 146–55.

Goodale, Katherine, *Behind the Scenes with Edwin Booth*, New York, 1931, repr., New York, 1969.

Gould, Thomas R., *The Tragedian: An Essay on the Histrionic Genius of Junius Brutus Booth*, New York, 1868.

Grant, G., *Essay on the Science of Acting*, London, 1828.

Greenblatt, Stephen, *Renaissance Self-fashioning from More to Shakespeare*, Chicago, 1980.

Grossman, Edwina Booth, *Edwin Booth: Recollections by His Daughter*, New York, 1894, repr., New York, 1969.

Guerrero, Ed, 'Black Stars in Exile: Paul Robeson, O. J. Simpson, and Othello', in Jeffrey C. Stewart, ed., *Paul Robeson: Artist and Citizen*, New Brunswick, N.J., and London, 1998.

Guthrie, Tyrone, *A Life in the Theatre*, London, 1961.

Habib, Imtiaz, *Shakespeare and Race: Postcolonial Praxis in the Early Modern Period*, Lanham, New York, Oxford, 2000.

Habicht, Werner, 'Shakespeare and the German Imagination: Cult, Controversy, and Performance', in Heather Kerr, Robin Eaden and Madge Mitton, eds, *Shakespeare: World Views*, Newark, Del., and London, 1996, pp. 87–101.

Hackett, James Henry, *Notes, Criticisms and Correspondence upon Shakespeare's Plays and Actors*, New York, 1863; repr. New York and London, 1968.

Hanmer, Thomas, ed., *The Works of William Shakespeare*, vol. 6, Oxford, 1744.

Hankey, Julie, *Othello: Plays in Performance*, Bristol, 1987.

Hare, Arnold, *George Frederick Cooke: The Actor and the Man*, London, 1980.

Hawkins, F. W., *The Life of Edmund Kean* (1869), repr. New York, 1969.

Hazlitt, William, *The Complete Works of William Hazlitt*, ed. P. P. Howe, 21 vols, London and Toronto, 1930–34, vols V and XVIII.

Henry Irving Shakespeare, The [*The Works of William Shakespeare*, ed. Henry Irving and Frank A. Marshall], vol. VI, London, 1889.

Hepokoski, James A., *Giuseppe Verdi: 'Otello'*, Cambridge, 1987.

Hiffernan, Paul, M.D. *Dramatic Genius: In Five Books*, London, printed for the author, 1770.

Highfill, Philip N., *A Biographical Dictionary of Actors, Actresses, Musicians, Dancers, Managers & Other Stage Personnel in London, 1660–1800*, 16 vols, Carbondale, Ill., 1973–93.

Hill, Aaron, *The Dramatic Works of Aaron Hill, Esq.*, 2 vols, London, 1760.

——, *The Works of the Late Aaron Hill, Esq.*, 4 vols, London, 1753.

Hill, Errol, *Shakespeare in Sable: A History of Black Shakespearean Actors*, Amherst, Mass., 1984.

[Hill, John], *The Actor: A Treatise on the Art of Playing*, London, 1750.

Hillebrand, Harold N., *Edmund Kean*, New York, 1933, repr. 1966.

Hodgdon, Barbara, 'Kiss Me Deadly; or, The Des/Demonized Spectacle', in *Othello: New Perspectives*, ed. Virginia Mason Vaughan and Kent Cartwright, Rutherford, Madison, Teaneck, London and Toronto, 1991, pp. 214–55.

——, 'Race-ing Othello, Re-engendering White-out', in L. Boose and R. Burt, eds, *Shakespeare the Movie: Popularizing the Plays on Film, TV, and Video*, London, 1997.

Hogan, Charles Beecher, *Shakespeare in the Theatre, 1701–1800*, 2 vols, Oxford, 1952, 1957.

Holmes, Martin, *Shakespeare and Burbage: The Sound of Shakespeare as Devised to Suit the Voice and Talents of His Principal Player*, London and Totowa, N.J., 1978.

Honigmann, E. A. J., *The Texts of 'Othello' and Shakespearean Revision*, London and New York, 1996.

Hortmann, Wilhelm, 'Changing Modes in *Hamlet* Production: Rediscovering Shakespeare after the Iconoclasts', in Werner Habicht, D. J. Palmer and Roger Pringle, eds, *Images of Shakespeare*, Newark, Del., and London, 1988.

——, *Shakespeare on the German Stage: The Twentieth Century*, Cambridge, 1998.

Hoyt, Edwin P., *Paul Robeson: The American Othello*, Cleveland, 1967.

Hütter, Martina, Patrick Li, Dietrich Schwanitz and Birgit Susemihl, 'Theaterschau Nord: Othello–Theater als Lichterkette', *Jahrbuch 1994 der Deutsche Shakespeare-Gesellschaft/DSG West*, Bochum, 1994, pp. 160–8.

Hyman, Earle, '"*Othello*" or, Ego in Love, Sex and War', in Kaul, pp. 23–8.

Ireland, John, *Letters and Poems by the Late Mr Henderson, with Anecdotes of His Life*, London, 1766.

Jackson, C. Bernard, *Iago*, in Woodie King Jr, ed., *The National Black Drama Anthology*, New York and London, 1995, pp. 47–99.

Jackson, Russell, and Robert Smallwood, *Players of Shakespeare 2*, Cambridge, 1985.

Jacobs, Alfred, 'Orson Welles's *Othello*: Shakespeare Meets Film Noir', in Jonathan Bate, Jill L. Levenson and Dieter Mehl, eds, *Shakespeare and the Twentieth Century*, Newark, Del., and London, 1998, pp. 113–24.

Jacobsohn, Siegfried, *Max Reinhardt*, Berlin, 1921.

James, Henry, *The Scenic Art*, ed. Allan Wade, New York, 1957.

Jarro (G. Picinni), *L'Otello di Guglielmo Shakespeare*, Florence, 1888.

Johnson-Haddad, Miranda, 'The Shakespeare Theatre *Othello*', *Shakespeare Bulletin* 16.2 (Spring 1998), 9–11.

Johnson, David, *Shakespeare in South Africa*, Oxford, 1996.

Johnson, Lemuel A., *Shakespeare in Africa (& Other Venues): Import and the Appropriation of Culture*, Trenton, N.J., 1998.

Jones, Elwyn, 'Bringing *Othello* to Television', *Radio Times*, 9 December 1955, p. 5.

Jones, James Earl, and Penelope Niven, *James Earl Jones: Voices and Silences*, New York, 1993.

Jorgens, Jack J., *Shakespeare on Film*, Bloomington, Ind., 1977.

Kachler, K. G., 'Leopold Biberti als Darsteller des Othello', *Shakespeare Jahrbuch 1973*, 131–43.

Kaleidoscope, presented by Natalie Wheen, BBC Radio 4, British Library Sound Archive, n.d. [1997?].

Kemble, Frances, *Records of a Girlhood*, New York, 1879.

——, *Records of Later Life*, New York, 1882.

Kendall, Madge, *Dramatic Opinions*, Boston, 1890.

Kennedy, Dennis, *Looking at Shakespeare: A Visual History of Twentieth-century Performance*, Cambridge, 1993.

Klepac, Richard L., *Mr Mathews at Home*, London, 1979.

Knight, William G., *A Major London 'Minor': The Surrey Theatre 1805–1865*, London, 1997.

Knutson, Roslyn, *The Repertory of Shakespeare's Company 1594–1613*, Fayetteville, Ark., 1991.

Koon, Helene, *How Shakespeare Won the West: Players and Performances in America's Gold Rush, 1849–1865*, Jefferson, N.C., 1989.

Kudláčková, Johana, 'Pět Podov Českého *Othella* na Scénách Národního Divadla' [Five Incarnations of the Czech Othello on the Stages of the National Theatre], National Theatre programme for *Othello*, Prague, 1998, pp. 76–87.

La Place, Pierre-Antoine, *Le théâtre anglois*, 8 vols, London, 1746, vol. I.

Leavis, F. R., 'Diabolic Intellect and the Noble Hero: or The Sentimentalist's Othello', *The Common Pursuit*, London, 1952; Harmondsworth, 1962, pp.136–59.

Leroy, Onésime, *Études sur la Personne et les écrits de J.-F. Ducis*, Paris, 1835.

Limon, Jerzy, 'A Polish Gentleman's Visit to London Theatres in 1820–1821', in Lois Potter and A. F. Kinney, eds, *Shakespeare: Text and Theatre*, Newark, Del., and London, 1999, pp. 109–19.

Lower, Charles B., 'Othello as Black on Southern Stages, Then and Now', in Philip C. Kolin, ed., *Shakespeare in the South: Essays on Performance*, Jackson, Miss., 1983.

MMTC, Appendix (Appendix of material collected but not used for Marshall and Stock, *Ira Aldridge*, in Mander Mitchinson Theatre Collection, folder on Ira Aldridge).

MacDonald, Joyce Green, 'Acting Black: Othello, Othello Burlesques, and the Performance of Blackness', *Theatre Journal* 46 (1993), 231–49.

McGuire, Philip C., 'Whose Work Is This? Loading the Bed in *Othello*', in Jay L. Halio and Hugh Richmond, eds, *Shakespearean Illuminations: Essays in Honor of Marvin Rosenberg*, Newark, Del., and London, 1998.

McKellen, Ian, *Acting Shakespeare* (reprint of souvenir programme of 31 August 1986).

——, *William Shakespeare's 'Richard III'*, Woodstock, N.Y., 1996.

McKernan, Luke, and Olwen Terris, eds, *Walking Shadows: Shakespeare in the National Film and Television Archive*, London, 1994.

MacLiammóir, Micheál, *Put Money in Thy Purse: The Filming of Orson Welles' Othello*, London, 1976.

McMillin, Scott, *Plays in Performance: Henry IV, Part One*, Manchester and New York, 1991.

Manvell, Roger, *Shakespeare and the Film*, London, 1971.

Marowitz, Charles, *An Othello*, in *Open Space Plays*, Harmondsworth, 1974.

Marshall, Herbert, and Mildred Stock, *Ira Aldridge, the Negro Tragedian*, London, 1958, and Washington, D.C., 1993.

Mason, Edward Tuckerman, *The Othello of Tommaso Salvini*, New York and London, 1890.

Matteo, Gino J., *Shakespeare's Othello: The Study and the Stage*, Salzburg, 1974.

Maurel, Victor, *Dix ans de Carrière*, Paris, 1897; repr. New York, 1977.

Mendes, Sam, Platform Performance at National Theatre, Cottesloe, 30 October 1997.

Merchant, Christina, 'Delacroix's Tragedy of Desdemona', *Shakespeare Survey* 21 (1968), 79–86.

Miller, John, *Ralph Richardson: The Authorized Biography*, London, 1995.

Monaco, Marion, *Shakespeare on the French Stage in the Eighteenth Century*, Paris, 1974.

Montagu, Jennifer, *The Expression of the Passions: The Origin and Influence of Charles le Brun's Conférence sur l'expression générale et particulière*, New Haven and London, 1994.

Morley, Henry, *The Journal of a London Playgoer*, London, 1866, 1891, repr. Leicester, 1974.

Morozov, Mikhail M., *Shakespeare on the Soviet Stage*, London, 1947.

Murphy, Arthur, *The Life of David Garrick, Esq.*, 2 vols, London, 1801.

N., W., 'Critical Remarks on the *Othello* of Shakespeare' in *The Bee, or Literary Weekly Intelligencer*, vol. I (ed. James Anderson), on 12, 19, 29 January and 2 February 1791, repr. Vickers, *Critical Heritage*, vol 5, London, 1981, pp. 556–66.

Neill, Michael, 'Unproper Beds: Race, Adultery, and the Hideous in *Othello*', *Shakespeare Quarterly* 40 (1989), 383–412.

Nels, Sophia, *Shakespeare na Sovyetskoy tsenem* [Shakespeare on the Soviet Stage], Moscow, 1960.

Odell, George C. D., *Shakespeare from Betterton to Irving*, 2 vols, New York, 1920.

Ogude, S. E., 'Literature and Racism: The Example of Othello', in Mythili Kaul, ed., *Othello, New Essays from Black Writers*, Washington, D.C., 1997.

Olivier, Laurence, *Confessions of an Actor*, London, 1982.

——, *On Acting*, London, 1986.

Orkin, Martin, *Shakespeare Against Apartheid*, Craighall, South Africa, 1987.

Osborne, Charles, *The Complete Operas of Verdi, An Interpretive Study of the Librettos and Music and their Relation to the Composer's Life*, New York, 1979.

Ostuzhev, Alexander, 'On *Othello*', in Roman Samarin and Alexander Nikolyukin, eds, *Shakespeare in the Soviet Union*, trans. Avril Pyman, Moscow, 1966.

Othello as Performed by Sig. Salvini and the American Company ... The only authorized edition with the Italian and English Text, New York, n.d. (Folger PR 2829 A28 Sh Coll.)

Oxberry's Dramatic Bibliography and Histrionic Anecdotes, London, 1825.

Pechter, Edward, *'Othello' and Interpretive Traditions*, Iowa City, 1999.

Pepys, Samuel, *Diary of Samuel Pepys*, ed. R. Latham and W. Matthews, 10 vols, London and Berkeley, 1970–83.

Phillips, Caryl, *The Nature of Blood*, London, 1997.

Potter, Lois, 'Colley Cibber: The Fop as Hero', in J. C. Hilson, M. M. B. Jones and J. R. Watson, eds, *Augustan Worlds*, Leicester, 1978, pp. 189–206.

Procter, B. W. [Barry Cornwall], *The Life of Edmund Kean*, London, 1835, repr. New York, 1969.

Quarshie, Hugh, *Second Thoughts About Othello* (International Shakespeare Association Occasional Paper no. 7), Chipping Campden, 1999.

Raby, Peter, *Fair Ophelia: A Life of Harriet Smithson Berlioz*, Cambridge, 1982.

Rede, Leman Thomas, *The Road to the Stage, or, the Performer's Preceptor*, London, 1827.

Ritorni, Carlo, *Commentarii della vita e delle opere coredrammatiche di Salvatore Vigano e della coregrafia e de corepei*, Milan, 1838.

Roach, Joseph, *The Player's Passion: Studies in the Science of Acting*, Newark, Del., and London, 1985.

Robson, William, *The Old Play-goer*, London, 1846, repr. 1969.

Rosenberg, Marvin, *The Masks of Othello: The Search for the Identity of Othello, Iago, and Desdemona by Three Centuries of Actors and Critics*, Berkeley and Los Angeles, 1964.

Roth, Philip, *I Married a Communist*, London, 1998.

Russo, Peggy, '*Othello* after O.J.: Never Say Never Again, Again', unpublished paper delivered at Folger Shakespeare Library, January 1999.

Salvini, Tommaso, *Leaves from the Autobiography of Tommaso Salvini*, New York, 1893; repr. New York, 1971.

Salvini Programme, The, at the Academy of Music, New York, 16 September 1873 (Billy Rose Theatre Collection, New York Public Library Performing Arts Collection, MWEZ + n.c. 6730).

Salvini text: *Othello, the Italian Version as Performed by Signor Salvini*, London, 1875.

Shattuck, Charles H., *Shakespeare on the American Stage: From the Hallams to Edwin Booth* [Washington, D.C.], 1976.

Shaw, George Bernard, *Our Theatres in the Nineties*, 3 vols, London, 1932.

——, *The Quintessence of Ibsenism, Collected Works*, vol. XIX, New York, 1931.

Shelley, Percy B., *The Letters of Percy Bysshe Shelley*, ed. Frederick L. Jones, 2 vols, Oxford, 1964.

Siddons, Henry, *Practical Illustrations of Rhetorical Gesture and Action, adapted to the English Drama from a work on the same subject by M. Engel*, London, 1807.

Siemon, James R., '"Nay, that's not next": *Othello* V.ii in Performance, 1760–1900', *Shakespeare Quarterly* 37 (1986), 38–51.

Singh, Jyotsna, 'The Postcolonial/Postmodern Shakespeare', in Heather Kerr, Robin Eaden and Madge Mitton, eds, *Shakespeare: World Views*, Newark, Del., and London, 1996.

Smallwood, Robert, 'Shakespeare Performances in England', *Shakespeare Survey* 51 (1998), 219–55.

Solomon, Rakesh H., 'Culture, Imperialism, and Nationalist Resistence: Performance in Colonial India', *Theatre Journal* 46 (1993), 323–47.

Spector, Susan, 'Margaret Webster's *Othello*: The Principal Players versus the Director', *Theatre History Studies* 6 (1986), 93–108.

Spevack, Marvin, *A Complete and Systematic Concordance to the Works of Shakespeare*, Hildesheim, 1968, vol. III.

Sprague, A. C., *Shakespeare and the Actors: The Stage Business in His Plays (1660–1905)*, Cambridge, Mass., 1944.

——, *Shakespearian Players and Performances*, Cambridge, Mass., 1953; London, 1954.

Stanislavski, Constantin, *Creating a Role*, trans. Elizabeth Reynolds Hapgood, ed. Hermine I. Popper, New York, 1989. First pub. in this trans. 1961.

——, *My Life in Art* [1924, trans. Hapgood], trans. J. J. Robbins, Cleveland and New York, 1956.

——, *Stanislavsky Produces Othello*, trans. Helen Nowak, London, 1948.

——, *Stanislavski's Legacy*, ed. and trans. Elizabeth Reynolds Hapgood, New York and London, 1968.

Starks, Lisa S., 'An Interview with Michael Maloney', *Post Script, Essays in Film and the Humanities*, 17 (1997), 79–87.

Stendhal (Henri Beyle), *Rome, Naples et Florence*, ed. Henri Martineau, 2 vols, Paris, 1927.

——, *Vie de Rossini*, ed. Henri Martineau, 2 vols, Paris, 1929.

Stone, Mary I., *Edwin Booth's Performances: The Mary Isabella Stone Commentaries*, ed. Daniel Watermeier, Ann Arbor, Mich., and London, 1990.

Stříbrný, Zdeněk, 'Shakespeare and Perestroika', *Prague Studies in English* XX (1993), 7–17.

——, *Shakespeare in Eastern Europe*, Oxford, 2000.

Sunde, Karen, *Kabuki Othello*, conceived and directed by Shozo Sato (playscript in Billy Rose Collection, New York Public Library, NCOF + 95 – 3035).

Suzman, Janet, *Othello Documentary* (www.onlineclassics.net/plays/main.html).

—, 'South Africa in *Othello*', in Jonathan Bate, Jill L. Levenson and Dieter Mehl, eds, *Shakespeare and the Twentieth Century*, Newark, Del., and London, 1998, pp. 23–40. (First published in *The Tanner Lectures on Human Values* 17, n.p., University of Utah Press, 1995.)

Temkin, Owsei, *The Falling Sickness: A History of Epilepsy from the Greeks to the Beginning of Modern Neurology*, Baltimore and London, 1945, rev. 1971.

Terry, Ellen, *Ellen Terry's Memoirs; with a preface, notes and additional biographical chapters by Edith Craig and Christopher St. John*, New York, 1932.

Thespian Praeceptor, The, London, 1811.

Thierry, Edouard, 'Salvini dans le rôle d'Othello', *Revue de France* (1877), 871–80.

Tillotson, Geoffrey, '*Othello* and *The Alchemist* at Oxford in 1610', *TLS*, 20 July 1933, p. 494.

Timpane, John, review of *Othello* by Levin Theater Company, Rutgers Arts Center, New Brunswick, N.J., 22 June–15 July 1990, *Shakespeare Bulletin* 9 (1991).

Towse, John Ranken, *Sixty Years of the Theater: An Old Critic's Memories*, New York and London, 1916.

Tynan, Kenneth, *Othello, by William Shakespeare: The National Theatre Production*, New York, 1967.

Vandenhoff, George, *Leaves from an Actor's Notebook*, London, 1860.

Vaughan, Virginia, *Othello: A Contextual History*, Cambridge, 1994.

The Verdi–Boito Correspondence, ed. Marcello Conti and Mario Medici, English-language edition by William Weaver, Chicago and London, 1994.

Vickers, Brian, ed., *Shakespeare: The Critical Heritage*, 6 vols, London, 1974–81.

Voltaire, François-Marie Arouet, *Zaïre*, ed. Eva Jacobs, *Complete Works of Voltaire*, vol. 8, Voltaire Foundation, Oxford, 1988.

Watermeier, Daniel, ed., *A Critical Edition of Selected Letters from Edwin Booth to William Winter*, PhD dissertation, University of Illinois, 1968.

Webster, Margaret, 'On Cutting Shakespeare – and Other Matters', *Theatre Annual* (1946), 29–36.

——, *Don't Put Your Daughter on the Stage*, New York, 1972.

Welles, Orson, and Peter Bogdanovich, *This Is Orson Welles*, ed. Jonathan Rosenbaum, London, 1993.

White, R. S., *Innocent Victims: Poetic Injustice in Shakespearean Tragedy*, Newcastle-upon-Tyne, 1982.

Williamson, Audrey, *Old Vic Drama: A Twelve Years' Study of Plays and Players*, London, 1948.

Wilmeth, Don B., *George Frederick Cooke, Machiavel of the Stage*, London and Westport, Conn., 1980.

Wingate, Charles E. L., *Shakespeare's Heroes on the Stage*, New York and Boston, 1896.

Winter, William, ed., *Shakespeare's Tragedy of Othello as Presented by Edwin Booth* (1878), Philadelphia, 1920.

——, *Life and Art of Edwin Booth*, New York and London, 1893. Folger copy grangerized: ART Vol. a6.

Winters, Shelley, *Shelley, Also Known as Shirley*, New York, 1980.

Woods, Leigh, *On Playing Shakespeare: Advice and Commentary from Actors and Actresses of the Past*, New York, Westport, Conn., and London, 1991.

Worrall, Patricia B., review of *Othello*, directed by Nancy Keystone, Georgia Shakespeare Festival 1997, *Shakespeare Bulletin* 17 (1999), 24.

Worthen, W. B., *Shakespeare and the Authority of Performance*, Cambridge, 1997.

Young, Edward, *Complete Prose and Poetry*, ed. James Nichols, 2 vols, London, 1854, repr. Hildesheim, 1968.

Zhang, Xiao Yang, *Shakespeare in China: A Comparative Study of Two Traditions and Cultures*, Newark, Del., and London, 1996.

INDEX

Othello and characters in *Othello* will not appear in this index. Plays are indexed under their authors, where known, and otherwise by title. Page numbers in italics refer to illustrations.

Hall, Mary, 90
Hampden, Walter, 90, 138
Hands, Terry, 164
Hankey, Julie, 24, 30, 44, 79, 88,
    153, 197, 199
Hanmer, Thomas, 17
Hare, Arnold, 19
Harewood, David, 198, *199*
Harrow, Lisa, 188
Hart, Charles, 12–13
Hart-Davies, Rupert, 125
Harwitt, Robert, 211
Hasso, Signe, 137, *137*
Hawkins, F. W., 74
Hazlitt, William, 14, 31, 32, 34, 35,
    38, 48
Heald, Anthony, 212
Heath, William, *62*
Henderson, John, 72–4, *73*, 76
Hicks, Thomas, 81
Hiffernan, Paul, 29
Highfill, Philip N., 73
Hiley, Jim, 172
Hill, Aaron, 25–6, 57, 58–9
Hill, Errol, 106, 157, 168
Hillebrand, Harold H., 34
Hilský, Martin, 201, 202
Holloway, Baliol, 90
Holm, Ian, 129
Holmes, Martin, 3
Honigmann, Ernst, 6, 10, 11, 210
Hopkins, Anthony, 135, 154, 155
Hortmann, Wilhelm, 200
Hoyt, Edwin P., 119, 129
Hudeček, Václav, 201
Huston, Walter, 91
Hütter, Miranda, 175, 200
Hyman, Earle, 132, 157, 167, 169

Ibsen, Henrik, *Ghosts*, 89
Ireland, John, 72, 73
Irving, Henry, 17, 19, 40, 81, 192;
    alternating with Booth, 31, 46,
    55, 83–4
    1876 *Othello*, 53, 88
Irving, Washington, 76

Jackson, C. Bernard, 170
Jackson, Henry, 5

Jackson, Robert Jason, 205
Jackson, Russell, 165, 198
Jacob, Irène, 193, *194*
Jacobi, Derek, 149, *149*
Jacobs, Alfred, 140
James, Emrys, 210
James, Henry, 40
Jannings, Emil, 97–8
Jarro (Picinni, G.), 75
John, Errol, 164
Johnson, David, 175
Johnson, Patrice, 180, *181*, *plate 2*
Johnson-Haddad, Miranda, 172,
    173
Jones, D. A. N., 172
Jones, Elwyn, 164
Jones, Ernest, *Hamlet and Oedipus*,
    92
Jones, James Earl, 147, 154, 160–
    4, *163*, 169–70
    comparisons with, 182, 212,
    213
    and Robeson, 157–8, 164
    views on racism, 147, 161, 169,
    184
Jones, Robert, 209
Jones, Robert Edmund, 91
Jonson, Ben, 27, *The Alchemist*, 3,
    7; *Poetaster*, 27; *Sejanus*, 7;
    Volpone, 7
Jorgens, Jack J., 100
Joyce, Rachel, 208
Julia, Raul, 167
Jurgons, Michael, 200

Kachler, K. G., 89
Kahn, Michael, 179
Kaiser, Oldřich, 202, *203*
Kani, John, 176–7, *plate 1*
Kanin, Garson, 136–8
Karajan, Herbert von, 103
Kean, Charles, 35, 108
Kean, Edmund, 19, 30, 40, 63, 94,
    108–9
    as Iago, 74–5, 77
    as Othello, 31–5, *33*, 77–8, 125
Keene, Theophilus, 71
Kelly, Jude, 179–81, 182, 186
Kemble, Charles, 50